M000188144

Shelley's Radical Stages

Dana Van Kooy draws critical attention to Percy Bysshe Shelley as a dramatist and argues that his dramas represent a critical paradigm of romanticism in which history is 'staged'. Reading Shelley's dramas as a series of radical stages – historical reenactments and theatrical reproductions – Van Kooy highlights the cultural significance of the drama and the theatre in shaping and contesting constructions of both the sovereign nation and the global empire in the post-Napoleonic era. This book is about the power of performance to challenge and reformulate cultural memories that were locked in historical narratives and in Britain's theatrical repertoire. It examines each of Shelley's dramas as a specific radical stage that reformulates the familiar cultural performances of war, revolution, slavery and domestic tyranny. Shelley's plays invite audiences to step away from these horrors and to imagine their lives as something other than a tragedy or a melodrama where characters are entrapped in cycles of violence or struck blind or silent by fear. Although Shelley's dramas are few in number they engage a larger cultural project of aesthetic and political reform that constituted a groundswell of activism that took place during the Romantic period.

Dana Van Kooy is an Assistant Professor of Transnational Literature, Literary Theory and Culture in the Humanities Department at Michigan Technological University, USA.

Shelley's Radical Stages

Performance and cultural memory in the post-Napoleonic era

Dana Van Kooy

Routledge
Taylor & Francis Group

LONDON AND NEW YORK

First published 2016
by Routledge
2 Park Square, Milton Park, Abingdon, Oxon OX14 4RN

and by Routledge
711 Third Avenue, New York, NY 10017

Routledge is an imprint of the Taylor & Francis Group, an informa business

British Library Cataloguing in Publication Data
A catalogue record for this book is available from the British Library

Library of Congress Cataloging-in-Publication Data
Van Kooy, Dana.
  Shelley's radical stages : performance and cultural memory in the post-
Napoleonic era / by Dana Van Kooy.
    pages cm
  Includes bibliographical references and index.
  1. Shelley, Percy Bysshe, 1792–1822–Dramatic works.   2. Shelley,
Percy Bysshe, 1792–1822–Criticism and interpretation.   3. English
drama–19th century–History and criticism.   4. Romanticism–Great
Britain.   I. Title.
  PR5442.D7V36 2016
  822'.709–dc23
  2015021926

ISBN: 978-1-4094-5715-2 (hbk)
ISBN: 978-1-315-60894-5 (ebk)

Typeset in Times New Roman
by Apex CoVantage, LLC

For David

Contents

Figures

Abbreviations

BL	*Biographia Literaria*, 2 vols in *The Collected Works of Samuel Taylor Coleridge*, eds James Engell and W. Jackson Bate. 14 vols. Princeton: Princeton University Press, 1969.
BLJ	*Bryon's Letters and Journal*, ed. Leslie A. Marchand. 12 vols. London: John Murray, 1973–82.
BSM	*The Bodleian Shelley Manuscripts*, eds Donald H. Reiman et al. 23 vols. New York: Garland, 1986–2002.
CPW	*Lord Byron: The Complete Poetical Works*, ed. Jerome J. McGann. 7 vols. Oxford: Clarendon Press, 1980–83.
CWWH	*The Complete Works of William Hazlitt*, ed. P.P. Howe. 21 vols. London: J.M. Dent and Sons, 1930–34.
Letters	*The Letters of Percy Bysshe Shelley*, ed. Frederick L. Jones. 2 vols. Oxford: Clarendon Press, 1964.
Poems	*The Poems of Shelley*, eds Kelvin Everest and Geoffrey Matthews. 4 vols. London and New York: Longman, 1989.
Poetical Works	*The Complete Poetical Works of Shelley*, ed. Thomas Hutchinson [1905], cor. G.M. Matthews. Oxford: Clarendon Press, 1970.
Prose Works	*The Prose Works of Percy Bysshe Shelley*, ed. E.B. Murray. vol. 1. Oxford: Clarendon Press, 1993; New York and London: Routledge, 2002.
Shelley's Prose	*Shelley's Prose: or the Trumpet of a Prophecy*, ed. David Lee Clark. Alburquerque: University of New Mexico Press.
SPP	*Shelley's Poetry and Prose*, eds Donald H. Reiman and Neil Fraistat. 2nd edn. New York: Norton, 2002.
SWLH	*The Selected Works of Leigh Hunt*, eds Robert Morrison, Michael Eberle-Sinatra, Jeffrey N. Cox, Greg Kucich, Charles Mahoney, John Strachan. 6 vols. London: Pickering & Chatto, 2003.
SWWH	*The Selected Works of William Hazlitt*, ed. Duncan Wu. 9 vols. London: Pickering & Chatto, 1998.

Acknowledgements

The title of this book came to me while sitting in a small room on the coast of England. It had been a blustery day, and I had just returned from a long hike along the beautiful coastline. This solo walk had occasionally been broken up with adventures in muddied trail ruts, episodes of bushwhacking through brambles with fellow travellers and finally a celebratory plunge into the sea. Needless to say, I was cold and tired by the time I reached my room and yet I remained inspired by what I had seen and what I had accomplished. In some ways, this vignette encapsulates the story of this book, except that I have had the pleasure of more companionship than I could have ever imagined on that day.

Most of this book was written while I was at the University of Colorado, Boulder. I have benefitted immeasurably from the friendship and the collegiality of the community at CU. Jeff Cox, Jill Heydt-Stevenson, Christopher Braider, Timothy Morton and Michael Gamer read this as a dissertation and I am grateful to their insightful commentary and suggestions. Terry Robinson read and commented on several versions of Chapter 1, and I will always be grateful for her enthusiasm and her long-standing friendship. Michele Speitz read and commented on Chapter 2. David Duff read several chapters in their earliest and most rudimentary forms. David Glimp read Chapter 3 and provided insightful commentary. Deven Parker took time from her own work to help me with mine, and Kirstyn Leuner has always listened attentively. Katherine Eggert, Nan Goodman, William Kuskin, Suzanne Magnanini, Padma Rangarajan, John Stevenson, Terry Toulouse, Paul Youngquist and Nicole Wright provided kind words of advice and critical input, perhaps without even knowing it. The English Department and the Program for Writing and Rhetoric provided me with opportunities to teach what I love and to discover that there is always more.

Conferences have provided me with a valuable venue for the presentation and the discussion of my work. I want to thank David Clark, Daniel O'Quinn, Julie Carlson, Marjorie Levinson, Daniel White, Steven Jones, Greg Kucich, Jeffrey Cass, Jerrold Hogle, David Worrall and Michael Macovski for their insight and their conversation. I owe a great deal to Jane Moody, who I can only wish to have known better. My most most-standing debt is to Tilottama Rajan.

Although I have only been here a short time, I want to thank those in the Humanities Department at Michigan Technological University who have made the long cold winter seem more like a joy-filled summer's day, in particular Kette Thomas, Erin Smith, Ron Strickland, Beatrice Smith, Alexandra Morrison, Scott Marratto, Stephanie Carpenter, Andrew Fiss, Laura Kasson Fiss and Stefka Hristova have, along with my students, energized and encouraged my endeavours.

Finally, I want to thank my family and friends. I am especially grateful to Gretchen Spiro and Michelle Anderson and the Crawford clan. Lisa Rivero surfaced out of the blue at a critical moment and both helped and inspired me. My family – the Van Kooys and the Halls – have been enthusiastic in their support. David and Dillon Hall: without your laughter and your patience, nothing would have happened.

The rest is jazz.

Introduction "something must be done . . . what yet I know not"

Radical performances in the Romantic period

Percy Bysshe Shelley (1792–1822) was born three years after the French Revolution began, and like many of his contemporaries, he was inspired by what had been its promise and haunted by its failures. Shelley died in a boating accident while living abroad in Italy, 10 years before the Great Reform Bill passed in 1832. Although Shelley died quite young, just prior to his thirtieth birthday, his extensive literary corpus has proven pivotal in defining the shifting cultural relevance of literature. While the Victorians praised him as a visionary lyric poet, he is, to quote Timothy Morton, increasingly acknowledged as

> a protean writer, working in almost every corner of cultural and literary space in the Romantic period: from the upper class to the radical underground; from heterosexual love poetry to prose on homosexuality; from very subtle figurations to pugnacious political verse; from lyric to drama.[1]

Shelley's writing responded to the forces of political conflict as well as those of personal loss. In Shelley's youth, Napoleon's armies threatened every European monarch and reached, often in conflict with British forces, to almost every corner of the world. The Napoleonic wars, Napoleon's defeat at Waterloo in 1815 and the revolts, popular uprisings and messianic movements of this period, created, according to C.A. Bayly, a general and critical disruption on a scale that had not been seen since the Mongol invasions of the thirteenth century.[2] Notwithstanding the period's political upheavals, which included the overthrow of the Bourbon monarchy, the decline of the Ottoman Empire and the formation of global political alignments, the post-Waterloo political order looked surprisingly similar to the *ancien régime* that had initially sparked revolutionary violence in France. The Ottoman Porte, the English and French monarchies and even the papacy emerged from this worldwide destruction like the survivors of Prospero's tempest: distressed by what seemed an apparent loss, but mysteriously renewed and revived, as if nothing had happened.

While there is an increasing amount of scholarship being done on Shelley's early collections of poetry in *Original Poetry of Victor and Cazire* and *Posthumous Fragments of Margaret Nicholson*, published in 1810, and his 1813 volume of 'Minor Poems' in the *Esdaile Notebook*, the bulk of Shelley's work was published in the post-Waterloo era and arguably the best of it was produced in the tempestuous era of Peterloo (1819).[3] Amongst these are Shelley's dramas, a collection of four complete plays and two fragments, composed between 1818 and his death in 1822. Generally speaking, Shelley's dramas are history plays; they stage the past in order to uncover the generic and/or ideological 'root', from the Latin *radix*, of contemporary social and political ills. Through the generic framework of the drama, Shelley sought to discover the revolutionary potential in the present moment, and as he writes in the first and fourth Acts of *Prometheus Unbound*, to transform 'fear and self-contempt and barren hope' into 'bright Visions' of real possibility (*PU*, I,8; IV,514). The dramatic form provided Shelley with an alternative means of producing a critical reflexivity that could potentially liberate his audiences, as he tells us in the Preface to *The Cenci*, by 'teaching the human heart, through its sympathies and antipathies, the knowledge of itself' (*SPP*, 142). Shelley's dramas contest the 'ghastly masquerade' of tyranny (*The Mask of Anarchy* I. 27), which he saw performed repeatedly in various cultural venues, including Britain's theatres, its streets, its courtrooms, newspapers and even in the halls of Parliament. As Stuart Curran aptly describes Shelley's dramas, they are 'records of mental liberation, by which ideas imply social action, [and] essences are caught in the process of embodying themselves in human form'; they are 'watchful [and] cautionary' and tell us to 'Beware – and be free'.[4] They enact personal and cultural mobility and stage social change and political transformation.

This book is about Shelley's radical dramas and about the power of performance in times of crises. Performance repeats, revises and actualizes what exists in the cultural imaginary; it reproduces and recreates identities, memories and histories: sometimes reinforcing or reifying norms, at other times providing the means of abandoning these scenes and opening the door to new possibilities.[5] *Shelley's Radical Stages* locates and identifies the often obscured or hidden connections that link different cultural performances and explains why one might resist fixed notions of cultural identity and history while another affixes an alternative meaning to these familiar performances. Composed over a period of five years, Shelley's plays often begin with a conventional tragic framework that would have been familiar to contemporary British audiences attending London's theatres. However, they also incorporate an epic perspective that renounces these tragedies and looks across a geographical expanse that stretches from Great Britain to its imperial interests in the Mediterranean, the Americas and the East, and encompasses British, Greek and Italian cultural history. *Hellas* and *Prometheus Unbound* turn most distinctly toward the future, creating radically new dramatic forms that, in Curran words, 'continually enlarge frames of reference so as to mediate between an internal psychological state and its enveloping political organization, between one mind and the whole of human culture'.[6]

Shelley's Radical Stages reimagines romanticism by radicalizing it: taking it back to its performative roots: most obviously, in drama, the theatre and print journalism but also in the halls of Parliament and courtrooms where laws are enacted. This study recognizes the performative quality of words that J.L. Austin discussed in his *How To Do Things With Words*,[7] where he argued that words do not merely describe the world around us; they do things. And just as words and their meanings circulate and adapt to various contexts, so too the key to comprehending how performances work is to trace how they migrate across historical periods and between geographical and cultural locales. Performances rarely exist as isolated events. Instead they are embedded in a genealogy that links scripted spaces to impromptu or improvizational spaces. Although Shelley's dramas are few in number, they need to be read as cultural performances that connect history to cultural memory through the mediums of the early nineteenth-century theatrical repertoire, the print culture of the radical and reform movements and the street scenes of political protest.

This perspective reorients our collective definition of the Romantic period and how we increasingly situate it within the concept of modernity.[8] Curran and others have placed Shelley's great epic vision,[9] which culminates with *Prometheus Unbound*, firmly within a poetic tradition. I also consider *Prometheus Unbound* Shelley's greatest accomplishment, but I regard his epic vision as inherently theatrical. Shelley's dramatic corpus constitutes a Brechtian epic theatre[10] that portrays and critiques the national and global crises of the period. Shelley's plays invite audiences to become more actively engaged, more a part of the performance – an active, thinking character rather than a passive spectator – and his stages, especially in the cases of *Hellas* and *Prometheus Unbound*, appear more presentational, more like the classical Greek theatre with its chorus and masked archetypal figures. Shelley's corpus reproduces myths, cultural memories, contemporary political crises, history, iconography, Greek tragedies, Shakespearean drama and a popular tale that dates back to the Italian Renaissance. It also contributes to a loosely conceived collective project of reform, whose lineaments can be traced in the pages of John and Leigh Hunt's *The Examiner* (1808–22), in William Cobbett's *The Political Register* (1802–36), T.J. Wooler's *The Black Dwarf* (1817–24) and in the more conservative essays printed in *Blackwood's Edinburgh Magazine* (1817/1818–1905). To fully understand both the significance and the scope of Shelley's dramas, it is important to contextualize them within the overlapping literary circles and reform movements of the period and within the cultural institutions of drama and the theatre. Jeffrey N. Cox has described this project as one of 'clearance and reclamation rather than an act of colonizing the past by the present'.[11] Essayists, poets, dramatists: these writers believed in the performative power of words to revive the past and to shape the future. Shelley's dramatic turn is symptomatic of the period's mobilization of literary talents around the theatre that constitutes what James Chandler has identified as a collective act of 'self-making, or – remaking'.[12] As the works of Cox and Chandler suggest, these cultural performances articulate a historicized self-awareness of the British nation and the British Empire. Dramas ranging from those of Joanna Baillie and Lord Byron to the State Theatricals penned by Wooler for *The Black Dwarf* function as complex social acts and reveal a web of human and cultural relations that spans across a historical and a global geographical continuum, while being located firmly within the Romantic period.

Throughout each of the following chapters, I address what Jane Moody has referred to as the 'complex, ambivalent interlacing of institution and performance' in the Romantic period by mapping the intersections between different dramatic formulations and theatrical praxes.[13] In contrast with Jacqueline Mulhallen's *The Theatre of Shelley* and Curran's comprehensive study, *Shelley's Cenci: Scorpions Ringed with Fire*, books that focus almost solely on questions of performability, I am more concerned with the concept of performativity. I share both Mulhallen's and Curran's view that Shelley's plays should be liberated from the dark closets of the mental theatre and the closed spaces of private theatricals. They need to be studied through the critical lenses of theatrical practices and theatre history and to some extent this book contributes to that ongoing project. But my central concern is to consider how Shelley's dramas reflect a key cultural practice during the Romantic period: one that shaped the public's historical perspective and facilitated its ability to imagine 'virtual' possibilities that were distinct from the familiar tragedies of history.[14] Situating *The Cenci, Oedipus Tyrannus; or, Swellfoot the Tyrant*, 'Charles the First', *Hellas* and *Prometheus Unbound* within a cultural context that extends beyond the doors of the theatre, onto the street and into the pages of print, *Shelley's Radical Stages* illustrates the emergence of a historical consciousness that offered audiences radically different ways of reading and experiencing cultural performances that occurred in and outside the theatre.

This reading of Shelley's oeuvre draws attention to his experimental dramaturgy and how it engages his audiences through inter-textual echoes and what Jacky Bratton refers to as inter-theatrical performance sites.[15] Merging together various textual and theatrical sites, Shelley's dramas embody a historical and a performative genealogy that compresses contemporary and historical events, literary reviews and theatrical productions into one complex and multi-faceted vision of reform. Nigel Leask in *British Romantic Writers and the East*, Steven Jones in *Shelley's Satire* and contributors to both *The Cambridge Companion to Shelley* and *The Unfamiliar Shelley* foreground Shelley's interest in politics and history, the relevance of national and global contexts to his work and the significance of his non-canonical fragments and marginalized texts. The figure of Percy Shelley that readers will encounter in these pages is closely aligned to the one that takes shape in these studies. Shelley is a visionary as well as an astute and pragmatic writer who remains keenly aware of the British government's collusion with patent theatres and its crackdown against dissident voices, especially through the legal chicanery evinced in its use of *agents provocateurs* and its prosecution of seditious and blasphemous libel cases. Shelley's active voice in cultural debates engages, amongst others, Baillie, Byron, Cobbett, William Godwin, the Hunt brothers, Hazlitt, William Hone, John Gibson Lockhart and Wooler. Far from being unworldly or philosophically obscure, his dramas allude to published political and aesthetic debates and employ popular culture – its music, its poetry, its performances. Each of Shelley's dramas function as a 'prismatic and many-sided mirror' (*A Defense of Poetry* 520) that reflects on conspiracy, regicide, civil war, revolution, empire and slavery. In most of his dramas, Shelley breaks with the high forms of tragedy to challenge cultural complacency about the dire need for reform. The one obvious exception is *The Cenci*, where he takes tragedy and his audience to a breaking point by vividly depicting how its performance entraps its characters and its audiences in a destructive anatomizing casuistry that condemns as criminals Beatrice Cenci and others who act out the unspeakable. *The Cenci* portrays how a vague cultural awareness of everyday violence reproduces mute performances that silence public outrage.

Reconfiguring romanticism and its histories

Romanticism is a historical period and a literary movement. The conventional narrative of romanticism has been Euro-centric and viewed almost exclusively in terms of the French Revolution (1789) and the battle at Waterloo (1815). This history, with its abbreviated historical timeline, tells two tales: how revolutionary activity gives way to an unprecedented escalation of violence, which eventually ends with the restoration of European monarchs and how the balance of global power shifted in the period from French to British control. This narrative constricts the geographical and chronological scope of history so as to portray the British Empire as a force of political order. However, the Romantic-period landscape has become increasingly diverse and complex. The almost-proverbial field of dancing daffodils is now riven by scenes of local and national riots; it has been marred by the ravages of war and immersed in the politics of global imperialism. Romanticism is, as David Simpson's most recent work on Wordsworth suggests, a site of social concern.[16] As the lens widens geographically and historically and the list of writers increases in terms of numbers and cultural diversity, the haunting images of poverty, war, death and homelessness come into focus. If 'Wordsworth's poetry insists that there is no comfortable place to stand and no easy way to feel good about oneself in the face of the social and material inequities that continue to perplex all efforts at justifying one's own place in the world',[17] then Shelley constructs performative spaces where audiences can confront and contest these scenes of global conflict and personal turmoil and – if only momentarily – abandon their uncertainty.

In several ways Shelley is working in a philosophical tradition that culminates today in the works of Giorgio Agamben, Judith Butler, Jacques Derrida and Jean-Luc Nancy. All of these writers are concerned with creating more liberating prospects and often build upon and critique the works of their forbears to accomplish their task. Abandon is one of the key terms I adopt from the work of Agamben and Nancy. Abandonment, as Nancy describes it, is a dialogical movement; it is founded upon negation, but it does not simply refer to giving up or renouncing some position. Acts of abandon interweave release and blithe engagement and allow for a break with the stultifying status quo in order to produce more liberating possibilities that had either been overlooked or deemed unrealistic. This insightful work helps elucidate what I believe to have been Shelley's social concerns and his attempt to oppose those paralysing doubts that devolve into skepticism and cynicism.

As the canvas of romanticism widens to one that is more philosophically nuanced and planetary in its scope, it allows for a certain fungibility in its chronological sequencing of events and its geographical placement of peoples. Effectively, we now have multiple romanticisms, a network of crisscrossing perspectives that destabilize the more reified and conventional historical narratives.[18] Within this broadened landscape the French Revolution still represents a national and international controversy about the possibilities for 'liberty, equality and fraternity'. As Michael Gamer and David Duff, amongst others have noted, the cultural debates that gave rise to revolutionary action and reform movements also instigated and promoted literary and cultural innovation that redefined the fields of history, aesthetics and philosophy and transformed the popular domains of entertainment.[19] The French Revolution ushered in a new age, one we now refer to as modernity and one that erupted into 'a war', as a writer to *The Times* notes in 1812, 'of no common description – a war of system against system, in which no choice is left us, but victory or extirpation'.[20] In the post-Napoleonic era both the French Revolution and Waterloo were saturated with mythic significance and each event functioned as a mobile signifier, informing and legitimizing revolutionary *and* reactionary positions. Many hoped that Waterloo would somehow mark an end to this era of war and revolutionary upheaval. But this battlefield with its paralysing images of dying and dead bodies proved to be a haunting testament of things to come. Waterloo brought the Napoleonic wars to an end but it failed to close the figurative Pandora's Box that this era of national and global violence had opened. In the aftermath of Waterloo, the Liverpool government sustained their iron-fisted control over the country by imposing counter-revolutionary measures like the Coercion Act (1817), effectively suspending *habeas corpus* and expanding its powers to ban what it viewed as seditious activities, including public meetings and demonstrations like that at Spa Fields in December of 1816 or the Blanketeers March (March, 1817). From a political perspective, the 'new' order that structured post-Napoleonic Britain and its global empire rested on the public's perception of disorder. The sharp up-tick in nationalist movements – Greece, Italy and South America – and religious fundamentalism around the world, including the Wahhabis, represented some of the responses to the widespread disruptive power of imperial force being wielded throughout the world. As the work of Agamben suggests, empires preserved their sovereignty by focusing the state's resources on internal and external threats, which were both real and manufactured. Exploiting their people's fears of revolutionary violence, each state – whether France, Britain or the Ottoman Empire – in various ways developed a paradigm of governance that relied upon sustaining a permanent state of emergency, or what Agamben refers to as a state of exception.[21] The British government exerted its control ostensibly through its judicial system, particularly by focusing public's attention on the 'threats' posed by dissent and political activism and the subsequent punishments, which ranged from debilitating fines to gruesome executions. The innumerable cases of treason and seditious and blasphemous libel attest to the role played by the judicial system in generating a perpetual state of political crisis. The 1794

Treason Trials, John and Leigh Hunt's prosecution for libel in December 1812, which resulted in a hefty fine of £500 and prison, and the Cato Street Conspiracy (1820) are some of the most visible examples.

Shelley and his contemporaries identified these oppressive policies as historical forms of oppression and instances of political theatre. Eighteenth-century historians, including William Robertson (*History of Scotland* [1759], *The History of the Emperor Charles V* [1769] and *The History of America* [1777]) and Edward Gibbon in his *The History of the Decline and Fall of the Roman Empire* (1776–88) had widened the historical field and indicted imperial acts of conquest and empire building. These histories inspired writers like Baillie, Bryon, Mary Mitford and Shelley to produce dramas that revisited familiar national tragedies and the global geography of empire, transforming these narratives into a performative dialectic of chronological and geographical stages.

This juxtaposition of geographic and chronological perspectives and the construction of progressive historical narratives in many ways defined the Scottish Enlightenment and would influence Hegel's *The Phenomenology of Spirit* (1807). As Chandler explains in *England in 1819*, this dialectic of time and space created the idea of

'states' that belong at once to two different, and to some extent competing, orders of temporality. On the one hand, each society is theorized as moving stepwise through a series of stages sequenced in an order that is more-or-less autonomous and stable. Insofar as stages are also 'ages', these sequencings can also be said to constitute temporal orders. On the other hand, this same historiographical discourse always implies a second temporality, one in which these different national times can be correlated and calendrically dated in respect to each other.[22]

What interests me most here is Chandler's conception of 'states' as stages. Historical 'states' represent competing cultural frameworks that can be staged. This comparative model of history draws attention to patterns of development as well as characteristic affinities between nations, between different forms of consciousness and between the past and the present. While this awareness of a historical situation is, as Chandler argues, endemic to romanticism, it is important to develop Chandler's insightful argument a step further, to make explicit the relationship between historical discourses and those of the theatre and the drama. As the still relatively recent work on the Romantic theatre demonstrates, the theatre existed as a pivotal cultural institution during this period. Theatrical performance influenced print culture, from news reporting and literary reviews to satiric caricature, and as such it produced a historical consciousness that was influenced by dramaturgical and theatrical practices.

As a series of radical stages, Shelley's dramas embody this paradigm of romanticism. Read individually and collectively, these dramas and others written in the period reconstruct familiar historical and theatrical stages. In the Preface to *Hellas*, for example, Shelley identifies his drama about Greece as engaging in one of several unfolding historical events. He portrays the contemporary moment as 'the age of the war of the oppressed against the oppressors' (*SPP*, 432) and he depicts this era as one set in motion long ago when two ancient civilizations clashed: Rome and Greece, 'the instructor [and] the conqueror' (*SPP*, 431). Among the cultural legacies Britain has inherited from this clash are its drama, its political system and its ideology. To contest this heritage, Shelley announces in his Preface to *Hellas* the emergence of a 'drama of the revival of liberty' (*SPP*, 432) and a 'new race [that] has arisen throughout Europe, nursed in the abhorrence of the opinions which are its chains' (*SPP*, 432).

Further evidence of this Romantic-period paradigm can be seen in the popular demand for topical and historical material, which took form in 'heroic-scale gallery paintings', panoramas and staged spectacles of famous military campaigns, Shakespearean drama and melodramatic adaptations such as those of Sir Walter Scott's novels.[23] In part, the public's growing concern with current events was due to the easier and more detailed access to news, particularly information about the various wars and revolutions occurring throughout the world. The speed with which these events were conveyed and sensationalized transformed them increasingly into 'everyday' events, which Mary Favret examines at length in her groundbreaking study, *War at a Distance*, and which Greg Kucich argues created an insatiable craving for every kind of historical performance.[24] The culture industry that emerged focused almost exclusively on responding to the 'burgeoning vogue for staging history'.[25] Because the newspapers were not yet illustrated, the theatre and other forms of cultural performance played an essential role in responding to this appetite for visual reproductions of contemporary and historical events.[26] Subsequently, as Kucich and Richard Altick have demonstrated, the theatre is notable for its unprecedented expenditures and its creative ingenuity.[27] This cultural investment in performance gave rise to a variety of historical dramas, including Coleridge and Robert Southey's *The Fall of Robespierre* (1794), Richard Brinsley Sheridan's *Pizarro* (1799), Joanna Baillie's *Count Basil* (1798), *Ethwald Part First and Second* (1802), *Constantine Paleologus* (1804) and *The Family Legend* (1810), John Keats and Charles Brown's *Otho the Great* (1819–1820), Shelley's *The Cenci* (1819), *Hellas* (1821), 'Charles the First', (unfinished fragment), Byron's *Marino Faliero* (1820) as well as *Sardanapalus* and *The Two Foscari* (1821), Felicia Hemans's *The Siege of Valencia* (1923) and Mitford's *Foscari: A Tragedy* (1826), *Rienzi* (1828) and *Charles the First* (1834). If we add to this list the myriad melodramas and pantomimes dealing with historical and military topics, and the stage adaptations of Scott's poetry and historical novels, which numbered more than 4,500,[28] it becomes clear what role the theatre performed in developing and revising modes of historical consciousness in this period. While some dramas adhered to dramatic conventions, others provided audiences with innovative strategies for reimagining the past and visualizing the future. In these instances, the militaristic pageantry and the familiar political intrigues were displaced by more nuanced performances that challenged the normative theatrical, political and social practices. At times, Julie Carlson argues in the case of Byron's history plays and Shelley's *The Cenci*, these dramas portrayed the 'tragic collapse of a hierarchical social order',[29] and the 'struggle with problems of governance that ensue when grounds for acting are up in the air'.[30]

The theatre produced the social mechanisms of performance, display and spectatorship; it engaged the ongoing social and political dramas unfolding as historical events, particularly the violent suppression of revolt and the exploits of war. As Gillian Russell explains, war extended 'the boundaries of what was theatrically possible'.[31] Patent theatres – in London, Drury Lane, Covent Garden and the Haymarket – and the minor or illegitimate theatres – those not granted a government patent to perform traditional, spoken-word drama – attracted audiences by staging exacting replicas of well-known events people would have read about in the newspapers. For example, Russell discusses how Astley's production of *Paris in an Uproar; or the Destruction of the Bastile* (1789) featured a scaled model of the city, and in 1804 Sadler's Wells employed shipwrights and riggers from the Royal Naval dockyard at Woolwich to construct battleships in its production of *The Siege of Gibraltar*.[32] However, despite the theatres' efforts to reproduce events with historical accuracy and verisimilitude and to represent the topography of war and empire, these performances tended to expose the 'instability of theatricality as a medium of political expression'.[33] Whereas the patent theatres often depicted history as tragedy, the non-patented theatres' reliance upon music and spectacle transformed history into farce, reflecting Karl Marx's famous injunction in *The Eighteenth Brumaire* 'that all facts and personages of great importance in world history occur, as it were, twice [. . .] the first time as tragedy, the second as farce'.[34] Shelley and other like-minded dramatists were keenly aware of how the drama and the theatre often perpetuated the paralysing realities of war and terror, unravelling the potential for historical clarity and presenting audiences with only the haunting absurdity that history was little more than an endless cycle of terror. Shelley was one among many in his circle to employ Britain's dramas and its history and, in the words of Marx, to find 'once more the spirit of revolution'.[35]

Cultural performances in and outside the theatre

Throughout the Romantic period theatrical performances were subject to the 1747 Licensing Act and the British patent system, which granted certain theatres status as Theatres Royal and a monopoly to perform spoken-word or 'legitimate' drama. Performances at the Theatres Royal were identified as 'legitimate' because their play texts were examined and licensed – that is, censored – prior to production by the Lord Chamberlain's Office.[36] John Larpent (1741–1824) and later, the playwright, George Colman the Younger (1762–1836) held the office of Examiner of Plays during the Romantic era. Other performance spaces – and they were myriad and included taverns and lecture halls in addition to Sadler's Wells, Astley's Amphitheatre and the Adelphi, Surrey (formerly, the Royal Circus), Coburg and Olympic Theatres – were identified as illegitimate or minor theatres. Despite the monopoly, competing theatres continuously vexed the patentees and challenged the elitism and the government control exerted through the patent system. As Moody argues in *Illegitimate Theatre*, the late eighteenth century marked a watershed for a fundamental cultural transformation in 'the nature of London theatre'.[37] Illegitimate theatre emerged as the 'theatre of physical peril, visual spectacle and ideological confrontation [that] challenged both the generic premises and the cultural dominance of legitimate drama'.[38] This constituted nothing less than a cultural revolution. The language, the dramatic subjects and the heroic characters of comedy and tragedy evolved to more closely resemble a corporeal dramaturgy: one we associate with pantomime, melodrama, extravaganza and burletta. Reflecting the social and political concerns of the period, many of these performances tended to highlight war and the threat of revolution. These cultural innovations changed how history was staged for British audiences and it certainly proved effective in shifting the critical and aesthetic values of Georgian England, but it was not necessarily efficacious in promoting political and social reforms. To the contrary, the theatre's incorporation of popular cultural forms and practices proved an apt means of containing transgressive scenes that ostensibly challenged the state and all forms of political and social authority.[39] But the potential for this revolution within the theatre was immense and playwrights like Shelley – attracted by its commercial success, its innovative spirit and its vital potential for disrupting conventional performances – were drawn to the drama and the theatre for precisely this reason.

Performance cuts across multiple venues and disciplines, including theatre, literature, media studies, philosophy and anthropology. Performance is extra-literary and it subverts the cultural hegemony of print texts while providing a poignant means for cultural critique. What is unique about performance is its role in cultural productions of every kind. Performance marks a critical convergence between human reflection and political action; it provides the means for acting out relationships between people and nations and it also circumscribes a space for representing history. The work of Joseph Roach and Judith Butler has shaped the field of performance studies. Roach argues that histories and geographical spaces are not discovered but rather invented, often by means of reproducing cultural traumas like war, genocide and slavery.[40] These productions do not lead to an absolute truth but they do reproduce an evolving relationship between places and the people who inhabit them. Performance, Roach observes, marks the erasure of events and people by prompting acts of recollection, revision and even redemption. Butler further politicizes performance and performative acts.[41] In her earlier work on gender constitution, she has argued that 'gender is an "act", broadly construed, which constructs the social fiction of its own psychological interiority [and] is made to comply with a model of truth and falsity, which not only contradicts its own performative fluidity, but serves a social policy of gender regulation and control'.[42] Butler's recognition that performance is both fluid and compliant with established models of normative belief and behaviour provides a key to understanding Romantic-period tragedies as well as the first scene of *Prometheus Unbound* where Prometheus summons the spirit of Jupiter to repeat his long-forgotten curse against Jove and must subsequently endure a punishing reprisal designed to inhibit similar performances.

Shelley's critical attitude toward the monarchy and slavery inspired him to write *Prometheus Unbound*, but many of the period's most powerful performances were inspired by Waterloo, which as Philip Shaw notes, is 'best remembered as a tragic defeat rather than a glorious triumph'.[43] Contemporary observers seemed to agree that Waterloo was nothing more or less than one of the greatest human tragedies. In his article, 'Victory of Waterloo – Bonaparte's Abdication', printed in *The Examiner* on 2 July 1815, Leigh Hunt – Shelley's friend and the editor and owner of *The Examiner* – presented his readers with a heart-wrenching dramatic sketch. Hunt's essay functions as a dramatic monologue. The emotional tone is sombre; there are no displays of elation, but rather a visceral attempt to come to terms with that 'mysterious evil, war, [which] has been hacking and sweeping away' (*SWLH*, 2. 32) family and friends for too long. Hunt's essay portrays his emotional exhaustion and his sense of loss upon hearing the news about Waterloo. This scene of mass annihilation, where approximately 40,000 people lost their lives in a matter of eight hours, was, in many ways, too familiar after almost a quarter century of war. Hunt and his audience were too aware of the costs of war, and yet, Hunt manages to give voice to the hope that rises like a phoenix out of the ashes of despair[44]:

> What are to us the common feelings of hostility or of triumph, when we think of all those old men cut down with irreverent violence, – of those in manhood suddenly dashed into all the impotent postures of lifelessness [. . .]. And what, at least is even all this to the survivors? – What is the happiness that is struck dead, to the misery that is left alive? – What is it all to the fatherless, the childless, the husbandless? – to the mind's eye haunted with faces it shall never see again, – to voices missed in the circle, – to vacant seats at table, – to widowed wakings in the morning, with the loved one never more to be in that bed? – But, – no further. We check ourselves, here, for our own sakes, and for the sake of others.
>
> (*SWLH*, 2. 33)

Hunt's vivid portrait of human grief and personal suffering does not succumb to histrionics but rather invites readers to imagine the lives of others. It is not solely one person's sorrow that he asks his readers to consider but human vulnerability and the need to mourn the losses one has sustained both as an individual and as part of an ever-expanding human community that reaches from a family to the nation and finally throughout the expanse of an empire to the world. Hunt's essay re-enacts personal grief as an act of public and national mourning.

This article encourages readers to reflect on their loss, and through this reflection Hunt transforms the awareness of human pain and suffering into an act of political intervention.[45] Hunt's performance contributes to what Roach identifies in a different context as 'the necessary business' of encouraging the British people to remember 'who and what they are'.[46] Some performances, Roach writes, have a 'powerful way of *making* [people] into who and what they are, and even into who and what they might someday be' (168). Hunt's periodical essays represent a performative tradition that reproduces and reformulates cultural memories into a politics of hope and forgiveness. While Hunt voices grief, he does not give way to paralysing despair. The emotional check at the end of the article – 'for our own sakes, and for the sake of others' – conveys a social need to keep up appearances: to resist the desire for an intemperate emotional release. Hunt's hesitation allows the narrative to falter, but this performative gesture creates a rhetorical space wherein Hunt shifts his audience's attention from the human tragedy of Waterloo toward a new possibility: expressing 'charity towards *all* our fellow creatures, not one excepted' (*SWLH*, 2. 33). Rewriting the final scene of tragedy, Hunt turns the isolating nightmare of bodies piling up onstage into a scene of reconciliation and inclusion.

Two years after Waterloo, J.M.W. Turner produced a similar performance in his painting, *The Field of Waterloo* (Figure I.1). This painting offers audiences a dramatic tableau that encourages viewers to reimagine Waterloo, not as a national victory, featuring the national standard flanked by images of defiant heroism and steadfast resistance, but rather as a gaping wound in the landscape that is illuminated by a flaming rocket in the background and by a torch held by an anonymous and almost indiscernible mass of humanity in the foreground.[47] As Shaw notes in his discussion of *The Field of Waterloo*, Turner's painting presents audiences with an image of the national wound inflicted upon all Britons by Waterloo. It also functions as a radical portrait of a 'new relationship' between the British state and its people. In line with the work of Judith Butler, Favret and Agamben, Shaw argues that Turner displays 'the vulnerable body that can be maimed and killed'.[48]

Figure I.1 J.M.W. Turner, *The Field of Waterloo*, oil on canvas, 1818, Tate, London

This image, he writes, 'disturbs the ideology that perpetuates war' and poses 'an unequivocal challenge to the ideology of sacrifice'.[49] Produced, as Simon Schama reminds us, at a time when Britain was still celebrating Waterloo as a monumental victory and toasting the Duke of Wellington while 'fending off demands for reform and for measures to cope with poverty and hunger',[50] *The Field of Waterloo* discloses the wounded vulnerability of a sustained national trauma. Turner, like Hunt, portrays the destruction of domestic peace as a national tragedy. Instead of imagining a family gathered together at a table, Turner presents viewers with a conglomerate mass of human bodies: women and children grieve for their dead fathers, husbands and brothers. The patriotic pomp of drums, flashy uniforms and sabres has dissolved into this massive lump of 'clay',[51] made just visible by candlelight. Turner's tableau in the foreground contests the image of victory signified by the shooting rocket in the background. The play of shadow and light, chiaroscuro, reproduces the gaps of emotional and economic disparity that divide the public and private spheres: the domestic interests of the people against the state's national agenda. Turner's painting represents a dramatic and a historical performance: a reconstruction of a traumatic historical memory. Turner's dramatic tableau memorializes not those named and ranked men pictured standing bravely in uniform on the mansion walls of Britain's elite, but those whose names would never be recorded in the annals of history and whose bodies would never be recovered from the battlefield. This performance reveals and criticizes the violence that configures the relationship between the nation's governing body and its people. Both Hunt and Turner memorialize human suffering and vulnerability, and their work also marks a shifting social attitude about how war and its dead would be remembered. Heroic triumphalism gave way, if only rhetorically in some instances, to more unsettling portraits and to public acknowledgements like that made by the Duke of Wellington in the aftermath of Waterloo where he ascribed victory ' "to the superior *physical* force and the *invincible constancy* of British soldiers" ' (*SWLH*, 2. 34).[52]

In the final pages of his *A Philosophical View of Reform*, Shelley creates a narrative performance, which, like Turner's and Hunt's, reconstructs the cultural trauma of war. Shelley composed this fragment in the aftermath of Peterloo in 1819 and here, as in many of his other writings, he concerns himself with the question of political resistance and the 'right of insurrection' (*Shelley's Prose*, 259). He describes war as 'a kind of superstition; the pageantry of arms and badges [that] corrupts the imagination of men' (*Shelley's Prose*, 260). These lines acknowledge the powerful symbolism of pageantry and badges as the signs of power and law. Both function as distracting shows of power that blind the populace to their own worth and well-being. Shelley, like Hunt and Turner, superimposes a scenic narrative of communal grief to contest the patriotic festivity that infuses the parades of soldiers marching off to war:

How far more appropriate would be the symbols of an inconsolable grief – muffled drums, and melancholy music, and arms reversed, and the livery of sorrow rather than of blood. When men mourn at funerals, for what do they mourn in comparison with the calamities which they hasten with all circumstance of festivity to suffer and to inflict! Visit in imagination the scene of a field of battle or a city taken by assault, collect into one group the groans and the distortions of the innumerable dying, the inconsolable grief and horror of their surviving friends, the hellish exultation, and unnatural drunkenness of destruction of the conquerors, the burning of the harvests and the obliteration of the traces of cultivation.

(*Shelley's Prose,* 260)

It was not difficult for Shelley's audiences to visit 'the scene of a field of battle'. These scenes were reproduced everywhere: on stage, in newspaper reports and as Jane Austen's characters in *Persuasion* reveal, it too was the stuff of gossip. Shelley, Hunt and Turner require their audiences to actively remember and visualize those who suffered and died, those who remain alive and those who are paralysed by grief. Visualizing these mirror images of themselves, they see what the ideologies of nationalism and patriotism obscure: the ghostly reflections of human alienation. These compelling emanations bring the virtual into sharp focus and ground it in the specific historical conditions of everyday experience.

Each of these performances stages history and each revitalizes the ghosts which haunt the cultural imaginary. None of the characters in these performances exist in a timeless existential dimension; rather, they are represented in a life-like tableau. Drama and theatrical productions shape these performances, giving them a different depth and a motion that 'clicks' like the first cinematic productions. In Shelley's dramas, characters constantly move, abandoning one scene for another, thereby disrupting the imaginative paralysis that threatens to reduce characters and audiences to alienated sleepwalkers navigating blindly through history. Shelley deploys these theatrical acts of 'abandon' in a way that resonates with the works of Agamben and Nancy. Each act provides audiences with an alternative framework through which to review cultural memories. While these performances are often founded upon familiar staged tragedies, Shelley's dynamic dramaturgy does not entrap either its characters or its audiences in those performances but rather attempts to liberate them by means of allowing them to abandon one form (tragedy) for another (romance, pantomime or melodrama).

Shelley's radical stages

More than other events in the nineteenth century, Peterloo unites the revolutionary energy of the French Revolution to the horrible devastation of war, particularly as it appeared on the field at Waterloo. A phrase coined by journalists to refer to the events that took place at St Peter's Field in Manchester on 16 August 1819, the Peterloo massacre denotes the peaceful gathering of unarmed men, women and children who assembled to protest the laws of Parliamentary representation. The reports vary but the upshot is that a group of seasoned veterans who had fought at Waterloo were sent in to disrupt the assembly; people were killed and injured and the subsequent public outcry can be compared to that which followed the Kent State shootings in 1970. After Peterloo, Shelley wrote a series of letters to Thomas Love Peacock and Charles Ollier, expressing his frustration with the recent news from Britain. Prior to hearing the news of Peterloo, Shelley described how the 'very disturbed state' of affairs was enough to make him 'tremble & wonder' (to Peacock, 24 August 1819; *Letters*, 2. 115). Shelley also conveys his hope that the 'higher orders' will act, but he realizes if they do not, it is likely that 'anarchy will only be the last flash before despotism' (*Letters*, 2. 115). This reference to anarchy and despotism is the seed that will within a matter of weeks sprout into his virulent response to Peterloo, *The Mask of Anarchy*. A poem that forgoes the sublime imagery of 'Mont Blanc' and the intellectual beauty of a hymn for the visceral poetic machinery of allegory and satire, *The Mask of Anarchy* envisions the inevitability – perhaps even the historical necessity – of violent revolution.[53] In William Keach's illuminating discussion of the poem, he notes the grotesque brutality wielded by those in power. Murder/Viscount Castlereagh (Foreign Secretary), Fraud/Baron Eldon (Lord Chancellor), Hypocrisy/Viscount Sidmouth (Home Secretary) and Anarchy commit one atrocity after another, but perhaps the most disturbing element about this 'ghastly masquerade' (*The Mask of Anarchy*, l. 27) is the freedom with which these monsters trample into 'a mire of blood/The adoring multitude' (*The Mask of Anarchy*, l. 40–41). Shelley depicts this violent scene as the speaker's dream vision and as a masquerading pageant of power.[54] No one resists Castlereagh as he tosses human hearts to his bloodhounds or as Eldon's tears fall as millstones and knock out children's brains. There was no love lost between Shelley and Eldon, who was known for weeping in public and who had denied Shelley custody of his children in Chancery court. The historical reference to bloodhounds aligns the British citizens at Peterloo with the Jamaican Maroons, who had fought the British and secured their freedom through a treaty but who had also been forced to fight the British again in the Second Maroon War (1795), when they were hunted down in a genocidal campaign by Cuban dogs. Shelley's point is that neither the Magna Carta nor a treaty will guarantee a people's rights and secure their freedom.

Shelley confesses to Ollier that 'the torrent of my indignation has not yet done boiling in my veins. I wait anxiously [to] hear how the Country will express its sense of this bloody murderous oppression of its destroyers. "Something must be done . . . What yet I know not"' (6 September 1819; *Letters* 2. 117). Closing his letter with lines from his recently penned drama, *The Cenci*, Shelley adopts the character and the voice of Beatrice Cenci. As I discuss in the first chapter, Shelley condemns Beatrice Cenci for her act of patricide, but it is significant that in this moment, Shelley identifies with her. The limits of non-violence and the necessity of self-defense are clearly delineated here: you cannot let those in power kill you. Self-defense is a moral imperative. In addition to drawing the proverbial line in the sand, Shelley's letter reflects his turn to the drama at this critical historical moment and his political alignment with those harassed and oppressed people who witnessed and endured unspeakable acts.

The Mask of Anarchy as well as his letters, essays, poetry and dramas compel readers to remember that the Romantic period may well have begun with the storming of the Bastille on 14 July 1789 and concluded with the passage of the Reform Act in 1832, but it was an era defined by the savagery of war, the barbarity of slavery and the tyranny of reactionary politics. As our view of Romantic-period writers has shifted, becoming more inclusive of women, dramatists and figures like Olaudah Equiano, Mary Prince and Mirza Abu-Taleb Khan, so too our perspective of romanticism – as a period and an aesthetic – has shifted in terms of its geography and chronology. The compelling momentum of history that powers the studies of eighteenth- and nineteenth-century literature in conjunction with the pressing need in literature departments to globalize British and American literature has in the past two decades changed the field and its practitioners.

Shelley's Radical Stages examines romanticism as a historical period, an extraordinary era of aesthetic experimentation and what Paul Youngquist has recently termed a 'cultural enterprise'.[55] But the tale of romanticism is not a romance nor is it always a tragedy. But the resilience of reactionary power structures in this period was formidable. Throughout the early nineteenth century, conservative policies were deeply ingrained within the period's cultural productions from theatre to newsprint and literary reviews. Writers like Shelley were aware of the government's 'proclivity for aesthetizing politics' and countered its ability to make 'states and people media in the hands of tyrant-creators'.[56] As *the* cultural institution of the period, London theatres regularly opened their doors to more than 10,000 viewers on performance nights. While Britain was at war with France, the British government exerted its control over many forms of cultural production, including the theatre and print media, and easily justified its acts of censorship and its aggressive legal prosecution of printers and publishers.[57] As Colley argues, the 'recurrent, protracted, and increasingly demanding' forces of war forged Britain, both as a nation and a global empire and, according to David Bell, resulted in the first total war.[58] The increased size of European empires was matched only by the escalation of violence, creating an urgency amongst poets, dramatists, reformers and radicals to respond to the dehumanizing atrocities committed in the name of 'glory [. . .] and gold' (*The Mask of Anarchy*, l. 65) and sanctioned by 'GOD, AND KING, AND LAW' (*The Mask of Anarchy*, l. 37). By the end of the Napoleonic wars in 1815, freedom seemed as elusive as ever for those millions who remained enslaved throughout the world. The war between France and Britain was over, but war – under its various monikers – continued by other means and in other locations. To borrow Michel de Certeau's phrase, war had become a practice of everyday life.[59] Favret describes this seemingly interminable experience in terms of its chronology and its ever-expanding geographical scope as a condition of 'chilling numbness' that accompanies 'the long winter of wartime'.[60] Inducing despair, psychological and political paralysis, this 'ubiquitous system'[61] proved all too Real, to adapt Slavoj Žižek's and Jacques Lacan's term, as an un-representable trauma.[62] Cultural performances taking place in print, on stage, in the halls of Parliament and on city streets subjected this experience to complex acts of prestidigitation. At one moment a person might glimpse the precariousness of life; in the next, the desire to sweeten one's tea might blind them to terrors of slavery associated with the sugar industry. It is not difficult to see how these cultural negotiations would produce a complex: a psychological conflict leading to abnormal behaviour and, taking the word to its etymological root, *complexus*, a plaiting or weaving together of material realities and cultural practices, which were reflected in the period's dominant ideologies. Often the subject of melodramas, the most popular theatrical form in the period, war, slavery and revolt were made to appear 'at once unremarkable and nearly imperceptible; something nonevident that could not always be made evident. Felt and unfelt, impersonal and intimate'.[63]

This vision of romanticism requires a new grasp of history and a better understanding of the cultural performances that shaped this complex weave of aesthetic and political practices. *Shelley's Radical Stages* draws attention to a performance dynamic in Shelley's dramas that constitutes an alternative way of reviewing history for the purposes of unveiling these harsh realities and instigating reform. Shelley critiqued the disturbing violence that marks the post-Waterloo era by producing a series of radical stages, which challenged the conventions of theatrical productions and reconceived traditional models of history. Each of his plays presents audiences with an alternative historical performance wherein, to quote T.S. Eliot, the past is 'altered by the present as much as the present is directed by the past'.[64] Following the recent scholarship that emphasizes the communal nature of romanticism,[65] my project examines Shelley, his dramas, the dramas of his contemporaries and those extant in the repertoire, along with the published essays of those in his circle as well as the more radical and populist work being done by Cobbett, Wooler and Hone. These writers, like Shelley, responded to the conservative and reactionary shows of sovereignty and power that influenced the performances taking place in the government-licensed patent theatres. Shelley's relatively small corpus of dramatic work thus becomes representative of a larger collective effort that extended beyond his immediate circle. Wholly aware of the centrality of the theatre and the drama as *the* means of cultural production, these writers adopt and adapt dramatic forms to counter the ubiquitous violence that defined Britain as a nation and as a global empire.

This book is divided into two parts: Theatres of National Tragedy and Epic Stages of Power and Liberation. Part One – composed of three chapters – addresses *The Cenci, Oedipus Tyrannus; or Swellfoot the Tyrant*, and the fragment, 'Charles the First'. Reflecting a pervasive cultural concern with tragedy as a dramatic form as well as a framework for portraying history, these dramas represent Shelley's active experimentation with popular national narratives. In each instance Shelley locates British tragedies within a nationalist and a historical milieu. Although this practice of aligning tragedy and history is hardly unusual – we see it, for example, in Shakespearean drama – Shelley's dramas constitute multi-faceted performances that reflect layers of sedimented meanings, revealing a Romantic hermeneutic that utilizes dramatic forms and theatrical practices to contend against the complex ideological structures that sustain domestic violence and national discord, even civil war.

The first chapter examines Shelley's most familiar drama, *The Cenci* (1819). This is the story of Beatrice Cenci, an Italian young woman who lived in the late sixteenth century. Shelley first read about her after his visit to the Cenci Palace in Rome, where he had her story copied from an archived manuscript and her portrait reproduced from a drawing then attributed to Guido Reni (1575–1642). Initially, this drama, which stages the taboo acts of incest and patricide, might appear unrelated to Britain's national tragedies in the early nineteenth century. But focusing on the repetitious play of mute performances staged within the drama and their resonance with legal proceedings against journalists for seditious and blasphemous libel and cases of treason involving the government's employment of *agents provocateurs*, I make the case that British audiences would have been quite familiar the basic lineaments of her story. The taboos that circumscribe Beatrice Cenci's role as a character acting out mute(d) performances in some ways point to the cultural debate about who could and could not speak in different theatrical spaces. Read as a reproduction of contemporary legal cases, *The Cenci* compels its audiences to question the often complicitous and unnatural relationship between the state and its citizens: specifically, when the government and its judicial system are able to secure the public's silence and thus its complicity in unspeakable and obscene (necessarily performed offstage) crimes that implicate the government in framing and provoking acts of treason against itself. Written for Covent Garden but never performed, this drama critiques the theatre's formulaic production of tragedy and resuscitates the disturbing archetypal scenes of incest and parricide from Sophocles' *Antigone*, Shakespeare's *King Lear* and Walpole's *The Mysterious Mother* as mute performances that constitute a genealogy of tragedies that have informed the British people's cultural sensibilities about who and who is not a criminal.

In Chapter 2, I turn to Shelley's *Oedipus Tyrannus; or, Swellfoot the Tyrant*, a burlesque two-Act tragedy, which Shelley composed in response to the Queen Caroline affair in 1820. The domestic disputes between Caroline and her husband, the Prince Regent, spilled over into the streets when he directed Parliament to issue a Bill of Pains and Penalties, essentially placing her on trial for adultery, in order to keep her from claiming her rights as Queen after George III's death. Although the affair is often dismissed as a ridiculous scandal full of mummery and conceit, the trial, as Steven Jones observes, produced nothing less than an 'image of civil war' that destabilized, if only for a short time, the English monarchy.[66] Shelley's juxtaposition of Sophoclean tragedy with the street theatre of protests that erupted when the Prince Regent attempted to divorce his wife prior to taking the Crown highlights the interplay between political and theatrical tragedies. In this case, the unfolding British tragedy renders Liberty, the green bag and the whole of the Caroline affair as 'plaything[s] of the imagination', a phrase

Mary Shelley used to describe *Swellfoot* and one whose meaning this performance inverts through a series of allusions to *Blackwood's Edinburgh Magazine* and its editor, John Gibson Lockhart. A familiar allegorical character and the ideological lynchpin that sustained British patriotism, Liberty, for Shelley and other reformers had been become little more than a tragic character sacrificed to the powerful interests of the monarch and the empire. In *Swellfoot* Liberty's quest to liberate both the 'learned pigs' and the 'swinish multitude' is, to quote from Hazlitt in his 'Review of *Coriolanus*', 'sport to the few and death to the many' (*SWWH*, 3. 182). Shelley thus portrays the British people's romance with Dame Liberty as no more successful than the royal marriage of the Prince Regent to Caroline of Brunswick. In both cases, all that remained was a ghostly figure that embodied a long history of personal and political deception.

Chapter 3 addresses Shelley's dramatic fragment, 'Charles the First'. Shelley intended that this play, once completed be publicly performed.[67] As such, it is very much engaged with dramatic and theatrical traditions and how the stage and its actors, like the historical tragedies about monarchs, produce a politics of memory that gives life to 'titleless nothing[s]', 'lifeless idol[s]' or 'enchanted phantom[s]'. Breaking with theatrical convention, Shelley does not write a tragedy, but he does, like William Havard (1737) and Mary Mitford (1825), write in imitation of Shakespeare. 'Charles the First' stages a period of political controversy, focusing on the royal command for a performance of *The Triumph of Peace*, a masque written by James Shirley and Inigo Jones in 1634, 15 years prior to the King's execution. Shelley's performance critiques how royal iconography and radical iconoclasm shape the politics of memory that informed historical accounts as well as the actor John Philip Kemble's famous performances, which arguably propped up the British monarchy, despite the George III's debilitating illness and the dissolute activities of the Prince Regent. Shelley's dramatic fragment unveils an alternative politics of memory based upon Godwin's *Essay on Sepulchres*: one through which audiences can resuscitate and speak to those haunting ghosts that shape history and the as yet indistinct future.

Part Two – Epic Stages of Power and Liberation – moves in terms of genre from the closed world of tragedy to the more expansive and liberating performances of Shelley's lyric dramas, *Hellas* and *Prometheus Unbound*. It also shifts away from the insular and ethnocentric interests of the nation to the cosmopolitan issues of empire and the universal concern for freedom. In *Prometheus Unbound* and *Hellas*, Shelley responds more fully to the problems set forth in the other plays, offering liberating alternatives to the debilitating cultural and political paralysis that structures the historical tragedies of Beatrice Cenci, Queen Caroline and Charles I.

My discussion of *Hellas* in Chapter 4 explores how Shelley contested the ideological strictures imposed on the East by the discourses of classicism, Orientalism and Hellenism. An adaptation of Aeschylus's *Persians*, *Hellas*, as Shelley's attempt to contravene in the cultural debate about contemporary Greece, looks back to the emergence of Western empires in Greek and Roman epics and histories. Shelley's *Hellas* reconfigures tragedy and represents a drama that is more in line with contemporary melodrama, one that integrated elaborate spectacles of sight and sound to tantalize the audience's senses. Rather than promoting the synthesis of the ideal with the real, or as in the case of many melodramas, sequestering the imperial project within the confines of scenes featuring domestic tranquillity, Shelley sustains cultural tensions in a theatrical formulation that resists resolution and advances cultural critique.

With *Prometheus Unbound* – the focus of my final chapter – Shelley once again rewrites Aeschylean tragedy, transforming the mythic act of Jupiter's subjugation of Prometheus into a heroic quest in which Prometheus and his companions, Panthea and Ione embark on an odyssey to rediscover their freedom. The drama, continuously shifting its genre to reflect different forms of critical awareness, demonstrates how liberation can be achieved only through intermittent and momentary acts of abandon. Nancy's and Agamben's insights about 'abandon' provide an avenue for my analysis of Shelley's drama and the Promethean images that were popularized in slave debates and through the translations and the accompanying illustrations of Aeschylus's work. Responding to the reactionary ideology in the original text of *Prometheus Bound*, *Prometheus Unbound* contests and revises this tragic formulation through its allusions to the anti-slavery and abolitionists tracts. While abolitionist pamphlets and poems idealized Prometheus as a heroic figure, Shelley, as he does with many of his characters, humanizes him. *Prometheus Unbound* progresses from classical tragedy in the first Act through the stages of romance, the masque and the pantomime, culminating in Act 4 with an imaginative entertainment, an erotic dance between the earth and the moon. Each shifting generic lens creates a scene where characters act with abandon: travelling from one genre and one ideological landscape to the next. So, for example, Shelley's masque portrays Jupiter's power play and his declaration of absolute power. However, with the appearance of Demogorgon, this formal display of power turns into pantomime, which stages the comic deposition of Jupiter through the stage's trap door. Shelley thus employs high and low dramatic forms, creating visible links between Aeschylean tragedy and the contemporary repertoire of pantomime to depict his characters' liberating journeys. Each subsequent act thus liberates the plot and its characters – and perhaps even the audience – from the staid cultural formulations that inhibit political and theatrical reforms. In contrast with many contemporary dramas, many of which were bound to oppressive plots and stock characters, *Prometheus Unbound* reformulates theatrical performance and opens the door to alternative reformulations of history, tragedy and myth.

Shelley's dramas challenge oppressive violence in all its forms. Most centrally they focus on the theatrical and cultural performances that render mundane the experiences of war. The structure of feeling that Raymond Williams characterizes as the lived experiences of a particular age or generation effectively materialized or realized the ideology that gave imperialism its economic, militaristic and cultural impact. The complex layering of Shelley's performances functioned both to extend the bounds of theatrical praxes and dramatic convention and to reveal its limitations. The genealogical and epic dimensions of his dramas allowed Shelley to weave together the seemingly disparate elements of history, religion, economics and politics into a coherent picture that could be mediated and restructured through his deployment and mixing of various genres and dramatic forms. Adapting ancient and contemporary theatrical praxes and deploying irony and parody as a means of calling attention to these and other contextual frameworks, Shelley represents the various 'states' of the human condition as comparable to historical stages. While the truth exists within this dynamic, I do not believe it was Shelley's purpose to delineate that truth for his audiences. What perhaps compelled him most in writing his dramas was the idea of creating a liberating hermeneutic that mirrored and challenged the British public's appetite for what Wordsworth identified as 'frantic novels, sickly and stupid German Tragedies, and deluges of idle and extravagant stories and verse', which 'the rapid communication of intelligence hourly gratifie[d]'.[68] *The Cenci, Swellfoot the Tyrant*, 'Charles the First', *Hellas* and *Prometheus Unbound* deconstruct displays of power as masquerades and encourage audiences to abandon the imaginative paralysis that fed despair and rendered the future nothing more than a mirror of the past. Shelley's dramas constitute an alternative constellation of cultural performances that invite audiences to step away from the horrors of war and to redefine their roles in terms other than those which entrap characters in tragedy or condemn them to the Manichean worldview of melodrama where characters were struck silent or blinded by fear.

Notes

1 Timothy Morton, 'Introduction', in Timothy Morton (ed.), *The Cambridge Companion to Shelley* (Cambridge, 2006), p. 11.
2 C.A. Bayly, *Imperial Meridian: The British Empire and the World 1780–1830* (London; New York, 1989), pp. 164–5.
3 David Duff's ' "The Casket of My Unknown Mind": The 1813 Volume of Minor Poems', in Alan Weinberg and Timothy Webb (eds), *The Unfamiliar Shelley* (Farnham, 2009), pp. 41–67. Stuart Curran in his *Shelley's Annus Mirabilis* (Pasadena, 1975) identifies 1819 as the pivotal year in Shelley's career.
4 See Stuart Curran's 'Shelleyan Drama', *The Romantic Theatre: An International Symposium*, ed. Richard Allen Cave (New York, 1986), pp. 61–77, pp. 76–7.
5 Some of the most influential work on performance includes that of the anthropologist, Victor Turner, *From Ritual to Theatre: The Human Seriousness of Play* (New York, 1982); Judith Butler, *Gender Trouble: Feminism and the Subversion of Identity* (New York, 1999); Joseph Roach, *Cities of the Dead; Circum-Atlantic Performance* (New York, 1996); and Richard Schechner, *Between Theater and Anthropology* (Philadelphia, 1985). Jean-Luc Nancy's conception of abandon and abandonment informs my discussion: 'Abandoned Being', in *The Birth to Presence*, trans. Brian Holmes and others (Stanford, 1998), pp. 36–7.
6 Stuart Curran, *Poetic Form and British Romanticism* (New York, 1986), p. 199.
7 J.L. Austin, *How To Do Things With Words*, eds J.O. Urmson and Marina Sbisà (Cambridge, 1962).
8 Amongst some of the examples of this turn are these works: Peter Otto, *Multiplying Worlds: Romanticism, Modernity, and the Emergence of Virtual Reality* (New York, 2011) and David Simpson, *Wordsworth, Commodification, and Social Concern: The Poetics of Modernity* (Cambridge, 2009).
9 Curran, *Shelley's Annus Mirabilis*. Following Harold Bloom and his *Shelley's Mythmaking* (New Haven, 1959), Curran defines the significance of 1819 in terms of Shelley's ability to formulate an epic vision.

10 Bertolt Brecht, 'A Short Organum for the Theatre', in Terry Eagleton and Drew Milne (eds), *Marxist Literary Theory: A Reader* (London, 1996), pp. 107–35. See also *Brecht on Theatre*, ed. and trans. John Willett (New York, 1964). As Timothy Morton reminds us in his 'Receptions' chapter in *The Cambridge Companion to Shelley*, ed. Timothy Morton (Cambridge, 2006), pp. 35–41, p. 39 and p. 35, Brecht translated Shelley's *The Mask of Anarchy* in 1938 and identified Shelley as his brother.

11 Jeffrey N. Cox, *Poetry and Politics in the Cockney School: Keats, Shelley, Hunt and their Circle* (Cambridge, 1998), p. 3.

12 James Chandler, *England in 1819: The Politics of Literary Culture and the Case of Romantic Historicism* (Chicago, 1998), p. 5.

13 Jane Moody, '"Fine Word, Legitimate!": Toward a Theatrical History of Romanticism', *Texas Studies in Literature and Language* 38.3–4 (Fall/Winter, 1996): pp. 223–44, p. 224.

14 In his article, 'The Death of Tragedy; or, the Birth of Melodrama', in Tracy C. Davis and Peter Holland (eds), *The Performing Century: Nineteenth-Century Theatre's History* (New York, 2007), pp. 161–81, Jeffrey N. Cox briefly refers to the Romantic theatre as one that offered '"virtualities" rather than staged realities' (179). See also J. Jennifer Jones, 'Absorbing Hesitation: Wordsworth and the Theory of the Panorama', *Studies in Romanticism* 45.3 (Fall 2006): pp. 357–75.

15 Jacky Bratton, *New Readings in Theatre History* (Cambridge, 2003).

16 David Simpson, *Wordsworth, Commodification, and Social Concern.*

17 David Simpson, *Wordsworth, Commodification, and Social Concern*, p. 39.

18 Some examples of this critical work include, Srinivas Aravamudan, *Tropicopolitans: Colonialism and Agency, 1688–1804* (Durham, 1999), Marilyn Butler, *Romantics, Rebels and Reactionaries: English Literature and its Background, 1760–1830* (1982; New York, 1981), Nigel Leask, *Romantic Writers and the East: Anxieties of Empire* (Cambridge, 2004), Sari Makdisi, *Romantic Imperialism: Universal Empire and the Culture of Modernity* (Cambridge, 1998), Marcus Wood, *Blind Memory: Visual Representations of Slavery in England and America, 1780–1865* (Manchester, 2000) and his *The Horrible Gift of Freedom: Atlantic Slavery and the Representation of Emancipation* (Athens, GA, 2010), and Paul Youngquist's edited collection, *Race, Romanticism, and the Atlantic* (Farnham, 2013).

19 In *Romanticism and the Gothic: Genre, Reception, and Canon Formation* (Cambridge, 2000), pp. 1–10, Michael Gamer provides an extensive discussion of the shifting critical notions of romanticism. Central to his discussion is his identification of the Romantic with the genre. David Duff offers a similar overview in his essay, 'From Revolution to Romanticism: The Historical Context to 1800', in Duncan Wu (ed.), *A Companion to Romanticism* (London, 1999), pp. 23–34.

20 'To The Editor Of The Times', *The Times* (London, 15 Feb. 1812), 3+. *The Times Digital Archive.* Web. 2 July 2012.

21 Giorgio Agamben, *State of Exception*, trans. Kevin Attell (Chicago, 2005) and *Homo Sacer: Sovereign Power and Bare Life,* trans. Daniel Heller-Roazen (Stanford, 1998).

22 James Chandler, *England in 1819*, p. 128.

23 Philip Bolton discusses the popularity of theatrical adaptations of Scott's novels and poetry in *Scott Dramatized* (New York, 1992). Richard D. Altick in *The Shows of London* (Cambridge, 1978), p. 176, writes extensively about this cultural turn to history.

24 Mary A. Favret, *War at a Distance: Romanticism and the Making of Modern Wartime* (Princeton, 2010).

25 Greg Kucich, 'Baillie, Mitford, and the "Different Track" of Women's Historical Drama on the Romantic Stage', in Lilla Maria Crisafulli and Keir Elam (eds), *Women's Romantic Theatre and Drama: History, Agency, and Performativity* (Farnham, 2010), pp. 21–41, p. 27. Jeffrey N. Cox discusses speed in the performance of melodrama in his 'The Death of Tragedy; or, the Birth of Melodrama', particularly, 169ff. Paul Virilio

explores speed at length and in different contexts in *Speed and Politics: An Essay on Dromology*, trans. Mark Polizzotti (1977; Los Angeles, 2006).

26 Altick, *The Shows of London*, p. 176.

27 Altick, *The Shows of London*, p. 176; Kucich, 'Baillie, Mitford, and the "Different Track"', p. 27.

28 Philip Bolton in *Scott Dramatized* lists more than 4,500 stage adaptations of Scott's novels and poetry throughout the United Kingdom.

29 Jeffrey N. Cox, *In the Shadows of Romance: Romantic Tragic Drama in Germany, England, and France* (Athens, OH, 1987), p. 128.

30 Julie A. Carlson, *In the Theatre of Romanticism: Coleridge, Nationalism, Women* (Cambridge, 1994), p. 182.

31 Gillian Russell, *The Theatres of War: Performance, Politics, and Society, 1793–1815* (Oxford, 1995), p. 72. See also her discussion of war and the theatre, pp. 15–21.

32 Russell, *The Theatres of War*, p. 71.

33 Russell, *The Theatres of War*, p. 94.

34 I refer to the opening lines of Karl Marx's *The Eighteenth Brumaire of Louis Bonaparte* (1963; New York, 1994), p. 15.

35 Marx, *The Eighteenth Brumaire*, p. 15.

36 In contrast, censorship of written texts occurred post-publication with the government's legal action directed towards publishers and printers rather than the writers.

37 Jane Moody, *Illegitimate Theatre in London, 1770–1840* (Cambridge, 2000), p. 10.

38 Moody, *Illegitimate Theatre*, p. 10.

39 Jeffrey N. Cox writes about this conservative turn, particularly with regard to the melodrama in 'The ideological Tack of Melodrama', in Michael Hays and Anatasia Nikolopoulou (eds), *Melodrama: The Cultural Emergence of a Genre* (1996; New York, 1999), pp. 167–89. A similar claim is made about slave drama in Dana Van Kooy and Jeffrey N. Cox's article, 'Melodramatic Slaves', *Modern Drama* 55.4 (Winter 2012): pp. 459–75. In contrast, Leigh Hunt in a series of articles (*The Examiner*, X, 5 January and 26 January 1817, *SWLH*, 2. 81–6 and 2. 94–5) insists pantomime is *the* most liberating alternative to comedy and tragedy (*SWLH*, 2. 84).

40 Roach, *Cities of the Dead*.

41 Judith Butler, 'Performative Acts and Gender Constitution: An Essay in Phenomenology and Feminist Theory', *Theatre Journal* vol. 40, no. 4 (December, 1988): pp. 519–31. Also relevant: *Antigone's Claim: Kinship Between Life and Death* (New York, 2000) and *Precarious Life: The Powers of Mourning and Violence* (London, 2004).

42 Butler, 'Performative Acts', p. 528.

43 Philip Shaw, *Waterloo and the Romantic Imagination* (New York, 2002), p. 1.

44 For discussions of Waterloo in this context, see David Simpson's *9/11: The Culture of Commemoration* (Chicago, 2006), pp. 25–8. For a more general examination of mourning and violence, see Judith Butler's *Precarious Life*.

45 See John W. Kronik, 'Editor's Note', *PMLA* 107 (1992), p. 425.

46 Joseph R. Roach, 'Slave Spectacles and Tragic Octoroons: A Cultural Genealogy of Antebellum Performance', *Theatre Survey* 33 (November 1992): pp. 167–87, p. 168.

47 Shaw, *Waterloo and the Romantic Imagination*, pp. 19–29.

48 Shaw, *Waterloo and the Romantic Imagination*, p. 22.

49 Shaw, *Waterloo and the Romantic Imagination*, p. 22, p. 21.

50 Simon Schama, 'Turner, Painting Up a Storm', in *The Power of Art* (New York, 2006), p. 266.

51 Significantly, when Turner's painting was first exhibited, the catalogue included a quote from Byron's *Childe Harold's Pilgrimage*:

> The thunder-clouds close o'er it, which when rent
> The earth is covered thick with other clay,

Which her own clay shall cover, heap'd and pent,
Rider and horse, – friend, foe, – in one red burial blent!

(*CPW*, 3. 28.249–52).

52 David Simpson in *9/11: The Culture of Commemoration* (Chicago, 2006) discusses the changing public attitudes toward war and its fallen soldiers, specifically noting how in the aftermath of Waterloo, there was more concern about erecting public memorials to all the dead. Cox reads Keats's *Ode on a Grecian Urn* in a similar light in his *Poetry and Politics*, p. 165.

53 For example, William Hone's *The Political House that Jack Built* (London, 1819), which purportedly sold 100,000 copies by year's end. See also, Steven Jones's discussion of the poem in his *Shelley's Satire: Violence, Exhortation, and Authority* (DeKalb, IL, 1994), pp. 94–123.

54 William Keach, *Arbitrary Power: Romanticism, Language, Politics* (Princeton, 2004), p. 145. This discussion of Shelley's *The Masque of Anarchy* pivots on the issue of non-violence, pp. 144–9 and it obviously shapes my own thoughts about the poem.

55 Paul Youngquist, 'Introduction', *Race, Romanticism, and the Atlantic*, p. 1.

56 Joseph Roach, 'Introduction', in Janelle G. Reinelt and Joseph R. Roach (eds), *Critical Theory and Performance* (Ann Arbor, 1992), pp. 293–8, p. 297. Roach, with these words, is specifically referring to Walter Benjamin's response to fascism, but they seemed similarly apt in this historic and aesthetic context.

57 Gamer, Michael, 'Authors in Effect: Lewis, Scott, and the Gothic Drama', *English Literary History* 66 (1999): pp. 831–61. Gamer discusses the interplay of seditious and blasphemous libel cases and theatrical performance censorship in this essay.

58 Linda Colley, *Britons: Forging the Nation 1707–1837* (New Haven, 1992), p. 322. David A. Bell, *The First Total War: Napoleon's Europe and the Birth of Warfare as We Know It* (New York, 2007).

59 Michel de Certeau, *The Practice of Everyday Life*, trans. Steven Rendall (Berkeley, 1988).

60 Mary A. Favret, *War at a Distance*, p. 29.

61 Favret, *War at a Distance*, p. 29.

62 See Slavoj Žižek's *The Sublime Object of Ideology* (New York, 1989) and his *Looking Awry: An Introduction to Jacques Lacan through Popular Culture* (Boston, 2000). W.J.T. Mitchell provides an insightful discussion of this dynamic – although he is focused on race – in *Seeing Through Race* (Boston, 2012), pp. 16–17. Mitchell defines complex by taking it to its root, *complexus.*

63 Favret, *War at a Distance*, p. 29.

64 T.S. Eliot, 'Tradition and Individual Talent', in *Selected Essays* (New York, 1950), p. 5.

65 For example, Cox's *Poetry and Politics* and Gillian Russell, *Women, Sociability and Theatre in Georgian London* (Cambridge, 2007).

66 Jones, *Shelley's Satire*, p. 125.

67 Nora Crook brings this to our attention in 'Shelley's Late Fragmentary Plays: "Charles the First" and the "Unfinished Drama"', in *The Unfamiliar Shelley*, pp. 297–311, p. 298.

68 William Wordsworth, Preface to *Lyrical Ballads* (1800) in Michael Gamer and Dahlia Porter (eds), *Lyrical Ballads, 1798 and 1800* (Peterborough, Ontario, 2008), p. 177.

Part I
Theatres of national tragedy

1 Acting out the unspeakable

Mute performances in *The Cenci*

[I]f you cannot change the explicit set of ideological rules, you can try to change the underlying set of obscene unwritten rules
—Slavoj Žižek, *Welcome to the Desert of the Real*, p. 32

In the following three chapters I examine Percy Shelley's engagement with Britain's theatres of national tragedy. The word theatre is multivalent and encompasses the physical space for dramatic performances, the quality of theatrical productions, the profession of writing, acting, directing and producing plays, and more generally refers to an area where events unfold. Shelley composed his dramas in one of the most politically volatile periods of the post-Napoleonic era. The global conflict between France and Britain was over but a cold-war politics fraught with intrigue, paranoia and the conspiracies of spies and counter-spies defined the British nation. Demobilized soldiers came home to a country on the verge of political and economic collapse. Bad harvest compounded with an economy riddled with debt, exacerbating class tensions and giving way to a voracious consumer society that devoured everything and everyone left in its wake. The French Revolution and the Napoleonic wars mutated the period's emancipatory politics and dampened its revolutionary potency. Britain's romance with liberty gave way to personal and national tragedies on a scale that is sadly less difficult for us to imagine than it was for Shelley and his contemporaries. Attempting to keep hope alive in the midst of pervasive scenes of devastation, Shelley responded with a series of plays that illustrated and contested the conventions of representation and description that determined the formal patterns of British power and revolutionary action. In this chapter I focus on how Shelley in *The Cenci* directed his attention to social and political taboos and narrative portraits of theatrical characters and historical figures as multifarious mute performances, which at different times proved oppressive and liberating.

Shelley describes *The Cenci* (1819) in his Preface as a tale of 'national and universal interest' (*SPP*, 141). While the drama's long-standing popularity, its ability to captivate 'all ranks of people' and, he writes, its 'fitness' for the theatre (*SPP*, 141–2) suggest its universal appeal, it is not immediately clear how the play can be read as a British national tragedy. Set in Italy during the Counter-Reformation of

1599, *The Cenci* portrays a succession of violent acts that quickly accumulate critical mass when murder and conspiratorial collusion give way to incestuous rape and then patricide. The fierce crosscurrents of domestic violence in this drama link treason and the taboo in the 'appalling fray'[1] of early nineteenth-century British politics. In *The Cenci* and *Laon and Cythna* Shelley incorporates the taboo act of incest to comment on the systemic injustices that remain unchecked by any moral authority or political order. *The Cenci*'s more harrowing plot illustrates the dangerous volatility of characters subject to a reactionary regime and it dramatizes the difficulty of securing justice under such conditions. Darker than his poem, the drama raises questions about who can speak and under what circumstances they will be heard. *The Cenci* addresses this issue through mute performances that act out the unspeakable: the taboos of incest and patricide, which function within the domestic sphere as mirrors for the political taboos of treason and libel. These performances define Shelley's most compelling experiment with tragedy and they embody his most poignant critique of Britain's social structure, its politics and its justice system in the post-Waterloo era. As a Gothic tragedy, *The Cenci* dramatizes how an oppressive governing body reproduces substitutes of itself by instigating the very acts of violence that validate its existence. The system institutionalizes criminal complicity, which Sophocles describes in these terms in *Antigone*: 'Each of us was the criminal but no one/Manifestly so; all denied knowledge of it'.[2] *The Cenci*'s depiction of the underlying social complicity in proscribed acts – from rape and murder to conspiracy – brings to light how cultural ideologies structure and sustain the scandalous and awful power of the state.[3]

Much of the focus in this chapter is directed toward the character, Beatrice Cenci. Like her predecessors, Cordelia in Shakespeare's *King Lear* and Sophocles' Antigone, she speaks and acts from the position of the scandalous opposition. All three characters are, to adopt a phrase from Friedrich Schlegel, 'diabolic'.[4] The Greek root *diabolos* makes clear their dual roles as accusers and slanderers. Each character calls others to account for their actions; they invoke the law, but it is turned against them. The tyranny that transforms accusations into slanders and criminalizes those seeking justice ultimately compels them to act out the unspeakable. Cordelia is married off unceremoniously to the King of France and commits treason by leading an invasion of her country. Beatrice Cenci, silenced by her father's incestuous rape, plots his death, and then forces others into a complicitous and conspiratorial silence. Antigone defies the law to bury her brother, a traitor in Creon's State. What any of these characters represents is far from clear, but as Judith Butler writes, each one commits a 'deed that *is* and *is not* her own, a trespass on the norms of kinship and gender that exposes the precarious character of those norms, their sudden and disturbing transferability, and their capacity to be reiterated in contexts and in ways that are not fully to be anticipated'.[5] Their actions confound the audience's expectations while, at the same time, alerting them to the widespread systemic injustice that pervades each society. Their precarious existence exposes the oppressive and regulative force of the silence in which the taboo is embedded. These characters and their actions link the domestic sphere and the larger domain of the State. While it is commonplace to consider incest and patricide as taboo, these characters make clear how treason and seditious and blasphemous libel fit within this rubric. Custom routinely prohibits the discussion of incest or treason. In the Romantic period, libel was associated with the radical press and with the 'criticism of the government'. Seditious and blasphemous libel cases were both identified as 'violation[s] of the social order'.[6] The two laws were virtually interchangeable and rendered as criminal almost any attempt to verbally challenge the government, the Church or religious doctrine. As with taboos, it was prohibitively difficult to speak publically about these laws, and yet, any transgression immediately actuated the full force of society and its laws against those who dared to challenge the government or question the Church.

Within *The Cenci*, Beatrice Cenci speaks out repeatedly against her father and a system that condemns her to a torturous life. She is an erudite and charismatic character, lauded by others, but very few listen to her and no one will protect her. Her position mirrors that of many radical journalists and political activists in the Romantic period. And like an *agent provocateur*, she is a compromised figure: a person identified with a radical cause but who has been turned by the government into a spy and who will entrap others in conspiracies they might never have imagined or acted upon. Beatrice's words and her actions contest normative social and political practices while raising questions about the intelligibility of the system in which people act and live. Shelley's muted performances in *The Cenci* challenge the purview of social and political taboos that disfigure familial and social relationships and reconfigure laws and other cultural narratives like tragedy in ways that undermine our conceptions of justice and fairness.

Evoking a 'revolution in the passions' and 'revolutions in opinion'

Tragedy has long been associated with the unspeakable taboo but not with the accompanying silence. Speechless characters, mute performances and dumbshow or mime might appear momentarily in a tragedy like *Hamlet*, but silence's real province is pantomime, burlesque and melodrama. During the Romantic period the question of who could speak and under what circumstances was at the heart of a volatile cultural debate between London's theatres. On one side were the patent theatres: in London, Covent Garden, Drury Lane and the Haymarket. Theatres Royal, as they were designated, held a government patent or license to perform spoken-word drama: the comedies, tragedies and farces of the repertoire. Other theatres – the so-called minor playhouses, including the Surrey, Adelphi, Coburg, and Olympic theatres – could only produce illegitimate drama: pantomimes, musical drama and burlesques.

The patent system, which dates back to the Restoration of Charles II and the distribution of patents to Thomas Killigrew and William Davenant in 1662, established a government-controlled cultural monopoly. Patents elevated the theatre to the status of a cultural institution and transformed the morally suspect domain of theatrical performance into a politically sanctioned diversion.[7] Further 'legitimizing' spoken-word drama, the Licensing Act of 1737 forced the patent theatres to submit their play scripts to the pre-performance censorship of the Lord

Chamberlain's Examiner of Plays. This legislation and the Act of 1752 established a firm cultural gap between London's many theatres – a gap that actors, managers and playwrights would repeatedly contest until 1843 when the patent monopoly was abolished. The turbulent politics of the British theatre intensified with the French Revolution, the introduction of both the German drama and the French '*mélo-drame*' to the English stage at the turn of the century[8] and the Napoleonic wars. Jane Moody's field-changing study of illegitimate theatre makes clear that the Romantic period witnessed a theatrical revolution. Legitimate, spoken-word drama slowly made way for a new type of theatrical performance that challenged conventional genre hierarchies and the dominance of the patent houses. The rivalry between theatres and between legitimacy and illegitimacy played out in a competition between spoken-word drama and mute performances. Physical movement, sensationalized emotion, costumes, dazzling stage sets, music and dancing transformed the theatre into a space of physical risk, political confrontation and visual spectacle. The power of language was subverted by a visual rhetoric of bodily movement and emotional excess.

Leigh Hunt, writer and editor for *The Examiner* and Shelley's friend to whom he dedicated *The Cenci*, was very aware of the patent theatres' 'unspoken' collusion with the government, and he and other writers for the weekly disputed it repeatedly.[9] *The Cenci* dramatizes this critique insofar as its diverse performances enable Shelley to contend against the State and its institutions, including the Theatres Royal, which when compared with the courtroom, the monarchy and Parliament, proved one of the most visible and culturally relevant provinces within the government's jurisdiction. Shelley's drama opposes the conventions for staging tragedies and the theatre's prescribed roles for women on stage while it simultaneously challenges Britain's reactionary government by acting out the taboo, what Slavoj Žižek refers to as 'the obscene unwritten rules' (epigraph) that structure and obscure social and political practices.

Although Shelley wrote *The Cenci* for performance at Covent Garden and in the tradition of Shakespeare's *King Lear* and Sophocles' *Antigone*, he also produced a drama that contested the social, political and cultural norms. The unspeakable – the taboo – permeates every aspect of the play. In a plot that turns darker with each passing scene, characters lose their voices: sometimes they are stunned into silence, sometimes they register their resistance through their silence and sometimes they acknowledge their complicity by remaining silent. The widespread ineffectiveness of verbal appeal in the drama directs its characters to communicate through mute performances. *The Cenci* thereby acts out the minor theatres' proscribed performances and, like them, it challenges the legitimacy of those in power. Employing the tactics of illegitimate drama through the legitimate framework of tragedy, Shelley exposes the underlying culture of conspiratorial intrigue that defined both Britain's social and political structure and its cultural institutions. The play dramatizes this type of collusion repeatedly. Most clearly, we see this in the Church's silence throughout most of the play. The Church refuses to charge – verbally accuse – Count Cenci for any of his brutal crimes. He pays for this silence through the purchase of costly indulgences but he also makes clear to figures like

Cardinal Camillo that this forbearance implicates the Church. In other instances, Count Cenci's threats silence those who verbalize their outrage. For example, in the famous banquet scene Cenci imposes a complicit silence on his indignant guests with the warning that his 'revenge/Is as the sealed commission of a king/ That kills, and none dare name the murderer' (I, iii, 96–8). Everyone falls silent. Beatrice stands alone as her father's sole accuser.

The Cenci's mute performances resonate with conspiratorial and taboo acts. Throughout this chapter I present a genealogy of these performances by turning to and building upon Judith Butler's discussion of incest and political action in *Antigone's Claim* and John Barrell's study of treason and regicide in *Imagining the King's Death*. Butler's critique stems from her earlier work where she identifies gender as 'a performative accomplishment compelled by social sanction and taboo'.[10] Performance, she argues, puts forward 'a compelling illusion, an object of *belief*' while it also offers 'the possibility of contesting its reified status'.[11] For Butler, it is critical to question how performances become simultaneously regulative and yet so mundane that everyone appears 'to believe and to perform in the mode of belief'.[12] Taking cues from Jacques Lacan, Hegel and Claude Lévi-Strauss, she identifies the taboo as an unspeakable act, as the site of an arbitrary power that is often extended by society in political terms far beyond its province of prohibiting incest, fratricide and patricide. The taboo becomes the means of justifying punitive acts of ostracism or violence that often go unchallenged because of the taboo's status as an unquestioned cultural absolute.

Butler's insights become more obviously relevant to my reading of *The Cenci* when set alongside Barrell's work. In his study of the 1790s treason trials, Barrell reminds us that the British government effectively invented modern treason as a figurative and an imaginative act, transforming 'misdemeanours in the early months of 1794 [. . .] to high treason at the end of the year'.[13] The Treasonable Practices Act expanded the definition of treason extensively for the purposes of 'taming, if not [. . .] silencing, radical authors and booksellers'.[14] From the government's perspective there existed no real need to invoke this Act directly in court because it would have been too contentious. The Act's inherent threat made seditious and blasphemous libel cases more likely to be prosecuted and thus a more effective means of silencing the radical opposition. For Shelley, Hunt and others writing and acting on behalf of political reform in the early nineteenth century, these were critical court cases. Hunt and his brother, John Hunt were convicted and sentenced to prison for libel in 1812–13. In 1817 the stakes were higher in the government's case against James Watson, a Spencean activist,[15] who, along with Arthur Thistlewood, Thomas Preston and John Hopper, was arrested and charged with High Treason after the Spa Fields riot (2 December 1816). The government's case collapsed, and Watson was acquitted when John Castle's role as an *agent provocateur* was exposed. But, as Hunt notes in the pages of *The Examiner*, the line between radical activists and government spies can be hair thin. No one in Hunt's opinion is innocent in these cases and the government perhaps least of all insofar as it staged the trial and the execution of radicals to elevate the public's terror.[16]

The Cenci dramatizes unspeakable acts and it represents Shelley's attempt to give a voice to those radicals like Thistlewood who, in Hunt's words,

> was a man of desperate fortune and restless character, who was nevertheless too honest, in one sense of the word, to mend them by giving up his opinions; and whose politics were exasperated by the united effects of poverty, spies, resentment, and the Manchester sabrings [Peterloo].
>
> (*SWLH*, 2. 255)

Shelley and Hunt did not condone Thistlewood's actions; however, they had no desire to demonize him either. Considering the parallels between Thistlewood and Beatrice Cenci, it is important to remember that both writers would have insisted that 'the mere punishment proves nothing, and settles nothing. Men must look deeper. They must think of the first causes, and of the circumstances that lead to such mutual violence' (*SWLH*, 2. 253). Shelley's tragedy and Hunt's articles expose the social and political injustices that remain obscured by *shows* of power: revealing how these *shows* impose a complicitous silence that perpetuates domestic violence within the family and throughout the nation.

In his 1795 essay, *Perpetual Peace*, Immanuel Kant demonstrated the dire human and material costs of 'domestic' conflicts. How are such hostilities brought to an end? And, as David Clark writes, 'What comes *after*?'[17] Kant's essay examines the destructive dynamics of war and how war becomes a metaphysical condition. For Kant, war is total,[18] and peace is combat perpetuated by other means. Examining the rhetoric of peace, Kant realized how the perpetual violence of wartime implicated everyone, contaminated everything in an entangled milieu of destruction that permeates every mundane action and every thought. The insidious nature of power and the government's violent and aggressive acts towards its people and others threatened to transform the nation and the world into a vast graveyard, extinguishing individuals and families, and, as Clark argues, the very fact of right itself.[19] This situation, William Hazlitt insisted in a slightly different context, could slay the 'mind of the nation'[20] by imposing complicitous silence upon the people while, at the same time, inciting them to recall – to remember, to recite or repeat – violence as the absolute and unquestioned condition of being.

In his Preface, Shelley compares *The Cenci* with 'the deepest and the sublimest tragic compositions, *King Lear* and the two plays in which the tale of Œdipus is told' (*SPP*, 142). Like Shakespeare's *King Lear*, this drama tells the story of a powerful family's demise, and how Count Cenci, with more malicious intent than Lear, instigates a series of atrocities that reveal the destructive and terrifying dynamics that underlie the State's absolute and arbitrary power.[21] Both plays make visible the untenable conditions that lead to civil war. Whereas Edgar sums up *King Lear* as a 'sad time' (*King Lear*, V,iii,322),[22] Shelley describes his drama in his dedication to Leigh Hunt as a 'sad reality' (*SPP*, 140). Franco Moretti claims in his discussion of *King Lear* that Edgar's speech 'is the most extraordinary – and appropriate – of anticlimaxes'.[23] 'The close of *King Lear*', he writes, 'makes clear that no one is any longer capable of giving meaning to the tragic process;

no speech is equal to it, and therein lies the tragedy'.[24] Do such statements mark a nostalgic longing for the restoration of a traditional order as Moretti argues? Or do they echo the emotional fatigue exacted by two of the most harrowing tragedies in the British literary tradition? The references to a 'sad time' and a 'sad reality' point to the general tendency to elide the tragic with tragedy. Anyone who has taught Shakespeare or any tragedy has, like Helene Foley and Jean Howard, asked the question: what do car bombings, global warming and school shootings have to do with tragedy as a literary phenomenon?[25] The point of the question is not to make light of the tragic elements of everyday life, but to mark the difference between the two terms and to consider what we expect from tragedy. Do we want to view 'the thing itself; unaccommodated man' (*King Lear*, III,iv,98–9)? Do we anticipate the 'promised end' or 'an image of that horror' (*King Lear*, V,iii,63–4)? Should the good be rewarded and the bad be punished? What if the play takes us, in Nietzsche's famous terms, beyond good and evil? In the following paragraphs I consider how tragedy functioned as a cultural performance in the Romantic period. George Steiner famously located tragedy's demise within this era of revolutionary upheaval,[26] and while few today would adhere to this view, it does raise the question of how the form changed, especially with regard to its depiction of the taboo and the tragic.

Tragedy, like all dramatic modes, has evolved since its first performances on the Greek stage. Its formal elements and the circumstances of its production change in accordance with the demands of the marketplace and those of history. In the Romantic period tragedy still adhered to Horatio's formulaic catalogue, staging 'carnal, bloody, and unnatural acts,/[. . .] accidental judgements [sic], casual slaughters,/[and] deaths put on by cunning and forced cause' (*Hamlet*, V,ii,325–7); it also, as Jeffrey N. Cox notes, responded 'to the perceived collapse of traditional providential and hierarchical order'.[27] Horatio's catalogue nonchalantly references a series of violent acts that range in severity from the taboo to the accidental. Following the tradition of classical Sophoclean tragedy, Shelley's *The Cenci* turns on the revelations of incest and patricide. More clearly than its predecessor it also portrays more mundane tragic and scandalous acts.

Throughout the eighteenth and nineteenth centuries, dramatists like Horace Walpole, Joanna Baillie and Byron integrated incest into their sensationalist plots and Gothic tragedies. Walpole's *The Mysterious Mother* (1768) was published privately.[28] Baillie's *De Monfort* (1798), staged initially at Drury Lane in 1800, only alludes to incest by depicting the affection between siblings through the lens of jealousy. Byron in *Manfred* (1817) is more explicit, and like Walpole's drama, it was not staged. Few writers were willing to challenge their audiences' assumed and professed moral principles; however, this delicacy was not universal and these works, which pivoted on the revelation of incestuous acts and desires, were successful. Each of these dramatists realized that incest functioned to elevate the sensationalism of tragedy by increasing the audience's terror and shocking their moral sensibilities.

Walpole, for example, claims in his Postscript that he 'palliate[s] the crime' as much as possible in *The Mysterious Mother* by portraying the Countess as a sympathetic character and by suppressing the incestuous scene until the last possible moment in the play.[29] As I discuss later with regard to David Hume's historical portraits in *The History of England*, Shelley and Walpole employ the narrative technique of contrasting the character's qualities and their conduct. This encourages audiences to express sympathy for disreputable characters who cannot be identified as heroic. Walpole's description of how the Countess commits incest with her son when she is filled with 'grief, disappointment, and a conflict of passions' provides readers with a set of mitigating circumstances. Further vindicating her, he adds, these circumstances 'might be supposed to have thrown her reason off its guard, and exposed her to the danger under which she fell'.[30] Walpole thus redirects the audience's attention away from incest by inviting them to consider the Countess's desperation when committing incest and her remorse after the fact.

While Walpole casts his character in a sentimental light, thereby weakening the emotional charge of the taboo in his drama, he also insists that incest produces 'great situations', 'lofty characters' and the necessary contrasts that intrigue audiences and delineate meaning:

> I found it so truly tragic in the two essential springs of terror and pity, that I could not resist the impulse of adapting it to the scene [. . .]. I saw too that it would admit of great situations, of lofty characters, and of those sudden and unforeseen strokes, which have singular effect in operating a revolution in the passions, and in interesting the spectator. It was capable of furnishing not only a contrast of characters, but a contrast of vice and virtue in the same character [. . .].[31]

Walpole confesses his fascination with the taboo and justifies his 'impulse' to incorporate incest into his plot because, as he writes, it catapults the play's action, creating powerful dramatic turns, 'which have [a] singular effect in operating a revolution in the passions'. The taboo, Walpole argues, defines tragedy and its characters. His allusion to Aristotle's *Poetics* and his references to Oedipus and Orestes emphasize the traditional association between tragedy and incest in classical drama. Despite Walpole's persistent claims that incest and parricide are 'truly horrid' and revolting subjects, he also states that the 'Greek poet would have made no scruple of exhibiting it [in] the theatre' and that 'our delicacy [is] more apt to be shocked than our good nature'.[32] Walpole treads a fine line throughout the Postscript. He claims the public reaction to the taboo is little more than a *de rigueur* performance. Then he justifies the incest subplot as a 'story founded on an event in real life' before once again insisting that his 'moral is just'.[33] Walpole's wavering stance suggests his nervous reluctance to discuss the taboo. It also invites readers to consider Walpole's authorial performance, and how he navigates the rhetoric of the taboo to reformulate tragedy for his own purposes.

The Mysterious Mother challenges bowdlerized texts like Nahum Tate's *King Lear*[34] by reclaiming and repurposing the taboo. Walpole's appropriation of the seminal, archetypal taboos in Sophoclean tragedy and his ability to recast these acts within the formal parameters of Gothic drama encouraged dramatists to challenge the theatrical conventions of eighteenth-century tragedy. Both Baillie and Shelley followed Walpole in aspiring to create a 'revolution in the passions'. Baillie in her Introduction to the *Plays on the Passions*[35] called for social and political reform and insisted that rousing human passions was 'our best and most powerful instructor' because it awakens the audience's 'sympathetick curiosity'.[36] Baillie, like Shelley, believed that drama's 'highest moral purpose' resided in 'teaching the human heart, through its sympathies and antipathies, the knowledge of itself' and that self-knowledge fostered wisdom, justice, sincerity, tolerance and kindness (*SPP*, 142).

Not surprisingly, Shelley identified incest in terms similar to those used by Walpole: as a trope and a means of 'operating a revolution in the passions'. Writing to Maria Gisborne, Shelley explains that incest is

> like many other *incorrect* things a very poetical circumstance. It may be the excess of love or of hate. It may be that defiance of every thing for the sake of another which clothes itself in the glory of highest heroism, or it may be that cynical rage which confounding the good & bad in existing opinions breaks through them for the purpose of rioting in selfishness and antipathy.
>
> (16 November, 1819; *Letters* 2. 154, emphasis in original)

Incest functions as a double-sided trope, representing two distinct experiences: love and hate. Shelley's essay, 'On Love' and his poem, *Laon and Cythna; or, The Revolution of the Golden City: A Vision of the Nineteenth Century* (1817), reissued two months later as *The Revolt of Islam*,[37] challenge the taboo's power to regulate and promote social norms. In both works Shelley identifies love as 'the sole law which should govern the moral world' (*Poetical Works*, 37). Love creates sympathy and it is 'the bond and the sanction which connects not only man with man, but every thing which exists' (*SPP*, 504). The beloved is 'a miniature as it were of our entire self, yet deprived of all that we condemn or despise [. . .]' (*SPP*, 504). Laon and Cythna, brother and sister in the unrevised poem, represent for each other this 'ideal prototype of every thing excellent or lovely' (*SPP*, 504). Each sees the other as a mirror image, purged of its flaws and imperfections and as such the locus of their affection and their erotic desire. Paul Hamilton describes Shelley's conception of love as 'erotic self-definition', a process, he argues, whereby '[w]e grow enamoured of anything upon which we can project a reflection of ourselves that enhances us [. . .]'.[38] These remarks make clearer the slippery slope Shelley creates between love and incestuous love. *Laon and Cythna* portrays incest as a non-normative form of love that facilitates the process of self-discovery and the development of self-respect. In this context incest epitomizes 'the most daring and uncommon impulses of the imagination, [and as such it has the capacity to awaken] an immense nation from their slavery and degradation to a true sense of moral dignity and freedom [. . .]' (*Poetical Works*, 32).

Writing *The Cenci* as a tragedy and with an eye to theatrical production, Shelley situates incest and parricide within a normative context; they are atrocities, horrifying acts to be alluded to but not staged. '[C]onfounding the good & bad', incest in *The Cenci* stages 'that cynical rage' of brutal violence. The 'divine beauty in life' is displaced by the 'monster for which the corruption of society for ever brings forth new food which it devours in secret' (*SPP*, 521). Both texts portray the 'revulsion occasioned by the atrocities of the demagogues, and the re-establishment of successive tyrannies [. . .]' in an attempt to encourage those reformers who had remained resolute, buoyed by their 'indefatigable hope, and [their] long-suffering and long-believing courage' (*Poetical Works*, 35).

Shelley made a concerted effort in his writing to explore how social and moral constraints proscribe and invalidate many alternative formulations of personal and social relationships. As Barbara Groseclose and Monica Brzezinski Potkay remind us, Shelley diverged from the written account of the Cenci family, the Italian 'Relazione', specifically adding the element of incest to the story.[39] Depicting the incestuous relationship between Laon and Cythna, Shelley, like Butler in *Antigone's Claim*, challenges the taboo's power to regulate social norms. He appears to realize, as did Lévi-Strauss, that incest regulates kinship structures by existing 'on the threshold of culture, in culture, and [. . .] as [. . .] culture itself'.[40] Writers like Shelley, Byron, Baillie and Walpole approach the taboo as a cultural nexus point, a liminal space where they can negotiate between an explicit set of rules – the law, for example – and the intrinsic and often contradictory socio-cultural premises upon which those rules are based.[41] The taboo in tragedy can, as Walpole suggests, produce a 'revolution in the passions' and this, Shelley believed, could lead to 'revolutions in opinion' (*SPP*, 515).

Speaking pictures and the wordless expression of tragedy

The Cenci functions both as a tragedy and as a historical drama. As such it portrays taboos – incest and parricide – as representative of a specific historic configuration of power and oppression. Part of an extensive tradition of Romantic-period historical drama, Shelley's *The Cenci* – like Joanna Baillie's *Constantine Paleologus* (1804), Byron's *Marino Faliero* (1821), Felicia Hemans's *The Siege of Valencia* (1823) and Mary Russell Mitford's *Charles the First* (1834), amongst many others written and performed at the time – responds to a growing public demand to see recent and more distant historical events staged. According to Richard Altick, 'it fell to two forms of entertainment, the theatre and the new panorama, to give pictorial realization to [contemporary and historical] events'.[42] Historical drama, as Greg Kucich notes, proved particularly compelling 'as a powerful vehicle for engaging in the turbulent politics of the revolutionary era and the post-Napoleonic years'.[43] Moreover these writers 'develop[ed] revisionary modes of historical understanding that trenchantly address[ed] the politics of the present'.[44] Changes in eighteenth-century historiography and the popularity of the panorama, heroic-scale gallery paintings and historical portraiture inspired dramatists to experiment with ways of amplifying the sentimental register of their performances.

Mark Salber Phillips makes these connections clearer with his observation that painting 'was a key word in the vocabulary of historical criticism' in that it aestheticized the reading of historical narratives and transformed 'reading into a kind of historical spectatorship'.[45] David Hume (1711–76), arguably following Giorgio Vasari (1511–74) in his *The Lives of the Artists* and Plutarch in his *Parallel Lives* (1517), wrote his multi-volume *The History of England: From the Invasion of Julius Caesar to The Revolution in 1688* as a series of character studies. Written in the mid-eighteenth century (1754–61), Hume's history offers readers narrative portraits of England's most renowned monarchs: Queen Mary, Elizabeth I, and Charles I, among others. These distinct narratives blended history with autobiography and fiction (Phillips, 203) and employed tactics usually reserved for the gallery or the theatre: producing visually striking images that included minute details and unmistakable character contrasts. As I discuss in more detail in the following chapters this merging of genres and venues fed the public's interest in paintings that depicted famous actors in scenes that were historical, literary and theatrical: for example, Sir Thomas Lawrence's portrait of the actor, John Philip Kemble as Coriolanus (Figure 3.2). This painting linked Plutarch's *History*, Shakespeare's drama, the star-power of the contemporary theatre and the crises tied to George III's illness and the Regency. It also exemplifies how the drama and the theatre functioned as a cultural nexus between history and painting, reorganizing the field of cultural representation and raising questions about how pictures speak.

Many of these historical dramas, including Shelley's *The Cenci*, can be characterized as 'narratives of enlightenment'.[46] Karen O'Brien adopts this phrase to describe eighteenth-century historical narratives that appealed to cultural sensibilities and national interests and effectively employed literary and theatrical techniques to reformulate traditional historical accounts. Hume demonstrates his awareness of literary genres and the importance of character tension in his portrait of Queen Mary, where he acknowledges that 'an enumeration of her qualities might carry the appearance of a panegyric; an account of her conduct must, in some parts, wear the aspect of severe satire and invective'.[47] Hume adopts the dramatist's technique of using genre to distinguish a character's qualities from their actions. This tactic builds sympathy between the reader and the historical figure and, in the case of Hume's investigation of the Scottish Queen's betrayal of Queen Elizabeth, it effectively exonerates her of treason.[48] Not surprisingly, Hume's historiography prompted a generation of writers to experiment with the 'affective possibilities'[49] of portraiture, which allowed them to capitalize on the popularity of historical topics while also providing new avenues for 'participating discursively in national politics'.[50]

Shelley's depiction of history in *The Cenci* unsettles audiences. The drama's ability to generate the irrational quality of a nightmare that collapses into a credible, albeit 'unimaginable' reality recreates the conspiratorial intrigue that marked this era. Throughout the play characters *act up* and *act out*. These 'diabolic', accusatory and libellous performances rely on the wordless expression of characters: a threatening look, fear and paralysing confusion. Shelley prepares his readers for this performance in his Preface, where he offers a succession of narrative portraits, speaking pictures. In the first of these he outlines the plot and introduces the two main characters:

> The story is, that an old man having spent his life in debauchery and wickedness, conceived at length an implacable hatred towards his children; which shewed itself towards one daughter under the form of an incestuous passion, aggravated by every circumstance of cruelty and violence. This daughter, after long and vain attempts to escape from what she considered a perpetual contamination both of body and mind, at length plotted with her mother-in-law and brother to murder their common tyrant. The young maiden who was urged to this tremendous deed by an impulse which overpowered its horror, was evidently a most gentle and amiable being, a creature formed to adorn and be admired, and thus violently thwarted from her nature by the necessity of circumstance and opinion.
>
> (*SPP*, 141)

Shelley's prose summarizes the story in unambiguous terms that make for the appearance of a straightforward narrative. Whereas the play's title, with its Anglicized neutral gender that defaults to the masculine character, foregrounds Count Cenci, this account splits the narrative evenly between Francesco Cenci and his daughter. Count Cenci gets first billing, but Shelley depicts him as a rather flat character. Action – particularly, violence and cruelty – and passion define him. In contrast Beatrice Cenci's image weaves together psychic conflict into a portrait of abnormal, criminal behaviour. The list of her qualities identifies her as a heroine; she is long-suffering, gentle and amiable. But the narrative turns into tragedy when she acts on 'impulse'. The 'necessity of circumstance and opinion' transforms her into tragic heroine as well as a criminal and an outcast guilty of patricide. Both characters commit unlawful actions but the complexity of Beatrice's character puts her in the spotlight.

Shelley sustains this focus on Beatrice Cenci throughout the Preface, recreating a fascinating portrait that has stimulated curiosity and awakened the reader's sympathy. In the following narrative portrait Shelley describes his copy of a painting attributed to Guido Reni (1575–1642): one purportedly taken while she was in prison awaiting trial. After centuries of scrutiny the painting has become less germane insofar as scholars no longer believe it is Reni's or that its subject is Beatrice Cenci.[51] It has nonetheless influenced assessments of Beatrice's character and played a pivotal role in appraisals of Shelley as a writer and a dramatist. Shelley introduces this painting to his readers through this vignette: 'I had a copy of Guido's picture of Beatrice which is preserved in the Colonna Palace, and my servant instantly recognized it as the portrait of *La Cenci*' (*SPP*, 141). Shelley's statement testifies to the painting's universal appeal and its status as a cultural icon. Like Walpole he emphasizes the story's historicity and more than Walpole he is able to provide his audiences with a material marker of its 'truth'. The portrait is captivating in its attention to detail and its ability to bring to life both a dead historical figure and a work of art:

There is a fixed and pale composure upon the features: she seems sad and stricken down in spirit, yet the despair thus expressed is lightened by the patience of gentleness. Her head is bound with folds of white drapery from which the yellow strings of her golden hair escape, and fall about her neck. The moulding [sic] of her face is exquisitely delicate; the eye brows are distinct and arched: the lips have that permanent meaning of imagination and sensibility which suffering has not repressed and which it seems as if death scarcely could extinguish. Her forehead is large and clear; her eyes, which we are told were remarkable for their vivacity, are swollen with weeping and lusterless, but beautifully tender and serene. In the whole mien there is a simplicity and dignity which united with her exquisite loveliness and deep sorrow are inexpressibly pathetic. Beatrice Cenci appears to have been one of those rare persons in whom energy and gentleness dwell together without destroying one another: her nature was simple and profound. The crimes and miseries in which she was an actor and a sufferer are as the mask and the mantle in which circumstances clothed her for her impersonation on the scene of the world.

(*SPP*, 144)

Reading this one might recall Paulina's cautionary speech in *The Winter's Tale* where she tells Leontes and other members of the court to '[p]repare/To see life as lively mocked as ever/Still sleep mocked death. Behold and say 'tis well' (*The Winter's Tale*, V,iii,14–19). Both scenes represent the dramatis personae as living dramatic characters posing as a work of art. Shakespeare's play depicts what happens when a work of art comes alive: the audience's stunned silence is followed by conversations relating the casuistic explanations that weave tragedies and romances into a coherent history. Shelley reanimates Reni's painting by shattering its iconic stillness and infusing Beatrice Cenci with a sensibility that humanizes her. In the terms of *The Winter's Tale*, 'she's warm' (V,iii,109). Shelley's drama and the body of critical commentary that accompanies it constitute the casuistic attempts to respond to and clarify *The Cenci*'s meaning.

The duplication and repetition of these images point to the proliferation of this image in art, in drama, in cultural iconography and in history. The wordless expression of Reni's portrait and Shelley's speaking picture function as mute performances, which like their counterparts performed in London's illegitimate theatres, create an illusion that the audience can see everything. This has led to many critical misconceptions of Shelley and his character.

Influenced by Victorian interpretations, which label Shelley and other second-generation Romantics as over-emotional, ineffectual and even incoherent,[52] Richard Holmes proposes that we read this narrative description as Shelley's self-portrait. He writes, 'From the way Shelley described this portrait, it is obvious that not only was he deeply moved by it but also that he strongly emphathized with her personality'.[53] This commentary moves from an observation about Shelley's empathy for his character to the suggestion that there exists a 'striking resemblance between the Reni portrait of La Cenci and the [Amelia] Curran portrait of Shelley' (517), produced in 1819 (Figure 1.1). Citing a number of characteristics shared by both portraits – androgyny, broad, pale forehead, arched brows – Holmes argues that Shelley identified with Beatrice Cenci, and that 'Miss Curran seems to have discovered this in a strangely unconscious way in her painting' (517). Holmes collapses the

Figure 1.1 Amelia Curran, *Percy Bysshe Shelley*, oil on canvas, 1819, 23½ × 18¾ in. (597 mm × 476 mm), © National Portrait Gallery, London

distinction between the author and his character and interprets Shelley's narrative description of his protagonist as a cross-dressing self-portrait. This interpretation opens the door to the play's gender politics but it fails to acknowledge that Shelley, Baillie, Byron and others were often engaged a radical form of gender criticism that is more in line with Judith Butler's ideas of gender and performance. While this perspective still shapes our view of Shelley and our interpretation of his writing, it discounts his political and commercial savvy as well as his intellectual acuity.[54]

In a more recent reading of these lines Julie Carlson declares, 'Shelley literally sees himself in this picture, not simply in the pathos of (fe)male suffering but in Beatrice's actual physical features'.[55] Carlson is obviously influenced by Holmes but she adjusts the angle of the mirror to demonstrate how 'Shelley's captivation by this portrait captures the double logic of male romantic reactions to women on stage'.[56] Carlson's main argument is limited by this 'double logic', which essentially views Romantic-period drama through the polarized lens of melodrama. While Carlson teaches us a lot about Coleridge's and the era's 'theatre of remorse' and how theatrical and critical discourses have collapsed tragic and melodramatic performance traditions, her reading of this passage locates what is perhaps most disturbing about the play of mirror images in Shelley's narrative portrait. Carlson reduces this play of mirrors into a set of cultural and philosophical binaries, which, she argues, can be reduced in Shelley's Preface to one 'tell-tale phrase': 'energy and gentleness dwell together'. The contrast between Beatrice Cenci as the '*beau ideal*' and the terrifying image of her as '*la bella parricide*'[57] sets up a moral dilemma from which there is no clear path to resolution. The cascading play of recognition and disavowal reveals how portraiture stills performance at a critical juncture: making it impossible to 'distinguish [Beatrice's] "true" or ideal self from the contingencies of her situation because women in theatre are defined by "circumstance" and reduced to body parts'.[58] Shelley's portrait delineates his character as a beautiful woman caught in a horrifying dilemma, who, by the way, is just an actress manipulating the situation for effect. Carlson's reading proves almost as haunting as the play; however, it also illustrates how audiences read mute performances through a process of identifying and negotiating cultural binaries.

Stuart Curran notes that the Victorian, Henry Crabb Robinson, was 'struck' by Shelley's portrait, adding that Thomas De Quincey was the 'first commentator to emphasize the image patterns central to Shelley's dramatic conception: "The true motive of the selection of such a story was – not its darkness, but [. . .] the light which fights with the darkness [. . .] the glory of that suffering face immortalized by Guido"'.[59] Once again the portrait is being read in terms of the Manichaeistic struggle between good and evil that defined nineteenth-century melodrama and which continues to inform our critical responses to Shelley and romanticism. Curran's remarks also direct us to consider how the history of Reni's portrait and studies of portraiture inform interpretations of Shelley's narrative description.

Groseclose pursues this line of inquiry in 'The Incest Motif in Shelley's *The Cenci*', attempting to discern what might have been appealing to Shelley about Reni's portrait and how Shelley reconfigured the image for his own dramatic and theatrical purposes. Examining trends in Romantic-period portraiture, she maintains that Reni's painting 'rivaled Raphael's *Transfiguration* as the most famous picture in Rome' and that its attraction stemmed from its depiction of 'mournfulness, an attribute believed to endow mere physical beauty with spiritual distinction'.[60] Shelley's drama and its altered portrayal of Beatrice Cenci increased the mass-market appeal of Reni's painting, creating a mania for reproductions, which noticeably adapted to a shifting cultural demand for renditions that emphasized sensuality more than innocence.[61]

Each of these interpretations situates Shelley's narrative portrait at the 'crossroads of historical portraiture and theatrical performance', where 'aesthetics, ideology, and commerce' overlap.[62] But the anachronism of Victorian interests and sensibilities obscures Shelley's purpose in composing the Preface and his play, namely, to stage tragedy. To see this more clearly we need simply turn to the cultural context of theatrical reviews and celebrity portraiture. Amongst the most fashionable and marketable paintings in the period were those of actors, and Sarah Siddons (1755–1831), with nearly 400 portraits in addition to sculptures and drawings and innumerable narrative reproductions of her performances in reviews, caricatures and correspondence, represents one of the most accessible pictures of tragedy in the period.[63] Performing in the title role of Thomas Southerne's *Isabella, or the Fatal Marriage* at Drury Lane in 1782, Siddons established herself as the leading actress of the day. Her performances redefined the tragic roles of Isabella, Lady Macbeth and Queen Katherine in Shakespeare's *King Henry VIII*. Baillie, amongst other dramatists created characters for her, which arguably revolutionized the role of women on stage.[64] Reynolds's painting, *Sarah Siddons as the Tragic Muse* (1794; Figure 1.2), marked the apotheosis of Siddons into the cultural icon of tragedy. This portrait fused historical and allegorical elements, blurring conventional distinctions between reality and fiction and making visible the rhetorical pictorialism that rendered acting as an aesthetic object.[65]

Early in the summer of 1816 and four years after her retirement Siddons returned to the stage at Covent Garden for three performances. In late May she played Queen Katherine in a benefit performance for Mr and Mrs Charles Kemble. A week later she performed Lady Macbeth in a command performance for Princess Charlotte, who purportedly wanted to see Siddons in her most famous role and she returned again a few weeks later in the same role. Between the second and third performances William Hazlitt wrote his 'Miss Siddons' review, printed in *The Examiner* on 16 June 1816.[66] Hazlitt's review is yet another portrait of Siddons. What marks this essay is the way in which Hazlitt's description mirrors Reynolds's painting:

> She was regarded less with admiration than with wonder, as if a being of a superior order had dropped from another sphere to awe the world with the majesty of her appearance. She raised Tragedy to the skies, or brought it down from thence. It was something above nature. We can conceive of nothing grander. She embodied to our imagination the fables of mythology, of the heroic and deified mortals of elder time. [. . .] Power was seated on her brow, passion emanated from her breast as from a shrine. She was Tragedy personified. She was the stateliest ornament of the public mind.
>
> (*SWWH*, 3. 144)

Figure 1.2 Sir Joshua Reynolds, *Sarah Siddons as the Tragic Muse* (1784), oil on canvas, 94¼ × 58⅛ in. (239.4 × 147.6 cm), The Huntington Library, Art Collections, and Botanical Gardens. 21.2

Hazlitt refrains from a physical description of Siddons and he follows Reynolds in detailing her iconic, stately demeanour. Whereas Reynolds employs the chiaroscuro lighting associated with Raphael to reinforce her regality and her transcendent divinity, Hazlitt resorts to the syntax of art history, particularly the vocabulary of the sublime: wonder, majesty, superior. Hazlitt's account is illustrative and dramatic in its re-creation of tragedy's ethos.

In this essay, Hazlitt adopts a high moral tone that resonates with tragedy and with those critics who condemned theatrical innovation as well as the theatre's illicit pleasures. But if we take a closer look at Hazlitt's review, there is a hint of illicit pleasure when he describes the 'retired and lonely student' for whom 'her face shone as if an eye had appeared from heaven' (*SWLH*, 3. 144). There is also a whiff of contentiousness in Hazlitt's description, which mimics – almost to the point of parody – the grand style of Reynolds's striking tableau. Reynolds and Hazlitt identify Siddons through her statuesque poses, for which she and her brother, John Philip Kemble were famous. Hazlitt's description of Siddons is marked by his use of the past tense and his purpose for this becomes clearer when we read this passage about the actor's mortality:

> Players should be immortal, if their own wishes or ours could make them so; but they are not. They not only die like other people, but like other people they cease to be young, and are no longer themselves, even while living. [. . .] It is the common lot: players are only *not* exempt from it.
>
> (*SWWH* 3. 144)

Hazlitt humanizes Siddons by casting her as all too human in her desire to incarnate herself as a cultural icon by drawing his audience's attention to her mortality and to the way she 'laboured' (*SWWH* 3. 145) on stage. No longer 'natural', no longer able to appear on stage as 'an apparition', she assumes 'the style of parliamentary oratory' or lapses into 'the hurried familiar tone of common life' (*SWWH*, 3. 145). Hazlitt warns her that she cannot continue to *act* in this vein and if she does, he 'shall have to criticise [sic] her performances' (*SWWH*, 3. 146). Hazlitt's narrative portrait depicts Sarah Siddons as a historic iconic embodiment of tragedy, one that need not grace London's stages any more. That aesthetic, that style of acting and tragedy itself has given way to something less iconic.

When Shelley composed his Preface he might have been reflecting on Hazlitt's review of Sarah Siddons and considering how his character and his play were remaking tragedy: a form embedded in a complex matrix of cultural memories and aesthetic praxes. Both Shelley and Hazlitt offer readers a series of character constructions – reproductions, really – which humanize the character-actor. The proliferation of images destabilizes the traditional iconography of tragedy and its characters. As a mute performance, Shelley's portrait moves deftly from a description of a character in a painting to a compassionate assessment of that character and then abruptly shifts to a judgement that compels the audience to identify Beatrice Cenci as an actor. 'The crimes and miseries in which she was an actor and a sufferer', he concludes, 'are as the mask and the mantle in which circumstances clothed her for her impersonation on the scene of the world' (*SPP*, 144). The protean fusion of character and actor dissolves, in Mita Choudhury's words, into 'a masquerade of still and moving images'.[67] Shelley's narrative portrait and Hazlitt's review unmask the cultural iconography that circulates around tragic figures. Both writers expose how tragedy and tragic characters define the culture of political repression.

Diabolic performances

Shelley's letters demonstrate his desire to add his play to a list of the era's profitable theatrical performances. In a letter to Thomas Love Peacock, he describes *The Cenci* as 'certainly not inferior to any of the modern plays that have been acted, with the exception of *Remorse* [. . .]' and that it offer[s] 'better morality than Fazio, & better poetry than Bertram [. . .]' (20 July 1819, 20 April 1818; *Letters* 2. 102, 2. 8). Adapting Shakespearean and Sophoclean tragedy to a contemporary tradition that includes Walpole's *Mysterious Mother* (1768, not performed), Coleridge's *Remorse* (Drury Lane, 1813), Henry Hart Milman's *Fazio* (Surrey, 1816; Covent Garden 1818) and Robert Maturin's *Bertram* (Drury Lane, 1816), Shelley reconfigures tragedy into what Schlegel might have referred to as a 'diabolic genre'. Schlegel coined this phrase in a brief statement, where he proposed that 'modern' tragedy had displaced pagan 'fate' with 'God the Father, [and] more often the devil himself'.[68] *The Cenci* features the diabolic, the Greek *diabolos*, the accuser and the slanderer, and it dramatizes 'The strange horror of the accuser's tale,/Baffling belief, and overpowering speech; Scarce whispered, unimaginable, wrapt/in hideous hints' (*The Cenci*, III,i,162–6). Considering *The Cenci* as a diabolic performance, it becomes more obvious how Shelley's drama engages contemporary political issues and how it also challenges contemporary stage practices.

Shelley's drama opens with a vivid depiction of a lawful society's collapse into unlawful violence and the subsequent disfigurement of fundamental social relationships. The first exchange between Cardinal Camillo and Count Cenci reveals the Church's complicity in acts of assault and murder and how the Pope, the Cardinal and presumably other principal players have enriched themselves by allowing aristocratic malfactors like Francesco Cenci the opportunity to secure their 'perilous impunity with [. . .] gold' (*The Cenci*, I,i,6). While the Church is certainly implicated in the charges being levelled against Count Cenci, the dialogue summons a Mephistophelean character and places it directly in the reader's/viewer's line of sight. When the Cardinal attempts to intimidate him, Cenci responds with a self-incriminating report of his crimes:

> As to my character for what men call crime
> Seeing I please my senses as I list,
> And vindicate that right with force or guile,
> It is a public matter, and I care not
> If I discuss it with you. [. . .]

All men delight in sensual luxury,
All men enjoy revenge; and most exult
Over the tortures they can never feel –
Flattering their secret peace with others' pain.
But I delight in nothing else. I love
The sight of agony, and the sense of joy,
When this shall be another's, and that mine.
And I have no remorse and little fear,
Which are, I think, the checks of other men.
This mood has grown upon me, until now
Any design my captious fancy makes
The picture of its wish, and it forms none
But such as men like you would start to know,
Is as my natural food and rest debarred
Until it be accomplished.

The Cenci, I,i,68–91

This narrative self-portrait condemns Count Cenci before the audience has the opportunity to fully comprehend the unfolding plot. A consummate villain, Count Cenci's character – like Iago's and Edmund's – is a mass of conflicting qualities. We see into the workings of his shuffling and insidious mind as he aligns his actions with those of 'all men' and almost simultaneously he insists that his lack of remorse and fear make it possible for him to do what others cannot. His affected transparency is nothing more than an act of dissimulation. Audiences look on as his 'captious fancy' weaves a tangled web of awful criminality that is undermined by the rhetoric of his base and mean motives. It remains unclear if Count Cenci is a criminal mastermind or a thug who deludes himself and others. The spotlight on Count Cenci condemns him and the aristocracy. His disclosures make clear how he and others manipulate the judicial offices of the Church and State with their wealth and how their defiance of canon and civil laws expose the systemic injustices that haunt the drama's characters and its audiences.

Throughout this dialogue the audience moves between condemning the Church and vilifying the Count. The first scene creates a wave of indignation that continues to swell throughout Act I and into Act II. It is obvious from his first moments on stage that Count Cenci creates and embodies the intolerable situation of inescapable violence that Kant describes in *Perpetual Peace*. His status as a wealthy and powerful patriarch shields him throughout most of the play. The Church refuses to condemn him for his brutal crimes or to secure justice for its communicants. In every confrontation, he silences his accusers by making clear his intention to harm them physically or ruin their reputation. In terms of traditional stage characters, he represents a villainous Restoration libertine driven by a lust, hatred and revenge. Only his imagination and his age, he tells Cardinal Camillo, restrict his actions: 'Invention palls: – Aye, we must all grow old – ' (*The Cenci*, I,i,99). He confesses to the audience that he craves only one thing: to commit an act '[w]hose horror might make sharp [his] appetite' (*The Cenci*, I,i,101), but he has not yet imagined it. Count Cenci contemplates his 'darker purpose' (*King Lear*, I,i,34) in conspiratorial silence. Alone after Cardinal Camillo has left him in disgust, Cenci turns imaginatively to his children. Initially he reflects on his hatred toward his older sons and the Pope's recent order to support them financially. Hoping 'some accident might cut them off' (*The Cenci*, I,i,132), he imagines their deaths as well as his wife's. He then turns his attention to his daughter and at that moment he conceives an act that even 'thou most silent air [. . .] shalt not hear' (*The Cenci*, I,i,140).

This 'darker purpose' motivates characters in Shelley's drama as it does in Shakespeare's *King Lear*. Count Cenci sees himself as the scourge of God and a vindictive force, but it neither begins nor ends with him. Even as the Church fails to reform him with its offers of 'perilous impunity' (*The Cenci*, I,i,6), a papal order arrives demanding that the Count make a financial allowance for his two sons, Rocco and Cristofano, living in Salamanca. Two scenes earlier Count Cenci had imagined their deaths, but it appears that the Pope's intervention has thwarted his designs, and that the Count – notwithstanding former dispensations – may be brought to account for his crimes. As the Banquet scene (I,iii) begins it seems possible Count Cenci may yet be reformed. He has opened his home to his friends, kinsmen, Princes and Cardinals. He concedes,

> I have too long lived like an Anchorite,
> And in my absence from your merry meetings
> An evil word is gone abroad of me;
> But I hope that you, my noble friends,
> When you have shared the entertainment here,
> And heard the pious cause for which 'tis given,
> Will think me flesh and blood as well as you;
> Sinful indeed, for Adam made all so,
> But tender-hearted, meet and pitiful.
> *The Cenci,* I,iii,1–13

The guests are enthralled by this sea-change. Even Lucretia, his wife, believes some transformation has occurred, telling Beatrice, 'Fear not, Child,/He speaks too frankly' (*The Cenci*, I,iii,35). Beatrice alone voices her fear that this is merely a ruse but she cannot conceive her father's meaning.

When the Count reveals that he has invited everyone to celebrate his sons' deaths, the guests verbally register their outrage and disbelief. One attempts to depart; another is rendered silent by his fear of the Count; a third insists it must be a joke. Once they realize the full enormity of what has occurred, they all attempt to seize him, but they are immediately checked by his threat:

> Who moves? Who speaks?
> *(turning to the Company)*
> 'tis nothing,
> Enjoy yourselves. – Beware! For my revenge
> Is as the sealed commission of a king
> That kills and none dare name the murderer.
> *The Cenci,* I,iii,95–8

Cenci's threat silences the room. Beatrice entreats the guests to provide refuge for her and her family. She confesses how she has not only 'borne much, and kissed the sacred hand/Which crushed us to the earth', but has also 'excused much, doubted; and when no doubt/Remained, have sought patience, love and tears/To soften him [. . .]' (*The Cenci*, I,ii,111–16). Beatrice has been the dutiful daughter, subjecting herself to patriarchal authority while attempting to reform her father through 'love and tears'. She realizes her complicitous role in sustaining her father's tyranny. Too often and for far too long she has been naïve and hypocritical, acting as if his crimes were committed for some mysterious yet noble purpose and justifying his cruelty as 'paternal chastisement' (*The Cenci*, I,iii,113). Beatrice's pleas excite compassion and she succeeds in cowering her father but she cannot compel her neighbours or the authorities to act.

Beatrice's plea needs to be read as both a confession and an accusation. Society has condoned and enabled her father and his crimes. The Pope's and the Church's authority, God's sovereignty and the rule of law have been compromised by this persistent complicity and wilful manipulation of the facts. Most characters in this drama assert their innocence; even Beatrice succumbs to this default position at the play's conclusion. Michael Scrivener argues that Shelley's 'naïve' characters do not see the systemic violence that allows each 'actor to maintain his privileged status without questioning his role in the system of privilege'.[69] In part this is true, very few characters fully acknowledge the horror of the situation. But no one in Shelley's drama is allowed to be naïve, with the possible exception of Bernardo. Count Cenci forces Cardinal Camillo to acknowledge his collusion in the first scene, telling him 'you give out that you have half reformed me,/Therefore strong vanity will keep you silent/If fear should not; both will, I do not doubt' (*The Cenci*, I,i,74–6). Characters attempt to maintain their innocence by compelling one another to acknowledge their 'darkest purposes' (*The Cenci*, II,ii,113). If and when these 'darkest purposes' materialize in language, it is only as barely audible and suggestive murmurs. Characters render them visible through their actions, whose palpability makes them appear inexorable.

We soon discover the limitations of Count Cenci's character. While he obviously represents the faithlessness, the treachery and the duplicity of a traitor he also functions more as a catalyst – or in the terms of this chapter, an *agent provocateur* – who instigates others to commit unspeakable acts. In many ways Count Cenci personifies what the British government feared in the 1790s when it drafted the Treasonable Practices Bill: a person who would ignore moral codes and the law and act out what they imagined. When Shelley penned his drama in 1819, the government was perhaps even more distrustful of its citizens. Throughout the war it had become well-practiced in planting spies and turning radicals to informants, many of whom were directed to sow the seeds of treason by suggesting people *imagine* insurrection or a plot that could be construed as threatening the throne or the realm. Moving into the second Act it becomes clear how Count Cenci has influenced other characters. The Prelate, Orsino, attempts to translate the Cenci family's 'darkest purposes' into his 'dear purposes' (*The Cenci*, II,ii,146) as he spurs Giacomo's desperation and pressures him to give voice to his unspeakable desire to kill his father. When questioned, Giacomo attempts to remain silent:

> Ask me not what I think; the unwilling brain
> Feigns often what it would not; and we trust
> Imagination with such phantasies
> As the tongue dares not fashion into words,
> Which have no words, their horror makes them dim
> To the mind's eye. – My heart denies itself
> To think what you demand.
> *The Cenci*, II,ii,82–8

Giacomo's thoughts terrify him; he refuses to trust his imagination, let alone verbalize his 'phantasies'. The choice he confronts – to kill or be killed – induces a psychological and physical paralysis. Incapable of sustaining the unfathomable possibility of patricide, he conjures up an image of being 'lost in a midnight wood' and daring not to ask the way from a passerby 'lest he [. . .] be [. . .] a murderer' (*The Cenci*, II,ii,95–6). Giacomo will not trust himself or anyone else at this moment. As Giacomo leaves the stage Orsino chides him to either have better thoughts or to be 'more bold' (*The Cenci*, II,ii,104).

An adept in the 'trick' of 'self-anatomy' (*The Cenci*, II,ii,108, 110), Orsino fully comprehends what Giacomo refuses to conceptualize. Iago-like in his ability to mask his guile as friendly counsel, Orsino launches into an extended monologue about 'what must be thought, and may be done' (*The Cenci*, II,ii,112) and speaks to the possibility of murdering Count Cenci:

> Now, what harm
> If Cenci should be murdered? – Yet, if murdered,
> Wherefore by me? And what if I could take
> The profit, yet omit the sin and peril
> In such an action? [. . .]
> From the unraveled hopes of Giacomo
> I must work out my own dear purposes.
> I see, as from a tower, the end of all:
> Her father dead; her brother bound to me
> By a dark secret, surer than the grave;
> Her mother scared and unexpostulating
> From the dread manner of her wish atchieved [sic]:
> And she! – Once more take courage, my faint heart;
> What dares a friendless maiden matched with thee?
> *The Cenci*, II,ii,120–24, 145–53

In contrast with Giacomo, Orsino easily contemplates murder. He does not see it as either a forbidden taboo (patricide) or as an absolute religious and legal proscription; it is simply something one might do if properly motivated. Self-anatomy has given him psychological insight and an amoral perspective that caters to his unscrupulousness. Orsino imagines he can 'see [. . .] the end of all' and that he can influence events to his 'own dear purposes'. For Orsino and Giacomo the imagination is an active and creative power. Visualizing and verbalizing a concept gives it – at least potentially – a material form. They both believe in the power of *creatio ex nihilo*, to adapt a phrase from Christian cosmology, creating something out of nothing. Count Cenci describes his criminal actions in these terms; he imagines something and then enacts it. Orsino and Giacomo's dialogue reveals the extent to which Count Cenci represents the norm. His actions and his character have been reproduced with a disturbing ease and logic.

Orsino believes he can rise above this pervasive paradigm that structures this tragedy and achieve his 'peculiar ends/By some such plot of mingled good and ill' (*The Cenci*, V,i,77–80). He does not recognize the 'Power/Which graspt and snapped the threads of [his] device/And turned it to a net of ruin' (*The Cenci*, V,i,81–3) until too late. Blind to his own complicitous role, Orsino aligns himself neither with the victims like Giacomo nor, like Camillo, with the oppressive tyranny of the patriarchy. Orsino would murder the Count if prompted, but he understands how he might manipulate the situation and each of the characters involved to get what he really wants: Beatrice. Like the Count, Orsino is not interested in love or in pursuing an equitable and fulfilling relationship with Beatrice. Although he proclaims his love for her, Orsino seeks to force her to turn against herself and to acquiesce to living as his mistress.

Giacomo, Beatrice, Lucretia and Bernardo experience the moral dilemmas they encounter as nothing more than an infinitely long act of endurance. They have suffered too much and too often; life has been reduced to mere survival, a 'bare existence' where inviolable rights are subsumed by the violent political contention that Giorgio Agamben refers to as the state of exception.[70] The fact that others might have hope or imagine an alternative does not affect these characters; they are caught – imaginatively, politically, economically and spiritually – in a ring of fire and like scorpions sting themselves through their silence and their attempts to revenge their wrongs. *The Cenci*'s tragic form eclipses all other formal interventions that might disrupt the 'strange horror of the accuser's tale' (*The Cenci*, III,i,162).

In the midst of these plots and subplots Beatrice Cenci emerges from her father's shadow and commands the stage. As a star performer, she directs other characters and enthralls her audience.[71] In her first appearance of the drama, she commands Orsino to 'Pervert not truth' and charges him, 'You are a Priest,/Speak to me not of love' (*The Cenci*, I,ii,7–8). Orsino broaches the topic of their erstwhile love, suggesting that he may 'obtain/The dispensation of the Pope to marry' (*The Cenci*, I,ii,9–10). This character is no stranger to manipulating people for his own benefit, but Beatrice, with her words and her vibrant stage presence, foils his desire and his plans to make her his mistress. He confesses to the audience that he fears '[h]er subtle mind, her awe-inspiring gaze,/Whose beams anatomize me nerve by nerve/

And lay me bare, and make me blush to see/My hidden thoughts' (*The Cenci*, I,ii,84–7). Julie Carlson points out that Beatrice plays the role of 'a commanding actress'[72] more than she does that of her character. In this she is like her father, whom Jerrold Hogle has described as 'so much a theatrical character that his very significance – and certainly his continued power over others – depends on the reaction of an auditor'.[73] All eyes are fixed on her; she captivates her audience – on and off stage – and renders them spectators.[74]

Submitting the drama to Covent Garden, Shelley hoped that Eliza O'Neill (1791–1872) would perform the part of Beatrice Cenci and that Edmund Kean (1789–1833) would play Francesco Cenci, her father. O'Neill followed Sarah Siddons as the leading female tragedian of the period. Shelley was not alone in examining the gendered dynamics of power and performance. Joanna Baillie's *De Monfort* (1798) – written for Sarah Siddons – initially encourages the audience to identify the titular character as male; however, by play's end Jane De Monfort stands in the limelight. This elision of masculine and feminine characters is one way both *De Monfort* and *The Cenci* dramatize and critique the gendered theatrical and social conventions associated with dramatizing women. Both Shelley and Baillie created a feminine character that challenged gendered cultural norms. Endowed with self-awareness, these characters subvert the conventional stereotypes that render women passive, seductive and overly emotional.[75] While men in both plays attempt to coerce Beatrice Cenci and Jane De Monfort – either through violence or flirtatious flattery – into adhering to the script of their gendered expectations – these characters simply refuse to do so. Baillie's and Shelley's women do not liberate themselves but their actions reveal how Gothic and tragic performances entrap female characters within the oppressive ideology of male fantasies.

As the play's tragic heroine, Beatrice Cenci imagines herself as a matriarch who nurses and shields the innocent and defenseless and how she will stand '[l]ike a protecting presence [. . .] [the] only refuge and defence' against her 'father's moody wrath' (*The Cenci*, II,i,89–90, 46–9). Beatrice encounters many obstacles to enacting what she imagines. When she commits patricide, she discovers that the 'dry fixed eye ball' (*The Cenci*, I,i,111) of the patriarchy[76] has finally condemned her father. But its focus will alight on Count Cenci only for a moment before directing its full 'illuminating' force toward Beatrice and her family. Managed by the Inquisition, the prosecution will be relentless in its pursuit of judgement rather than the truth. Shelley's focus on Beatrice Cenci in his Preface makes clear that he was concerned with how audiences would follow the lead of the prosecution purely out of habit.

Beatrice, like Cythna, is a revolutionary figure. She stands against her father, Lucretia informs us, a check to 'his unnatural pride' and as a 'protecting presence [whose] firm mind/has been [a] refuge and defence [. . .]' (*The Cenci*, II,i,44–9). When the Count rapes her, even he staggers in disbelief at the atrocity he has committed. He cannot speak, but like a child 'with tottering steps' flees his daughter's presence (*The Cenci*, II,i,113). Beatrice realizes that she has 'endured a wrong so great and strange,/That neither life or death can give [her] rest'

(*The Cenci*, III,i,140–42). She cannot find solace in retreat nor can she appeal to a higher authority. 'There is no vindication and no law', she tells Orsino, '[w]hich can adjudge and execute the doom/Of that through which I suffer' (*The Cenci*, III,i,135–7). When Orsino advises her either to '[a]ccuse him of the deed, and let the law/Avenge thee', or 'endure' (*The Cenci*, III,i,152–3, 167), Beatrice dismisses this counsel as 'small profit' (*The Cenci*, III,i,169). The Church and the law, she realizes, are implicated in her father's actions. She resolves on a course of revenge and retaliation. As Shelley reminds us in the Preface, revenge, like retaliation and atonement, are 'pernicious mistakes', and although it would have been better if Beatrice had realized that she cannot be 'truly dishonored by the act of another', she would not have been a 'tragic character' (*SPP*, 142) if she had done so. Foregrounding Beatrice's identity as a theatrical character underscores the shortcomings of moralistic interpretations of the play and its characters.

Reading *The Cenci* as an 'accuser's tale' (*The Cenci*, III,i,163) transforms tragedy into something more familiar, more mundane, more in line with the familiar stories printed in newspapers and lived out in courtrooms. Responses to Shelley's drama prove how difficult it was and remains to oppose the prevailing *doxa* that condemns reformers and radicals as extremists and threats to the realm. Again, this is not to condone acts of terror or criminal behaviour but rather to adjust the lens and to see the larger picture. How can tragedy reveal and contest the oppressive tyranny directed against specific classes of people throughout the modern era? For Walpole and Shelley the taboo provided one means of readjusting tragedy's cultural register. Incest represented the diabolic – the accusatory and slanderous – relationship between people and between the state and its citizens. A violation of normative kinship relations, incest marks the abandonment and the betrayal of one person by another. If we expand the domestic sphere to include the nation, how should we view the government that employs *agents provocateurs* against its own people? Who can hold the nation accountable for its actions without being accused, slandered and condemned as unpatriotic or a traitor? Shelley's tragedy undermines 'legitimate' political and theatrical practices. His drama and his characters do not adhere to the stipulations of classical, Aristotlean dramaturgy. Beatrice and her father are not marked by an individual or unique tragic flaw. Self-anatomy defines their psychology, but no one in the play is immune to this 'trick'. None of Shelley's characters are heroic in a 'conventional' sense. His remarks in *A Defence of Poetry* make clear that he idealized humanity more than the deification of its 'peculiar errors' (*SPP*, 516). Shelley attempted in his play to unveil the difference between 'the truth and beauty of friendship [and] patriotism and preserving devotion to an object' (*SPP*, 516). Shelley's characters are all too human in being subject to the tragic violence that demarcates the mundane.

In her discussion of Lévi-Strauss's *The Elementary Structures of Kinship*, Butler's question about the unquestioned authority of taboos helps explain why Shelley depicted incest and the taboo in *The Cenci* and *Laon and Cythna*: 'Do such rules [taboos] produce conformity, or do they also produce a set of social configurations that exceed and defy the rules by which they are occasioned?'[77] Butler obviously does not question the atrocity of acts like incestuous rape but she encourages her readers to consider how taboos, as sequestered mores function politically and socially to dictate unnecessarily rigid conformity in other instances of associatively proscribed behaviour. Society unquestioningly links homosexuality and other non-normative sexual acts with incest as outrageous transgressions that require a severe punitive response. Because they function as universal and unilateral proscriptions, taboos provide governing – civil and/or religious – institutions with a means of deploying them prejudicially against marginalized groups. Shelley's essay 'On Love' suggests that he was concerned with the social proscription of homosexuality; *The Cenci* indicates that he was also troubled by the taboo's universal scope and how it could be deployed to inhibit, castigate and demonize the accused: whether they were women, criminals or simply political and religious dissidents.

Shelley had long been haunted by the call for violent revolution. In an early letter to Thomas Jefferson Hogg, he discusses the problem of how the law is all too often at odds with morality, politics and an individual's conscience. Clinching his argument with Hogg, Shelley declares, 'is the *Antigone* immoral[?] Did she wrong when she acted in direct [and] noble violation of the laws of a prejudiced society' (9 May 1811; *Letters* 1. 81). Shelley considers Creon's law as little more than the imposition of a regulative public opinion. The world, he writes, 'wallows in selfishness & every hateful passion'; its laws are a 'tempest of prejudice' (*Letters*, 1. 81). Writing 10 years later to John Gisborne from Pisa while composing *Hellas*, Shelley is still contemplating Antigone:

> You are right about Antigone – how sublime a picture of a woman! And what think you of the chorus's, & especially the lyrical complaints of the godlike victim? – and the menaces of Tiresias & their rapid fulfillment? Some of us have in a prior existence been in love with an Antigone, & that makes us find no full content in any mortal tie.
>
> (22 October 1821; *Letters* 2. 364)

Antigone, the ghostly apparition that seems more 'real' than Shelley's 'mortal ties', haunts *The Cenci*. Steeped as she is in the incestuous legacies of her father, Antigone hardly represents normative principles. However, as Butler observes, *Antigone* poses important questions about kinship and state-sponsored violence. Antigone mirrors the experience of being implicated in the power structure one opposes and, as such, points to a 'political possibility that emerges when the limits to representation and representability are exposed'.[78] *The Cenci* portrays the complicity of characters in acts of injustice as well as terror and revenge. Their specious acts of 'self-anatomy'[79] implicate everyone in the most heinous of crimes, despite their verbal protestations of innocence. In contrast with much of the critical casuistry that has been invoked to interpret *The Cenci*, I believe this play dramatizes truth rather than judgement. And the truth is not that one character is more guilty than another or that people should be paralysed by the fear of what might happen or what someone might imagine. The drama's mute and silent performances stage the 'accuser's tale': the play of accusation and slander that implicates everyone – and most particularly the governing body – in acting out the unspeakable dynamics of tyranny. *The Cenci* constructs an alternative form of tragedy, which at this moment of extreme political and cultural turmoil, existed in the space between legitimate and illegitimate theatrical performances.

Notes

1 Percy Shelley, *Laon and Cythna; Or, The Revolution of the Golden City: A Vision of the Nineteenth Century* in volume 2 of *Poems* (1.xi. 218). Monica Brzezinski Potkay in 'Incest as Theology in Shelley's *The Cenci*', *Wordsworth Circle* 35.2 (Spring 2004): pp. 57–65, reminds us that Shelley revised his poem at his publisher Charles Ollier's request because he was alarmed by the government's blasphemy charges against William Hone. She also notes that Mary Shelley's journal entry for 22 December 1817 suggests that Hone's three acquittals for blasphemy 'emboldened Shelley to go ahead with [. . .] *The Cenci*' (63).

2 Sophocles, *Antigone*, in trans. and eds David Grene and Richmond Lattimore, *Sophocles I*, Second Edition (Chicago, 1991), ll. 289–90.

3 Jacques Derrida discusses this power dynamic in his essay, 'Force of Law: The "Mystical Foundation of Authority"', in Drucilla Cornell, Michel Rosenfeld, David Gray Carlson (eds), *Deconstruction and the Possibility of Justice* (New York, 2002), pp. 3–67.

4 Friedrich Schlegel, *Philosophical Fragments*, trans., Peter Firchow (Minneapolis, 1991), p. 3. Significantly, Schlegel employs the term 'diabolic' to refer to a genre rather than a character type. Later in the chapter I will address Schlegel's primary use of the term.

5 Judith Butler, *Antigone's Claim: Kinship between Life and Death* (New York, 2000), p. 24.

6 Michael Scrivener defines these terms in his 'The Discourse of Treason, Sedition, and Blasphemy in British Political Trials, 1794–1820', *Romantic Circles* (March, 1999), http://www.rc.umd.edu/print/praxis/law/cscrivener/mscrv.htm, paragraph 4 and paragraph 6. Victoria Myers situates *The Cenci* in the context of blasphemy in her article, 'Blasphemy Trials and *The Cenci*: Parody as Performative', in Alexander Dick and Angela Esterhammer (eds), *Spheres of Action: Speech and Performance in Romantic Culture* (Toronto, 2009), pp. 100–123.

7 Jane Moody provides a historical overview of the patent system in *Illegitimate Theatre in London, 1770–1840* (Cambridge, 2000), pp. 10ff. It is significant to note that Shelley in *A Defence of Poetry* identified the 'grossest degradation of the drama [with] the reign of Charles II when all forms [. . .] became hymns to the triumph of kingly power over liberty and virtue' (*SPP*, 520).

8 August von Kotzebue (1761–1819) was one of the most famous German dramatists adapted to the English stage in this period. Elizabeth Inchbald's *Lovers' Vows* (1798) and Richard Brinsley Sheridan's *Pizarro* (1799) were two of the most famous English productions of Kotzebue's dramas. Thomas Holcroft is credited with bringing the first '*mélo-drame*' to England with *A Tale of Mystery* (1802), an adaptation of Guilbert de Pixérécourt's *Coelina; our, L'Enfant du mystére*.

9 Writers for *The Examiner*, including Thomas Barnes, William Hazlitt, and Hunt mocked and criticized the patent theatres on a regular basis. Certain productions of Shakespeare attracted their scrutiny in 1813 and again, in 1816–17, when Hazlitt sought to reveal the conspiratorial relationship between political and theatrical legitimacy. Moody discusses this at length in '"Fine word, Legitimate!": Toward a Theatrical History of Romanticism', *Texas Studies in Language and Literature*, 38.3–4 (Fall/Winter 1996): pp. 223–44, in *Illegitimate Theatre*, and in 'Romantic Shakespeare', in Stanley Wells

and Sarah Stanton (eds), *The Cambridge Companion to Shakespeare on Stage* (Cambridge, 2002), pp. 37–57.

10 Judith Butler, 'Performative Acts and Gender Constitution: An Essay in Phenomenology and Feminist Theory', *Theatre Journal* 40.4 (December, 1988): pp. 519–31, p. 520.

11 Butler, 'Performative Acts and Gender Constitution', p. 520.

12 Butler, 'Performative Acts and Gender Constitution', p. 520.

13 John Barrell, *Imagining the King's Death: Figurative Treason, Fantasies of Regicide 1793–1796* (Oxford, 2000), p. 45.

14 Barrell, *Imagining the King's Death*, p. 603.

15 Spenceans or the Society of Spencean Philanthropists were followers of the reformer Thomas Spence (1750–1814) who advocated for political reform through a land redistribution plan. He published lectures, pamphlets and the periodical, *Pig's Meat: Lessons for the Swinish Multitude* (1793–95).

16 In 1820 Hunt wrote a series of articles about the Cato Street Conspiracy, which culminate in 'Execution of the Conspirators', *The Examiner*, XIII, 7 May 1820, pp. 289–91. Rpt. *SWLH* 2. 252–6. Another relevant case was that of the Pentrich Rising or Derbyshire Insurrection (9 June 1817), which involved Oliver the spy. In this instance, Jeremiah Brandreth, Isaac Ludlam and William Turner were arrested and executed for treason. Barbara Groseclose makes the connection between this event and *The Cenci* in 'The Incest Motif in Shelley's *The Cenci*', *Comparative Drama* 19.3 (Fall 1985): pp. 222–39, p. 232. She also cites Shelley's response to this event in his essay, 'An Address to the People on the Death of the Princess Charlotte' (1817). Rpt. *Prose Works*, pp. 231–9, pp. 233–4.

17 David L. Clark, 'Unsocial Kant: The Philosopher and the Un-regarded War Dead', *Wordsworth Circle* 41/1 (Winter 2010): pp. 60–68, p. 61.

18 David A. Bell offers a historical view of total war in *The First Total War: Napoleon's Europe and the birth of Warfare as We Know It* (New York, 2007). Clark suggests that Kant was the first to use the term, total war, in 'Unsocial Kant', p. 62.

19 Immanuel Kant, *Perpetual Peace: A Philosophical Sketch*, trans. H.B. Nisbet and ed. Hans Reiss, *Kant: Political Writings* (Cambridge, 1970), pp. 93–130. David L. Clark, 'Schelling's wartime: philosophy and violence in the age of Napoleon', *European Romantic Review* 19/2 (April 2008): pp. 139–48, p. 141.

20 William Hazlitt, 'The Times Newspaper: On the Connection between Toad-eaters and Tyrants', *The Examiner* X, 12 January 1817, pp. 26–8, p. 27. Reprinted in *SWWH*, 4. 136–43, p. 140.

21 William Keach offers a compelling study of arbitrary power in his *Arbitrary Power: Romanticism, Language, Politics* (Princeton, 2004). The work of Giorgio Agamben also informs my discussion throughout this book, specifically, *State of Exception*, trans. Kevin Attell (Chicago, 2005) and *Homo Sacer: Sovereign Power and Bare Life*, trans. Daniel Heller-Roazen (Stanford, CA, 1995).

22 Throughout this chapter I reference the conflated text of *King Lear* in the Norton edition, *N*: see the list of abbreviations for full bibliographical details.

23 Franco Moretti, ' "A Huge Eclipse": Tragic Form and the Deconsecration of Sovereignty', in Stephen Greenblatt (ed.), *The Power of Forms in the English Renaissance* (Norman, OK, 1982), pp. 7–40, p. 17.

24 Moretti, ' "A Huge Eclipse": Tragic Form and the Deconsecration of Sovereignty', p. 17.

25 Helene P. Foley and Jean E. Howard, 'The Urgency of Tragedy Now', *PMLA* 129/4 (October, 2014): pp. 617–33.

26 George Steiner, *The Death of Tragedy* (New Haven, 1961). Jeffrey N. Cox contests this view in his *In the Shadows of Romance: Romantic Tragic Drama in Germany, England, and France* (Athens, OH, 1987), p. 3ff.

27 Cox, *In the Shadows of Romance*, p. 16.

28 In the Larpent version of the play, this tension is played out in Act II, scene iii. It appears as scene ii in the reproduction that is reprinted in *Seven Gothic Dramas*.

29 Horace Walpole, *The Mysterious Mother* in Paul Baines and Edward Burns (eds), *Five Romantic Plays, 1768–1821* (Oxford, 2000), p. 66. Also, Jeffrey N. Cox discusses Walpole's *The Mysterious Mother* in his 'Introduction' to *Seven Gothic Dramas, 1789–1825* (Columbus, OH, 1992), pp. 12–15.

30 Walpole, *The Mysterious Mother*, p. 66.

31 Walpole, *The Mysterious Mother*, p. 65.

32 Walpole, *The Mysterious Mother*, p. 65.

33 Horace Walpole, *The Mysterious Mother*, p. 65, p. 66.

34 Nahum Tate's edition of *King Lear* was first produced in 1681; Tate cut the character of the Fool and transformed the play into a tragicomedy, marking the progressive decline of tragedy in the Restoration period. While some critics condemned this version, Thomas Betterton, David Garrick and even John Philip Kemble performed in some version of Tate's *King Lear*.

35 Baillie's critique of the drama takes place in the Introductory Discourse appended to the first volume of *A Series of Plays: in which it is attempted to delineate the stronger passions of the mind. Each passion being the subject of a Tragedy and a Comedy* (1798). This edition has been edited and reprinted as *Plays on the Passions*, ed. Peter Duthie (Peterborough, 2001), pp. 67–113.

36 Baillie, *Plays on the Passions*, p. 74, p. 72.

37 Shelley was forced to suppress the incestuous relationship at the center of *Laon and Cythna* at the insistence of his publishers; he revised and reissued the poem as *The Revolt of Islam*.

38 Paul Hamilton, 'Literature and Philosophy', in Timothy Morton (ed.), *The Cambridge Companion to Shelley* (Cambridge, 2006), pp. 166–84, p. 183.

39 Groseclose, 'The Incest Motif', p. 222. Monica Brzezinski Potkay, 'Incest as Theology in Shelley's *The Cenci*', p. 57. Groseclose argues that 'parent-child incest is a symbol of tyrannical oppression [and that] the parricide must represent the possibility of eliminating tyranny through violence' (230). Potkay, in contrast, ties incest with Shelley's critique of Christian Theology.

40 Claude Lévi-Strauss, *The Elementary Structures of Kinship*, ed. Rodney Needham, trans. James Harle Bell and John Richard Von Sturmer (Boston, 1969), p. 12.

41 Judith Butler, *Gender Trouble: Feminism and the Subversion of Identity* (New York, 1999), pp. 52–5.

42 Altick, *The Shows of London* (Cambridge, 1978), p. 176.

43 Greg Kucich, 'Baillie, Mitford, and the "Different Track" of Women's Historical Drama on the Romantic Stage', in Lilla Maria Crisafulli and Keir Elam (eds), *Women's Romantic Theatre and Drama: History, Agency, and Performativity* (Farnham, 2010), p. 27.

44 Kucich, 'Baillie, Mitford, and the "Different Track"', p. 27. See also Greg Kuchich's 'Mary Shelley: Biographer', in Esther Schor (ed.), *The Cambridge Companion to Mary Shelley* (Cambridge, 2003), pp. 226–41.

45 Mark Salber Phillips, *Society and Sentiment: Genres of Historical Writing in Britain, 1740–1820* (Princeton, 2000), p. 202.

46 Karen O'Brien, *Narratives of Enlightenment: Cosmopolitan History from Voltaire to Gibbon* (Cambridge, 1997).

47 David Hume, *The History of England from the Invasion of Julius Caesar to the Revolution in 1688* (6 vols, Indianapolis, 1983), pp. 4. 252.

48 Mark Salber Phillips, *Society and Sentiment*, pp. 67–9.

49 Salber Phillips, *Society and Sentiment*, p. 93.

50 Kucich, 'Baillie, Mitford, and the "Different Track"', p. 28.

51 Groseclose, 'The Incest Motif in Shelley's *The Cenci*', p. 223.

52 Susan Wolfson follows how writers and their critics engaged in gender politics throughout the nineteenth century in *Borderlines: The Shiftings of Gender in British Romanticism* (Stanford, 2006).

53 Richard Holmes, *Shelley: The Pursuit* (1974; New York, 1987), p. 516.
54 Timothy Webb and Alan M. Weinberg critique this Shelleyan 'myth' in their 'Introduction' to *The Unfamiliar Shelley* (eds), Timothy Webb and Alan M Weinberg (Farnham, 2009), pp. 1–18.
55 Julie A. Carlson, *In the Theatre of Romanticism: Coleridge, Nationalism, Women* (Cambridge, 1994), p. 198.
56 Carlson, *In the Theatre of Romanticism*, p. 198.
57 Carlson, *In the Theatre of Romanticism*, p. 198.
58 Carlson, *In the Theatre of Romanticism*, p. 207.
59 Stuart Curran, *Shelley's Cenci: Scorpions Ringed with Fire* (Princeton, 1970), p. 20. Curran quotes from *Henry Crabb Robinson on Books and Their Writers*, (ed.) Edith Morley (3 vols, London, 1938), 2. 651 and from *Collected Writings of Thomas De Quincey*, (ed.) David Masson (13 vols, Edinburgh and London, 1897), 11. 376.
60 Groseclose, 'The Incest Motif in Shelley's *The Cenci*', p. 223.
61 Groseclose, 'The Incest Motif in Shelley's *The Cenci*', p. 235.
62 Heather McPherson, 'Picturing Tragedy: *Mrs. Siddons as the Tragic Muse Revisited*', *Eighteenth-Century Studies* 33.3 (2000): pp. 401–30, p. 401.
63 Throughout her career, Siddons sat for Thomas Gainsborough, Thomas Lawrence, George Romney and Sir Joshua Reynolds, amongst many others.
64 Cox, 'Introduction' to *Seven Gothic Dramas*, pp. 50–57.
65 McPherson, 'Picturing Tragedy', pp. 409–12.
66 William Hazlitt, 'Miss Siddons', *The Examiner*, IX, 16 June 1816, Rpt. *SWWH*, 3. 144–6.
67 Mita Choudhury, '*The Duenna* and Her Peers at Drury Lane', in Jack E. Derochi and Daniel J. Ennis (eds), *Richard Brinsley Sheridan: The Impresario in Political and Cultural Context* (Lewisburg, 2013), pp. 83–103, p. 97.
68 Friedrich Schlegel, *Philosophical Fragments*, p. 3.
69 Michael Scrivener, *Radical Shelley: The Philosophical Anarchism and Utopian thought of Percy Bysshe Shelley* (Princeton, 1982), p. 190.
70 Agamben, *State of Exception*.
71 In his 'Introduction' to *Seven Gothic Dramas*, p. 53, Jeffrey N. Cox discusses the phenomenon of Sarah Siddons as a star actress and how Baillie in *De Montfort* countermanded and exploited her star quality in her character, Jane DeMonfort, thereby facilitating a more nuanced exploration of gender and performance. Julie Carlson identifies Beatrice Cenci in these terms in her book, *In the Theatre of Romanticism*, p. 192.
72 Carlson, *In the Theatre of Romanticism*, p. 192.
73 Jerrold E. Hogle, *Shelley's Process: Radical Transference and the Development of His Major Works* (Oxford, 1988), p. 150.
74 Carlson, *In the Theatre of Romanticism*, p. 192.
75 Cox, 'Introduction' to *Seven Gothic Dramas*, pp. 56–7.
76 In 'Mrs. Siddons Looks Back in Anger: Feminist Historiography for Eighteenth-Century British Theater', in Janelle G. Reinelt and Joseph R. Roach (eds), *Critical Theory and Performance* (Ann Arbor, 1992), pp. 276–90, Ellen Donkin discusses the power of the male gaze in Romantic-period drama.
77 Butler, *Antigone's Claim*, p. 17.
78 Butler, *Antigone's Claim*, p. 2.
79 Jeffrey N. Cox offers a compelling discussion of self-anatomy in *The Cenci* in his *In the Shadows of Romance*, pp. 139–68.

2 'Plaything[s] of the imagination'

Liberty and the green bag in Shelley's *Swellfoot the Tyrant*

The Cenci is a riveting performance, a palpable tragedy, a historical drama, a character study and a performative testament to the desperation and despair felt by many Britons in the post-Waterloo era. This tragedy presents audiences with the impossibility of escaping either history's violent trajectory or the powerful vortex of cultural casuistry. After the political debacle of Peterloo in August of 1819 and the renewed calls for reform this event instigated, there were, according to William Keach, 'many reasons to believe in early 1820 that the prevailing winds of history still favored the old monarchical order [. . .]'.[1] Frustrated with the reactionary politics that defined British national policy in this period, reformers and more radical political activists could all agree with Beatrice Cenci when she tells her stepmother, Lucretia, 'Aye, something must be done;/What, yet I know not [. . .]' (*The Cenci*, III,i,86–7). Driven to desperate measures there were those like Beatrice who would attempt 'make/The thing that I have suffered but a shadow/In the dread lightning which avenges it [. . .]' (*The Cenci*, III,i,87–9). The pernicious and internecine violence Shelley dramatizes in *The Cenci* reflected the fact that British nation was on the verge of revolution. Tinder was scattered; sparks were flying; it seemed only a matter a time before it was all set ablaze.

In this period of elevated political tension Shelley directed his attention to Liberty and the task of delineating how it functioned politically and socially as a cultural fantasy. In 1820 Shelley penned his 'Ode to Liberty' in the spring and later published it with *Prometheus Unbound*. That year he also wrote and published anonymously his two-Act drama, *Oedipus Tyrannus; or, Swellfoot the Tyrant*. The edition was quickly withdrawn when the Society for the Suppression of Vice threatened legal action and had all printed copies destroyed.[2] Written earlier in the spring, his 'Ode to Liberty' responded to the 'tempestuous play' ('Ode to Liberty', XIX.285) of revolutionary and reactionary violence occurring at the time across Britain and throughout the world. The 'Ode to Liberty' narrates a history of liberty as told by 'A voice out of the deep' ('Ode to Liberty', I.15). Opening with a scene of primal and elemental chaos, where 'power from worst producing worse,/The spirit of the beasts' kindles ('Ode to Liberty', II.23–6) wars, the poem quickly moves out of the realm of myth and into historical time, where tyranny hangs 'o'er the populous [. . .],/Like one fierce cloud over a waste of waves' ('Ode to Liberty', III.38–40). After millennia, the spirit of Liberty is finally roused awake. Marking Liberty's presence, Athens appears as

> a city such as vision
> Builds from the purple crags and silver towers
> Of battlemented cloud, as in derision
> Of kingliest masonry: the ocean–floors
> Pave it; the evening sky pavilions it;
>   Its portals are inhabited
>   By thunder–zoned winds.
>   'Ode to Liberty', V.61–7

Shelley follows convention in depicting Liberty and Athens as classical-era ideals and he frames these abstractions through the aesthetic lens of the sublime: the city's portals, for example, are inhabited by the 'thunder-zoned winds'. As Keach notes, the poem enacts the tale of cyclical violence that can be traced to a moment when the 'veil of time and space' ('Ode to Liberty', VI.86) was torn and historical consciousness came into being. Throughout the remaining stanzas this cyclic narrative repeats itself with the virulence and the regularity that marks the volcanic activity occurring at the time near Naples and in eastern Sicily.[3] With every explosive event, there is a counter movement to 'impress' ('Ode to Liberty', XIII.194), 'repress' ('Ode to Liberty', XIV.209) and 'stamp' ('Ode to Liberty', XV.211). In the final stanza everything stops, 'and the spirit of that mighty singing' suddenly withdraws 'To its abyss' ('Ode to Liberty', XIX.271–2). Liberty comes to life in the storm that creates Athens and afterwards it sinks into the abyss with the falling summer rain. In the poem's final strains the 'waves which lately paved his watery way/[now] Hiss round a drowner's head in their tempestuous play' ('Ode to Liberty', XIX.284–5). The 'Ode to Liberty' portrays the 'serpent's path' that links liberty and tyranny, 'which the light air/Erases, and the flat sands close behind!' Liberty must cut the Gordian knot of which it forms a snaky part with tyranny. However, once 'the free [. . .] stamp the impious name/ Of KING into the dust!' ('Ode to Liberty', XV.211–12), Liberty too disappears under the waves of history.

Conventional thought contrasts tyranny and liberty, but in Shelley's ode the two conditions are linked indissolubly to form a *precarious* reality that relies, in Slavoj Žižek's words, 'on a delicate balance between reality-testing and the fantasy-frame'.[4] Liberty is embedded in the imaginative framework of cultural fantasy whereas tyranny epitomizes reality. Both can be depicted as allegorical characters that represent both a state of being and an active political force. Shelley's ode portrays the relationship between liberty and tyranny as interlocking and mutually destructive, one which mirrors the narrator's vision in *Laon and Cythna* (1817) of 'An Eagle and a Serpent wreathed in fight [. . .] Feather and scale inextricably blended' (*Poems*, 2. I.viii–ix.193, 201). Standing alone while contemplating this almost mythic scene of internecine conflict, the speaker laments the failures of the

French Revolution and, given the poem's date, the despair that accompanied the Napoleonic Wars: a decades-long global conflict that gave birth to the experience of modern wartime.[5]

A 'defiantly seditious and blasphemous poem', *Laon and Cythna*, according to Michael Scrivener, responds to William Hazlitt's 'Review of *Coriolanus*'. Hazlitt composed this essay in the aftermath of the Spa Fields riots on 2 December 1816, and it was printed in *The Examiner* on 15 December 1816.[6] In this provocative essay Hazlitt famously proclaimed, 'Poetry is right royal' (*SWLH*, 3. 181) and, in the words of Scrivener, he portrayed the relationship between poetry and politics as one of 'unbridgeable dichotomies' (Scrivener, 121). These ideas posed a significant challenge for Shelley and other reformers who believed poetry could alter social consciousness and effectively change the world. While I agree with Scrivener that Shelley might have been responding to this review when he wrote *Laon and Cythna*, there exists even more probability that Hazlitt's essay prompted and influenced Shelley while writing *Swellfoot the Tyrant*. The drama seems quite clearly to investigate and respond to Hazlitt's statement about how genre structures both the historical imagination and the possibilities for political reform in this fraught era of national upheaval:

> The history of mankind is a romance, a mask, a tragedy constructed upon the principles of *poetical justice*; it is a noble or royal hunt, in which what is sport to the few is death to the many, and in which the spectators halloo and encourage the strong to set upon the weak, and cry havoc in the chase, though they do not share in the spoil. We may depend upon it, that what men delight to read in books, they will put in practice in reality.
>
> (*SWWH*, 3.182)

To my knowledge no one has made this connection between *Swellfoot* and Hazlitt's review. Mary Shelley's note, which accompanied her inclusion of *Swellfoot* in the second edition of Shelley's collected works, has proven almost definitive. Here she describes how Shelley was inspired to write *Swellfoot* after reading aloud his 'Ode to Liberty' above the market square at the Baths of San Giuliano. His reading was apparently accompanied by the sounds of squealing pigs being brought to the market. At some point Shelley compared the grunting pigs to the chorus of frogs in Aristophanes' drama and 'one ludicrous association suggesting another [. . .], *Swellfoot* was begun' (*Poetical Works*, 410). Scholars have been generally skeptical about *Swellfoot* because of its obvious political significance and because it appears stylistically inconsistent with works like *Prometheus Unbound* and 'Mont Blanc'. If they acknowledge it at all, they quote Mary Shelley and refer to it dismissively as 'a mere plaything of the imagination' (*Poetical Works*, 410).

Timothy Morton interprets Mary Shelley's comment as a distraction for hostile readers.[7] The enmity the play encountered when first published anonymously suggests this is probably the case. However Mary Shelley's statement also resonates with a spoof written by John Gibson Lockhart, *Peter's Letters to his Kinfolk* in 1819, which situates the drama within a specific literary milieu and suggests there might be more to Mary Shelley's remark than Morton indicates. Morton's evolving commentary and articles written by Steven Jones, Samuel Gladden and others have opened the drama to rewarding discussions in recent years.[8] Most of this work has engaged questions about the relationship between cultural and political reform, sexual transgression and the issues of consumption and consumerism that are interwoven throughout the play. While Shelley adopts the satiric framework more often associated with the radical works of William Cobbett, T.J. Wooler and William Hone, he also writes *Swellfoot* with a knowing nod to the more reform-minded and intellectually and politically savvy readers of the period's most important journals and weeklies: the *Edinburgh Review*, *The Examiner* and the *Morning Chronicle*. *Swellfoot* stages the Queen Caroline affair, a royal scandal that captivated the nation in 1820, collapsing the event's tragic and romantic elements into a rollicking farce. The drama features a chorus of swine and caricatures of the King, the Queen, Lord Liverpool and Lord Castlereagh: Swellfoot, Iona Taurina, Purganax and Mammon. But one of the most problematic characters in the drama is Liberty, ostensibly Iona Taurina's doppelgänger. As the capital L suggests, she functions as an allegorical figure that allusively inhabits liberty's textual and historical legacies: promising freedom to radicals, change to reformers and a traditional and orderly stasis to conservatives. Throughout the drama Shelley examines a cultural and literary archive that had produced Liberty as a rhetorical figure and a liberation fantasy that defined the English as a people and a nation. Taking cues from Edmund Burke and Samuel Taylor Coleridge, amongst others contributing to the pamphlet wars of the 1790s and the culture wars of the early nineteenth century, Shelley casts Liberty as a wavering spectral appearance that never manifests fully as a material body. For Shelley the British people's romance with Liberty had no more substance than the marriage between the Prince Regent and Caroline of Brunswick. Like *Swellfoot* both romances were spoofs populated by caricatures. Liberty's tragic cultural framework – its 'circumvolving destiny' – perpetually deferred real political freedom.

National tragedies and public spectacles

The post-war years brought little in the way of political or economic relief to the British people. The period was marked by food shortages, economic inflation and other domestic crises. Within the halls of Parliament, radical MPs were increasingly isolated; fractions within the Whig party provided few opportunities for meaningful alliances and the whole project of reform seemed arrested by a pervasive pessimism.[9] Outside Parliament radical activity increased in the cities and especially in the provinces. There were demonstrations at Spa Fields (15 November and 2 December, 1816), Smithfield (21 July 1819), St Peter's field in Manchester (16 August, 1819) and throughout the duration of the Queen Caroline affair (June, 1820–July, 1821). In some cases these meetings devolved into violence: the riots at Spa Fields in December, the Peterloo Massacre in 1819 and the Cato Street Conspiracy (February–May, 1820). At Smithfield, Henry 'Orator' Hunt presided over a reform meeting, attracting a crowd of at least 10,000 and perhaps up to 80,000 people. Caricatures of this and other events limn the underlying economic and class tensions in satiric images that play upon the Hunt/hunt parallel and by representing bodies – human, animal and political – as consumable social constructions.[10] One caricature of Smithfield depicts 'Orator' Hunt as the Shakespearean character Bottom in *A Midsummer Night's Dream*. Portrayed with an ass's head, he speaks to an assembly of cattle, horses, sheep and pigs (Figure 2.1).[11] These satires deploy a Bakhtinian heteroglossy of 'high' and 'low' elements: ranging from Shakespearean performances and Burke's 'swinish multitude'[12] to the popular revelry of seasonal festivals and the marketplace where the occasional stock-auction would add a measure of chaos.

Reflecting the government's apprehension about these public demonstrations, Lord Sidmouth, the Home Secretary and a former Prime Minister, overreacted to Smithfield. He issued a letter instructing the country's lords-lieutenants to return to their counties and he placed the yeomanry on alert. The order for the Manchester Yeomanry to attack peaceful demonstrators at St Peter's Field in Manchester – resulting in Peterloo – demonstrates the government's anxiety and its paranoia about any public gathering. Parliament refused to launch a meaningful official investigation of the Peterloo Massacre and instead passed the Six Acts in December 1819. These laws curtailed the power of the press by increasing and

Figure 2.1 C. Williams, 'The Smithfield Parliament', 35 × 25 cm, etching, 1819, London Metropolitan Archives

extending the taxes on newspapers to include inexpensive 'penny' publications and they strengthened the laws against blasphemous and seditious libel. Radicals became increasingly desperate with every failure of the reform movement. Eventually, George Edwards, a radical turned government spy, who among others had infiltrated a group of radical Spenceans led by Arthur Thistlewood, prompted this group to conspire to overthrow the government in what has become known as the Cato Street Conspiracy.[13] Thistlewood had been implicated in the Spa Fields riots and released. Once apprehended, tried and convicted for the conspiracy at Cato Street, he along with co-conspirators William Davidson, James Ings, Richard Tidd and John Brunt were executed for treason. Due to public outrage about the government's use of *agents provocateurs*, Lord Sidmouth resisted calling Edwards to testify. Instead other conspirators were coerced into providing evidence. Leigh Hunt's lead article in *The Examiner* on 30 April 1820 details the 'bloody catastrophe' of this 'last act of the Cato-street tragedy'.[14]

From Shelley's perspective the government throughout this period acted as an *agent provocateur*, executing its 'Golden and sanguine laws which tempt and slay' ('England in 1819', l. 10). Moreover, in addition to the violence at Peterloo, there was still the problem of an 'old, mad, blind, despised and dying King' ('England in 1819', l. 1). The establishment of the Regency in 1811 had been designed to address the King's mental illness, but the Prince proved to be as ineffective as the incapacitated King. In his sonnet 'England in 1819', Shelley describes 'Princes' as 'the dregs of their dull race, [who] neither see nor feel nor know' (ll. 1–3). If the British people had heard the oracle in Shelley's 'Ode to Liberty' (XV, l. 216), they had yet to stamp 'the impious name/OF KING into the dust' ('Ode to Liberty', XV. 211–2). Freedom and Liberty functioned as little more than fleeting specters of hope amongst the 'trampled multitude[s]' (*The Mask of Anarchy*, l. 222).

With the death of George III on 29 January 1820, the scene shifted and the tragic events at Smithfield and Manchester gave way to the tawdry public spectacle of the Queen Caroline affair. Queen Caroline's unexpected return from the Continent in June of 1820, a few short weeks after the conviction of the Cato Street conspirators, sparked innumerable street scenes. People took to the streets throughout Britain in support of Queen Caroline – burning effigies, lighting fires and ringing bells – creating a street theatre that parodied courtly pomp, the judicial system and government ministers. Pamphleteers and radical journalists had traded on the theatre's popularity and its status as a central cultural institution: publishing caricatures like that of 'Orator' Hunt at Smithfield and Wooler's State Theatricals in *The Black Dwarf*.[15] Wooler proved adept at employing dramatic allusions and theatrical machinery to depict ministerial and monarchical activities as public theatre. His State Theatrical series played upon the slippery slope between truth and representation and acknowledged – as did Hone in his satires and Hazlitt in his essays – the vital role played by theatre in unveiling the state's penchant for masking the truth. These allusive matrices of satirical caricature portrayed politics as a mode of performance. In her discussion of Regency radicalism Moody points out that 'theatre was more than a convenient metaphor through which to imagine the illusions and deceits of Regency Government' because London's theatres had become 'identified as the cultural synecdoche of a corrupt political state'.[16] Satires crisscrossed political boundaries, amusing the reading public and slipping under the widely cast nets of censorship.

For example, J.L. Marks's satirical print of 1820 (Figure 2.2) depicts a well known scene from Shakespeare's *King Henry VIII* in which the King attempts to divorce his wife, Catherine of Aragon. In Marks's satire George IV substitutes for Henry VIII sitting on the dais under the canopy. Mirroring the British people's prejudice against Catholicism, the cardinals represent the government ministers, one of whom has his foot placed on Magna Charta while a barrister watches the proceedings with a Green Bag close to hand. The Green Bag, a central motif in Shelley's drama, was a device used by barristers to conceal the government's undisclosed 'evidence' in 'sensitive' cases of treason and seditious and blasphemous libel. Queen Caroline takes the part of Catherine of Aragon who was also forced into divorce proceedings and stands next to Alderman Wood, her counsel. The satire plays on obvious historical parallels between Henry VIII and the soon to be crowned George IV, situating both events within the popular context of Shakespearean drama. The satire also responds to and subverts George Henry Harlow's 1817 painting of the same scene (Figure 2.2).[17]

Harlow's painting reproduces this scene from the well-attended performances of the Kemble family at Covent Garden between 1806 and 1812. Set prior to

Figure 2.2 J.L. Marks, *King Henry VIII, Act II, Scene iv*, 34 × 24 cm, etching, c.1820, London Metropolitan Archives

Figure 2.3 George Henry Harlow, *The Court for the Trial of Queen Katherine*, 31 × 40 in., oil on canvas, 1817, Royal Shakespeare Company Collection in Stratford-upon-Avon

the era when Edmund Kean debuted as Shylock at Drury Lane in 1814, the oil painting, initially exhibited at the Royal Academy, celebrates the Kembles as the first family of London theatre. The younger brothers, Stephen and Charles Kemble, play the roles of King Henry and Thomas Cromwell. John Philip Kemble is featured playing the part of Cardinal Wolsey. Sarah Siddons, their sister, plays Queen Katherine who denounces Wolsey as her 'most malicious foe' and refuses to accept him as her judge (*All is True* or *Henry VIII*, II, iv, 81). Harlow's depiction memorializes the classical acting style of the Kemble family and the stately stage décor that arguably stabilized the troubled monarchy with its mad king and its profligate prince. Lawrence portrays Shakespearean drama and the Kemble family's roles in these performances as 'right royal' (*SWWH*, 3. 180–183), a phrase Hazlitt famously deployed in his 'Review of *Coriolanus*'.

Marks's satire capitalizes upon the historical and cultural parallels exhibited throughout the Queen Caroline affair and it subverts Lawrence's idealized portrait that collapses the distinction between the theatre's first family and the Royal family. Like Wooler's State Theatricals, this caricature inverts Lawrence's positive elision between the Kemble family and the monarchy and instead identifies those in power as actors performing in a play. Political parodies like those of

Marks and Wooler relied upon the audience's ability to recognize Shakespearean scenes and other theatrical allusions. When Kean took the stage at Drury Lane he revolutionized the theatre by subverting Kemble's statuesque performances and introducing an alternative range of emotions and acrobatic movements more in line with melodrama.[18] As the interplay between Lawrence's portrait and Marks's visual satire illustrates, the 'drama' of the Caroline affair was about more than the royal divorce proceedings. The affair encompassed a debate about the form and purpose of Britain's national culture: should it sustain the obvious charade of the royal family or critique it as a masquerade of power?

The 'drama' of the Caroline affair had been in production since 1795 when Caroline of Brunswick married the Prince. A marriage of financial and political expediency, the alliance provided the future George IV with much needed capital to pay his debts, and considering his sexual license and his previous secret marriage to the Catholic Maria Fitzherbert in 1785, it gave Parliament and the country some assurance regarding the possibility of a legitimate heir. However the two royals were ill-suited, and after Princess Caroline gave birth to their daughter, Charlotte, the couple separated. In the intervening years the Prince forbade contact between his daughter and his wife and initiated several investigations of his wife's fidelity. After 1814 Caroline left the country and lived abroad for six years until she returned to Dover to claim her position as queen consort. The Prince initiated divorce proceedings immediately and demanded that a Bill of Pains and Penalties be brought forward in the House of Lords. Considering the underlying charge of high treason, the action implicitly deprived her of her rights as his wife and as a citizen. When news of these proceedings spread, the outraged public took to the streets. Parliament withdrew the bill in November and effectively acquitted the Queen. After a celebratory procession in late November and public marches throughout January, it became apparent that neither she nor anyone within the reform movement would play a role in the new government. When Caroline accepted an annual pension of £50,000 – perhaps feeling there was no alternative but also taking an action she had resolved publicly to reject almost a year earlier – the populace, feeling betrayed, turned against her. By Coronation Day (July 1821), Londoners were cheering their new King, George IV. The Queen's attempt to disrupt the coronation ceremony by demanding entrance into Westminster Abbey failed when 20 prizefighters dressed as royal pages blocked her entry. The curtain dropped on Queen Caroline with the crowd hissing and mocking her. A short afterpiece followed when the Queen died within the month. Fearing more street demonstrations and possibly a violent outbreak, the government decided that she should be buried in Brunswick and that there would be no public ceremony recognizing her status as Queen. Moreover, the ministry refused to allow the Queen's funeral procession to enter London. For one final show, the populace rallied around *their* Queen and marched in the streets of Bristol, Manchester and Leeds, voicing their displeasure with the ministry's decision and their contempt for George IV. During the funeral procession, a crowd at Hyde Park Corner broke through the cordon of troops. Although the troops fired upon the public and two men were killed and several were wounded, the public succeeded in redirecting the procession through London. The city's residents paid tribute to Caroline for the last time.[19] This public defiance of the government's power to control the Queen's body marked the end of this long-running production.

The Caroline affair may have been a vastly entertaining spectacle, especially for those like Shelley living abroad, but it also proved a lightning rod for the reform movement: bringing together disparate groups with the shared interest of the Queen's case against the government. Reformers and government officials perceived the Caroline affair as more than the culmination of a domestic dispute between the Prince and his estranged wife. The affair raised the haunting spectre of civil war and brought the government to the point of crisis and it provided radicals with a 'legitimate' figure and a public face for their oppositional stance. As Steven Jones points out the

> image of civil war, with all its associations in English history, or of an anarchic frenzy around a disputed succession, lurked behind these debates and must have fed back into a series of popular demonstrations in support of the Queen after her return in the summer of 1820.
>
> (*Shelley's Satire*, 125–6)

Leigh Hunt, writing for *The Examiner*, wrote about the ongoing affair in terms that revealed the failures of England's judicial system. Too many people had suffered humiliation and injustice and like the Queen their lives had been subject to secret committees, the ensnaring Green Bag and the testimony of spies and informers. All of these people had been denied the right to a fair trial and their protests had been silenced. Her landmark case – though not so extraordinary from Hunt's perspective – put the judiciary and government ministers on public trial:

> [T]he means taken by the agents of the power Party – the Green Bag, the Secret Committee, &c. – are identical means which were lately used by the Oligarchy to deprive the people of their dearest rights. The People therefore are doing no more than protecting their own liberties when they oppose themselves to an attack of this illegal and unjust nature against the QUEEN; and they would be destitute of all love of justice, humanity, and decency, if they patiently suffered Ministers to trample on the remaining safeguards of *their* liberties [. . .]. [T]he English People must now either force Ministers to retract their present outrageous measures, or that right must again give way to might, and an enormous item be added to the swelled and rankling catalogue of our Political Wrongs.
>
> (*The Examiner*, XIII, 9 July 1820, p. 433)

Hunt considers the crisis as one in a series of national disturbances – the Spa Fields riots, the Pentridge Rising in Derbyshire led by Jeremiah Brandreth (June 1817), the Peterloo Massacre and the Cato Street Conspiracy. Caroline's behaviour may have been less than virtuous, but she was still *the* Queen, and as such, her title, her gender and her grievances became an appropriate means of challenging the oppressive practices that circumscribed and impeded political reform.[20] Hunt depicts the Queen's trial as too familiar. The hypocrisy, the lying and the cold-blooded plotting to entrap the Queen, Hunt argues, only 'add[s] to that mass of discontent and disgust [which gives] men further cause at once to fear and despise the system whose long corruptions compel it to encourage such disgraceful sacrifices of blood' (*The Examiner*, XIII, 30 April 1820, p. 273).

William Cobbett, one of the Queen's most outspoken supporters, took a different approach than Hunt and cast the affair as a Burkean romance in 'A Letter to Mr. Alderman Wood: Containing the Proverbs of "Absolute Wisdom;" or, A History of the Advice given to the Queen in the several periods of her long and unparalleled Prosecution'. Printed in *Cobbett's Weekly Political Register* on 17 June 1820, Cobbett adapts Edmund Burke's famous scene of the quintessential political romance in *Reflections on the Revolution in France* (1790):

> If thousands of swords ought to have flown from their scabbards to avenge the insult offered to the Queen of France, what ought to be the feelings of the people of England, at the insult offered to their own queen at St. Omers? However the age of chivalry is not wholly gone. The spirit of that age is still left in England, but it appears to live only in the breasts of the people; that people, which have been charged with a want of loyalty, with a want of reverence for the Throne, with a want of attachement [sic] to Kings and Queens; and who now are charged with factiousness and sedition, because they set up an unanimous shout of 'GOD SAVE THE QUEEN!'[21]

In his *Reflections on the Revolution in France*, Burke looks back 'sixteen or seventeen years' to contrast the misfortunes of Marie Antoinette subject to a revolutionary regime with his more 'delightful vision' of her former glory. The French Revolution marks the death of chivalry as a 'heroic enterprize', but Burke enacts it in this narrative performance.[22] Unlike Thomas Paine's rebuttal of Burke two decades earlier, Cobbett does not disdain romance as a 'theatrical representation, where facts are manufactured for the sake of show and accommodated to produce, through the weakness of sympathy, a weeping effect'.[23] He embraces Burke's elegiac celebration of chivalry as a popular ideological spectacle and celebrates those heroic and faithful knights who will protect the Queen's honour. His national romance features the proverbial scene of the English people fighting against injustice. Rather than following Paine and denying the power of Burke's spectacle, Cobbett recasts Burke's romance, replacing Marie Antoinette with Queen Caroline and the 'chivalric' gentry with the 'chivalric' common Englishman. Cobbett's letter reveals how adaptable romance could be and how quickly its political charge could shift from a conservative to a radical position and vice versa.

National romance

Of all the ways of describing either the royal marriage or the Caroline affair, none seems more inconceivable than that of romance. The royal family's scandal was devoid of heroic figures, scenes of personal or cultural transformation and an idyllic or pastoral landscape. And yet, the affair, like romance, was replete with a whole series of personal and political deceptions that were compounded by errors of judgement and innumerable temptations of a sexual and political nature.[24] Clearly engaging the romance tradition, Cobbett stages a powerful plea on the Queen's behalf in his open letter to Alderman Wood. Shelley, living in Italy, was aware of these and other responses to the affair. As he reveals in this letter to the Gisbornes, Shelley was both disgusted and amused by the unfolding event:

> How can the English endure the mountains of cant which are cast upon them about this vulgar cook–maid they call a Queen? It is scarcely less disgusting than the tyranny of her husband, who, on his side, uses a battery of the same cant. It is really time for the English to wean themselves from this nonsense, for really their situation is too momentous to justify them in attending to Punch and his Wife. Let the nation stand aside, and suffer them to beat till, like most combatants that are left to themselves, they would kiss and be friends.
>
> (30 June 1820; *Letters* 2. 207)

Shelley reproduces the antithesis between romance and reality to criticize the Caroline affair. He equates the couple's animosity for each other with the characters in the popular puppet show, *Punch and Judy*, which typically features a cast of characters, including Punch, who remains on stage throughout to nag, beat and ultimately kill the other characters: most often his wife, Judy, their baby, a clergyman, a policeman or a constable, a hangman and the devil. The topsy-turvy carnivalesque performance elides the domestic and political violence that is sometimes masked and, more often, glossed over by audiences of conventional romance. Shelley's ability to see the Queen Caroline affair in light of such overlap between the domestic and the political suggests that he took this event more seriously than is obvious. The affair represented the intrinsicate knot between tyranny and liberty and between radicals and the government and as such proved symptomatic of the contemporary national crises that had brought the country to the brink of revolution. The King and Queen's romance was mere 'mummery' and to hope that they 'would kiss and be friends' was both vain and farcical.

Almost a month later, Shelley returns to the topic of the Caroline affair in a letter to Thomas Medwin:

> I wonder what in the world the Queen has done. I should not wonder, after the whispers I have heard, to find that the Green Bag contained evidence that she had imitated Pasiphae, and that the Committee should recommend to Parliament a bill to exclude all Minotaurs from the succession. What silly stuff is this to employ a great nation about. I wish the King and Queen, like Punch and his wife, would fight out their disputes in person.
>
> (20 July 1820; *Letters*, 2. 220)

Shelley appears to be surveying the satiric possibilities offered by the Queen Caroline affair as he assembles an arsenal of classical allusions to create a palimpsest of references, which gesture toward a series of historical events – the Exclusion Crisis (1679–81), the 'Glorious Revolution' (1688) and the Hanoverian Succession (1714) – and a literary and mythic legacy of social and political violence. In addition to the repeated reference to *Punch and Judy*, Shelley alludes to the story of Pasiphae recorded in classical Greek and Roman texts. This juxtaposition of 'high' and 'low' discourses proves intrinsic to Shelley's dramatic and satiric conception in *Swellfoot*. Shelley plays the clown in this letter to Medwin. This figure, Mikhail Bakhtin observes in *The Dialogic Imagination*, appropriates the right to tease and confuse his audience, to hyperbolize life and to parody others, even to the point of betraying their prurient secrets to the public.[25] Shelley adopts a similar role in *Swellfoot*, producing his drama as a 'chronotope of theatrical space', to adopt Bakhtin's phrase, where characters are positioned to mirror specific historic events and mythological narratives. Like the political caricatures discussed earlier in the chapter, the Ovidian allusions in this letter and in *Swellfoot* register the instability produced by competing political allegiances during this political crisis. Pasiphae's story highlights the disturbing twists and turns of human action and human desire. It is helpful perhaps to recall that Pasiphae marries King Minos, who refuses to sacrifice a beautiful white bull to Poseidon; the god takes his revenge by cultivating in Pasiphae an unnatural longing for the bull; to satisfy these yearnings she orders Daedalus to build a structure which will enable her to consummate her salacious desire for her taurine lover. This act results in the birth of the Minotaur, a monstrous manifestation of the imperial force that is preserved in a labyrinth and sustained with human sacrifices. The myth reflects how those in power manipulate human desire and utilize human ingenuity for their own purposes.

Shelley appropriates this mythic narrative for *Swellfoot* and also adapts the witty and inventive forms of dramatic satire employed by Spence, Marks, Cobbett, Hone, Wooler and Hunt. Following Hunt, Shelley focuses his drama on the Queen's trial and oppressive state apparatuses, particularly the Green Bag. The drama's Advertisement functions as a dramatic frame and it evokes the mock advertisements produced and distributed by the London Corresponding Society (LCS) and the Society for Constitutional Information (SCI) in the 1790s. The appeal of mock advertisements, as John Barrell notes, is that they constitute a common language of satire that engages the interest and the knowledge of polite audiences while simultaneously appealing to vulgar and sometimes grotesque sensibilities.[26] Shelley sustains the interests of both audiences, integrating the classicism of 'learned pigs' with the ribald humour of the 'swinish multitude'. Alluding to Burke, Shelley follows Cobbett in returning to the loci of internecine political conflict during the early Romantic period: the Regency crisis (1788), the French Revolution (1789), the pamphlet war and the schism that occurred amongst the Whigs when Burke published his *Reflections on the Revolution in France*.

Swellfoot obviously focuses on the Queen Caroline affair. It also comments on the reform movement's failure to advocate successfully for reform during the 1790s and throughout the early nineteenth century. Shelley's letters indicate that he was critical of both the reform movement and of the ministry in their respective handling of Queen Caroline; both parties exploited Caroline's status as a private citizen and a national figure, staging their own version of a 'she-tragedy'. Popular during the late seventeenth and early eighteenth centuries, these dramas capitalized on the still relatively new sensation of actresses performing on stage after the Restoration (1660). 'She-tragedies', including Thomas Otway's *The Orphan* (1680), Thomas Southerne's *The Fatal Marriage* (1694) and Nicholas Rowe's *The Fair Penitent* (1703) and *Lady Jane Grey* (1715), shifted the spotlight from masculine heroes to the heroine's suffering and death. Adhering to this dramatic convention where these heroines were portrayed as both desirable and desiring and where the play turns on their transgression, their fall and their repentance, the ministry in its Bill of Pains and Penalties stressed the Queen's sexual license and the need for her to suffer for her illicit sexual affairs. In contrast, and similar to Rowe's *Lady Jane Grey*, the reformers cast Queen Caroline as a heroine, a martyr and a Queen. To sustain the Queen's status as a political symbol for reform, her supporters needed to emphasize her virtue; otherwise, they risked their cause being undermined by her immorality. Cobbett, like Burke in his depiction of Marie Antoinette, allows for the Queen's sexual desirability but divests her character of any female desire and eliminates any reference to her sexuality.[27] The Queen's very public record of illicit affairs made it difficult for reformers to maintain the moral high ground in the debate, particularly after Parliament dropped its charges against her.

Swellfoot alludes to she-tragedy as well as the more conventional tragedies: most notably, Sophocles' dramas and *King Lear*. Shelley also links his drama to the print politics of the period, creating a Woolerian State Theatrical with an accompanying mock advertisement. This nexus of mixed forms illustrates the symbiotic relationship between the press and theatrical culture. Aware of the synecdochical and metonymic figures of British political subjectivity, Shelley shrewdly dramatizes both the literal and the figurative bodies-politic by conflating the slapstick transformations of the harlequinade with the legerdemain of periodical spoofs, effectively unmasking the cultural and political authority amassed under multiple political, ethnic and cultural markers of legitimacy.

Spoofs, hoaxes and plagiarism

The Napoleonic wars ushered in a period of unprecedented violence throughout the world. These conflicts heightened the stakes of the ongoing culture wars within Britain's borders and for a number of reasons produced an increasingly professionalized literary culture. Periodicals publishing literary and theatrical reviews often included political commentary. This juxtaposition of political and aesthetic registers in conjunction with the social and political pressures to demonstrate one's patriotism led to the overt politicization of reviewing culture. Periodicals vied tenaciously with one another for readers, so much so that editors and writers sometimes resorted to personal attacks that resulted in lawsuits and occasionally, a deadly duel.[28]

John Gibson Lockhart provoked visceral cultural debate during this period by printing reviews that were both spoofs and publicity stunts. Most well known as

Sir Walter Scott's son-in-law, Lockhart proved to be one of the defining influences of early nineteenth-century Tory culture. He was an editor at *Blackwood's Edinburgh Review* and later at the *Quarterly Review*. He dubbed the 'Cockney school' and led the attack against the Hunt circle, especially Keats and Leigh Hunt.[29] Lockhart's editorial decisions undermined the more liberal *Edinburgh Review*'s promotion of Whiggish professionalism and its claim to cultural authority.[30] *Blackwood's* aggressive editorial posturing further politicized an already highly commercialized reviewing culture and, as Ian Duncan asserts in *Scott's Shadow*, allowed Lockhart and his cronies to transform 'the abstract, anonymous, judicial elitism of the Edinburgh reviewers into the masquerade of a boisterous coterie of "personalities"' (58). *Blackwood's* manufactured its legitimacy through stylized urbane satire, authorial masquerades and textual spoofs, all of which quickly became fashionable and commercially successful literary practices. The review accomplished this by using cryptographic ciphers (most notably, Z, who penned the reviews that smeared both Hunt and Keats as 'Cockneys') to obfuscate the identities of its contributors and by promoting 'authentic' and antiquarian fictions that stimulated the sales of Scott's works and other Scottish poets and novels like Hogg's *The Private Memoirs and Confessions of a Justified Sinner* (1824). In the case of Hogg's novel, *Blackwood's* promoted it by developing over a series of issues the character of the truculent Ettrick Shepherd, also known as James Hogg, who appears in the final pages of the novel, where playing the role developed for him in *Blackwood's* he declines to aid the literary gentlemen who have travelled into 'the romantic and now classical country'[31] in search of the mysterious memoir we have just finished reading. The narrator/editor orchestrates the spoof perfectly, insisting this text 'bears the stamp of authenticity in every line' while also confessing, 'yet, so often had I been hoaxed by the ingenious fancies displayed in that Magazine [*Blackwood's*], that when this relation met my eye, I did not believe it [. . .]' (226). The hoax perpetrated in *Blackwood's* and sustained by Hogg in his novel demonstrates the complexity of what was essentially an advertising ploy.

Shelley merges radical and Tory print practices in *Swellfoot*'s Advertisement, where he lampoons Tory antiquarianism and its attendant classicism, which Lockhart and other writers popularized in *Blackwood's*. One of the first steps in creating a hoax is to invent an editor who recovers a lost text. To validate the text the writer must situate it within a literary tradition, sometimes based upon an appreciation of classical texts, particularly Greek tragedy, and sometimes founded upon a conflation of historical facts and literary geography as is the case in Hogg's novel. *Swellfoot*'s Advertisement presents itself to readers as a classical drama. The antiquarian framework portrays the lost text as something between a mock translation and a forgery. This pseudo-translation comes across as a transparent forgery: a spoof.

Since the eighteenth century the British reading public had in turns both revelled in these controversies and argued heatedly about them. The forgeries of James Macpherson (1736–96), Thomas Chatterton (1752–70) and, within the theatre, William Henry Ireland's (1775–1835) discovery of a lost Shakespearean drama at the turn of the century fuelled cultural debates and cultural productions like Elizabeth Inchbald's *The Massacre* (1792). As pseudo-translations, *The Massacre* and *Swellfoot* navigate between liberal and conservative political positions. Deliberate and obvious parodies, these texts contribute to politically charged debates, disrupting reader's expectations without alienating their political sensibilities.[32] These dramas mix elements from illegitimate drama – farce, melodrama and pantomime, for example – with the drama's most noble form, tragedy, creating a text that did not mirror reality so much as call that reality into question. Both dramas reference obscure textual sources that Vita M. Mastrosilvestri, in an observation about *The Massacre*, identifies as 'historical reality itself' (167). *The Massacre*'s three-Act dramatization of intensifying violence begins with a verbal reference in the first Act and then fixes it as a physical object before unveiling it fully in the final Act.[33] Inchbald's drama reproduces the historical escalation of violence during the French revolutionary period. Shelley's *Swellfoot* reconfigures this historical trajectory in a more risible fashion that connects *Blackwood's* editorial hoaxes with radical caricatures and the rough festival culture of *Punch and Judy* performances.[34]

The Advertisement sketches the ruse of a found manuscript that has been edited and translated recently for a modern audience. The narrator depicts the document as both a literary relic and a commercial object. This antiquarian apparatus simulates the Tory classicism promoted in *Blackwood's* and as such it bestows a false air of legitimacy on this literary and economic venture. In this instance the author is displaced by the persona of a translator, keeping Shelley out of the limelight while allowing him to play the unobserved puppet-master who can satirize both the Scottish Tories and the divided Whigs. According to the Advertisement, *Swellfoot* is 'a remarkable piece of antiquity', which dramatizes 'the wonderful and appalling fortunes of the SWELLFOOT dynasty'. The translator identifies the recovered text as a lost tragedy and situates it within a classical tradition that is made to appear authentic in terms of geographical, historical and literary references. Appearing to date the text, the editor informs readers that it 'was evidently written by some *learned Theban*, and from its characteristic dullness, apparently before the duties on the importation of *Attic salt* had been repealed by the Boeotarchs'. There are a number of playful allusions in these lines for those 'learned pigs' in the audience. The phrase 'learned Theban' is King Lear's.[35] The anachronism marks the deliberate fictitiousness of this literary endeavour, but we are also being directed to recall the exchange between King Lear and Edgar, who at the moment is passing as Poor Tom:

LEAR. I'll take a word with this same learned Theban.
What is your study?
EDGAR. How to prevent the fiend, and to kill vermin.

(*King Lear*, III,iv,145–7)[36]

Edgar is disguised as the bedlamite, Poor Tom, to escape being wrongfully charged for the attempted murder of his father. As he tells Lear, his study is to prevent the fiend – his half-brother, Edmund – from taking his birthright and to kill the 'vermin' that have infected the kingdom. The 'learned Theban' is no more a canny sophist than he is a sage. Edgar has been falsely accused and unjustly disinherited. In the frame and on the run, he has been forced by a series of injustices to take the part of a radical reformer in an attempt to put things right again. Perhaps Shelley identified with Edgar in adopting the disguise of a translator to save his country from despair and civil war. More obviously, Edgar represents those like Queen Caroline and others – Jeremiah Brandreth, Arthur Thistlewood and even reformers like Cobbett, Hone, Hunt and Wooler – whose efforts for reform had been compromised by *agents provocateurs* and other forms of injustice.

The reference to the writer as a Theban also situates the drama within a fictional Sophoclean context. In terms of historical geography, the writer lives outside the democratic state of Athens and is aligned with Boeotia's Thebans: the major military power in Greece after Thebes defeated Sparta at Leuctra in 371 BCE. The Advertisement places the writer and the translator – who suppresses the seditious and blasphemous Chorus – firmly in the camp of the oppressors.[37] Given Edinburgh's identity in the period as the Athens of the North or Modern Athens, it also positions the author and the translator outside the established literary coteries of either the *Edinburgh Review* or *Blackwood's Magazine* and yet within a circle of writers whose work reconstructed classicism as a relevant contemporary aesthetic. *Blackwood's* published a series of articles in 1817 promoting antiquity, classicism and classical drama. These essays include 'On the Sculpture of the Greeks' and a four-part series entitled 'Remarks on Greek tragedy'.[38] In the first of these 'Remarks' the writer claims that the Greek theatre 'was not merely a place of public amusement, but rather a temple for the purification of national manners, and the worship of the gods [. . .]'(39).[39] For readers of Shelley's *A Defence of Poetry*, this statement strikes a familiar chord and reflects a shared concern for rehabilitating the classics. But it would be wrong to read *Swellfoot* in this light. *Swellfoot* parodies this nostalgic perspective and this attempt to recuperate the past. Written more in line with what Jeffrey N. Cox has identified as Cockney classicism, *Swellfoot* represents an irreverent parody that radicalizes conventional classicism.[40] The nature of the lampoon makes clear the historical and the cultural detachment from an idealized aesthetic. There is nothing pure or transcendent about *Swellfoot*. Incarnating the playful spirit of Cockney classicism, Shelley's Advertisement foregrounds the remoteness of the past and the impractical nature of any project to restore the imperial or epic matter of its heroic narratives.

The Advertisement's declaration that '[n]o liberty has been taken with the translation of this remarkable piece of antiquity, except the suppressing [of] a seditious and blasphemous Chorus of the Pigs and bulls at the last Act' echoes Shelley's concerns about seditious and blasphemous libel cases while writing *Swellfoot*. Other references, such as the etiology of Swellfoot/Hoydipouse/Oedipus belabour the text's authenticity as a literary artifact while the final claim – 'should the remaining portions of this Tragedy be found, entitled, *Swellfoot in Angaria,* and *Charité*, the Translator might be tempted to give them to the reading public' – is a bald promotion, signalling the literary venture's commercial interests. Although short, Shelley's Advertisement reproduces the standard authenticating devices one would have found in antiquarian and forged texts. Readers of *Blackwood's* and satiric radical journals would have identified this Advertisement easily as a spoof. Its mock-antiquarian guise was a periodical convention and sometimes a political necessity. But, what has been overlooked by critics who wish to dismiss this piece by quoting Mary Shelley's description of *Swellfoot* as 'a mere plaything of the imagination' is the fact that this Advertisement signals Shelley's participation in a larger cultural debate about literature's social and political efficacy. As Tilar Mazzeo points out, 'the legitimacy or illegitimacy of particular literary obligations masked a larger contest about how to come to critical judgment'.[41] Reviewers and journalists played the role of cultural gate-keepers, scrutinizing originality, individual genius, literary objectives and the author's place within a tradition that was increasingly determined by political and commercial interests.

The cultural dialogue acknowledged the politicization and commercialization of aesthetic praxes, Ian Duncan reminds us, and it traced the disintegration of the eighteenth-century ideal of a Republic of Letters to the French Revolution (*Scott's Shadow*, 45–69). The virulent political antagonism erupted into the pamphlet wars during the 1790s and it led literary-minded Whigs and Tories to re-examine what Byron referred to as the 'very *poetry* of politics' (*BLJ*, 8. 47). Byron's statement invites us to consider poetry as both a literary work and a quality or characteristic that defines politics. There were, of course, various ways that radical poetic and literary experiments structured political debates throughout the period. In the eighteenth century, pseudo-translations proved one of the most radical and politically relevant forms of poetic composition. James Macpherson's Ossian poems and Chatterton's pseudo-medieval poetry, both published in the 1760s, brought together the arts of antiquarian textual reconstruction and scholarly translation. The Ossian controversy pitted Hugh Blair, a Scottish minister and scholar who believed in the authenticity of the Ossian poems, against the renowned Samuel Johnson. Questions of textual legitimacy in these cases focused tightly on the politics of colonialism, empire and the possibilities for sustaining one's cultural heritage as well as a coherent national identity under such conditions. Like those printed in *Blackwood's*, these cases of plagiarism animated political discussions and influenced writers from Wooler to Shelley who experimented with what Mazzeo refers to as 'models of appropriation, assimilation, and narrative or lyric mastery' in their attempts to shape the 'processes of interpretive judgment' (*Plagiarism*, 182).

Swellfoot demonstrates Shelley's interest in these debates and his willingness to display his ability to masterfully mimic and synthesize these cultural practices. Shelley's reflexive parody of the tactics wielded in the periodical press cuts both ways. The reconstruction of antiquarian texts, especially in the cases of Chatterton and Macpherson, but also within the context of *Blackwood's* spoofs and Wooler's State Theatricals, had formed a readership on the alert for markers of (in)authenticity. Often satiric, spoofs and hoaxes remained popular because they reconstructed 'imagined communities' that for various political reasons were suppressed.[42] A pseudo-translation of a classical drama, *Swellfoot* reclaims classicism through a satiric eye.[43] Satire upsets normative cultural narratives and represents a subversive intervention. In this instance Shelley's Advertisement as a pseudo-translation undermines classicism's 'aura' – its 'power and allure'[44] – by calling attention to material and historical problems that accompany the discovery of classical scrolls and other *objets d'art*. Commercial and scholarly interests mask the cultural and political compromises that occur when 'lost' artifacts are retrieved and reclaimed by imperial interests. A convergence of 'classical allusions and popular forms' (Jones, *Shelley's Satire* 132), Shelley's *Swellfoot* mixes Aristophanic comedy, Sophoclean tragedy and Dionysian festival performances to produce a mock-tragedy that links classical Greek drama to the more populist traditions of English satire. This 'multilayered referential allusiveness' (Jones, 134), a phrase Jones employs to describe *Swellfoot*, integrates a gallimaufry of forms that brings the political crises surrounding the Queen Caroline affair into focus.

Spectres and spectacles of liberty

Swellfoot's opening stage direction portrays a scene that is both grotesque and eerily familiar:

> A magnificent Temple, built of thigh–bones and death's–heads, and tiled with scalps. Over the Altar the statue of Famine, veiled; a number of Boars, Sows, and Suckling–Pigs, crowned with thistle, shamrock, and oak, sitting on the steps, and clinging round the Altar of the Temple.

There is nothing subtle about his imagery, as Timothy Morton makes clear in 'Porcine Poetics' (281). To adopt Giorgio Agamben's concept, the cost of the temple's magnificence is all too visible in its display of 'bare life' (*Homo Sacer*, 85). These bodies do not manifest any recognizable humanity; they are merely construction materials – disposable and consumable – and this makes it shockingly clear that their lives have no political significance and that killing them does not constitute a crime. Agamben, significantly, does not equate bare life with either the biological nature of humanity (*zoe*) or with humanity's political identity (*bios*); rather, this always-expendable life exists within a 'zone of indistinction and continuous transition' (*Homo Sacer*, 109). This liminal space provides bare life with its *raison d'être*. While the political function of *homo sacer* changes throughout the historical record, it initially plays a paradoxical albeit pivotal role in the construction of sovereignty and sovereign power. Banished from the *polis*, *homo sacer* functions both as the necessary counterpart to sovereignty and the target of its *awful* – awe-inspiring and horrific – violence. A sovereign's ability to commit acts of violence that exceed the force of law while justifying them as necessary to the State's preservation legitimizes and authorizes their absolute and arbitrary power. Constructed of 'thigh – bones and death's – heads, and tiled with scalps', Famine's temple represents the incorporation of bare life into political and religious discourses. The temple visually mirrors how violent atrocities – genocide as racially and ethnically motivated killing – delineate citizenship.

On stage Famine remains veiled on the altar as Shelley spotlights Burke's 'swinish multitude'. They sit on the steps of the temple and cling – persistently and stubbornly faithful – to the altar. The swine reflect the twofold reality of leechlike princes who parasitically feed upon the country's resources and the 'citizenry' who have been 'starved and stabbed' by their oppressors ('England in 1819' ll. 5–7). With *Swellfoot* and in his sonnet, 'England in 1819', Shelley juxtaposes a sympathetic perspective of the people's suffering with a critique of those who both accept and impose this oppression. Alluding to Burke, Shelley targets the patriotism and the nationalism that sustain the biopolitics of sovereign power and undermine social and political relationships. The image of the swine 'crowned with thistle, shamrock, and oak' illustrates the national interests that constitute and divide the three kingdoms – Scotland, Ireland and England – within the United Kingdom. As Shelley notes in his 1817 *A Proposal for Putting Reform to the Vote throughout the Kingdom*, the 'prerogatives of Parliament constitute a sovereignty which is exercised in contempt of the people, [and it] is the object of Reformers to restore the people to a sovereignty thus held in their contempt' (*Prose Works*, 171). Shelley was keenly aware of how the monarch and his ministry prohibited reform and how their scorn of the common Briton condemned them as slavish and wretched. Burke's reference to a 'swinish multitude' reinforced these conventional notions of class hegemony. But what if the people could choose? Would they choose reform? Or had the people succumbed wholly to being 'degraded and ignorant and famished' (*Prose Works*, 171), as Shelley put it? Had 'Custom' converted the public to despotism and transformed each individual to a slave who, in Hazlitt's words,

> has no other hope or consolation, clings to the apparition of royal magnificence, which insults his misery and his despair; stares through the hollow eyes of famine at the insolence of pride and luxury which has occasioned it and hugs his chains the closer, because he has nothing else left.
> ('On the Connexion between Toad-eaters and Tyrants', *SWWH*, 4. 139)

Shelley and Hazlitt contested and exposed this disturbing relationship between the oppressed and the oppressor. Burke's powerful conservative vision reified the British people's romance with tradition and custom, which could and often did blind the populace to their own necessity and convinced them to sustain the repressive power structure for the sake of patriotic and nationalist sentiments.

The play itself opens with Swellfoot stepping onto the stage as a recognizable caricature of George IV. His opening monologue directed to 'Thou supreme Goddess' quickly slips into an encomium of his own image. His speech elides the identity of the monarch with the goddess, Famine and creates a causal relationship between the proverbial excesses of the Court and the nation's dire poverty. This caricature portrays the monarchy as a tyrannous and an all-consuming body that carelessly feeds in luxury while others suffer in the throes of Famine's grisly reality. The reflection of Swellfoot as he stands in front of a mirror and the audience, contemplating himself with satisfaction, reveals how self-absorbed he is with his corpulent body. A site of relentless parody, the King's body – grossly overfed and covered in the richest fabrics – is monumental:

> [T]his kingly paunch
> Swells like a sail before a favouring breeze,
> And these most sacred nether promontories
> Lie satisfied with layers of fat; and these
> Boeotian cheeks, like Egypt's pyramid,
> (Nor with less toil were their foundations laid).
> Sustain the cone of my untroubled brain,
> That point, the emblem of a pointless nothing!
>   *Poetical Works, Swellfoot* I, i, 3–10

The narrative self-portrait functions as a Sophoclean burlesque: contrasting Oedipus' fatherly concern for his people with Swellfoot's oblivious egotism and it criticizes the blindness of all monarchs. This portrait reveals what Shelley had argued for his unpublished *A Philosophical Review of Reform*: history has been a succession of tyrants who have made a bedfellow of war, using it as a prop to justify their greed for power and their 'need' or 'right' to impoverish and oppress their people (*Shelley's Prose*, 230–261).

The scene parodies the 'monumental' figure of George IV by shifting the lens from tragedy to farce. Shelley's portentous character mimics the myriad popular caricatures ridiculing the Prince Regent throughout the period. Ian Duncan has written about how the duplication and repetition of the monarch's body in print and on stage transformed the sovereign image into a simulacrum.[45] Parody yields quickly to pastiche just as stage practices and industrial-speed print technology expose the artifice of sovereign power for everyone to see. The King's image is everywhere and subsequently nowhere. Shelley's caricature ridicules the court's attempts to improve the monarch's image in the Romantic period. The more nebulous and insubstantial George III or the Prince Regent appeared, the more punctilious and grandiose court traditions became. But these shows of power could not support the underlying inauthenticity of an image subject to constant reproduction.

As I discussed in earlier sections of this chapter, artists often employed theatrical motifs in their caricatures for wider appeal and more effect. Robert Cruikshank's '*REFLECTION – to be or not to be?*', dated 11 February 1820 (Figure 2.4), presents the Prince Regent as the soon-to-be crowned George IV. Looking into the mirror in this moment of performative triumph, the visible face in the mirror is the more dignified Queen's, who is obviously standing further behind the King. The King's face is obscured by a full view of his backside. Much like Hamlet – the play is echoed in the print's title – who is haunted by his father's ghost, the Regent appears startled by the Queen's ghostly presence in *his* mirror. Cruikshank's print obscures the 'kingly paunch' because it features the 'most sacred nether promontories, [which]/Lie satisfied in layers of fat'. The Regent's 'Boeotian cheeks' are just visible in the mirror. The Prince's physical body was the subject of relentless

Figure 2.4 Robert Cruikshank, *REFLECTION – to be or not to be?*, 34 × 23.3 cm, etching, 11 February 1820, Courtesy of The Lewis Walpole Library, Yale University

jokes and ridicule and was reproduced incessantly to undermine the sovereignty and the legitimacy of the British monarchy. As in *Hamlet*, the question posed by the print and by Shelley's drama is whether the Regent will retain his crown in the brief interim before the official coronation ceremony. The popular outcry against the excesses of the court in conjunction with the dark future that 'look[ed] as black as death [and]/Dark as the frown of Hell' (*Swellfoot,* I, i, 96–7) suggested a tragic outcome.

Shelley develops this tragic trajectory throughout Act I and quickly shifts the audience's focus from the self-satisfied monarch to the 'unhappy nation' (*Swellfoot*, 1.1.60). Shelley fuses Burke's iconic 'swinish multitude' and the biblical story of the Gadarean swine through allusions to Aristophanes, producing a reverberating echo between scenes and characters that renders tragedy farcical. This dynamic appears initially as a series of grunts and squeals ranging from 'Eigh!' to 'Aigh!' to 'Ugh!'. This cacophony interrupts Swellfoot's monologue. Steven Jones identifies this noisy intrusion as a bathetic parody of Aristophanes' chorus of frogs that annoys Dionysius (*Shelley's Satire*, 137). These noises mimic the depiction of woe in Greek tragedy and they constitute a pastiche of human revulsion and contemptuous loathing. Shelley intensifies Burke's imagery of the 'swinish multitude', depicting pigs imitating 'humans imitating animals'.[46] Imitation and consumption elide in this cannibalistic frenzy where the abject sensations render everything and everyone disposable. The question is whether this pastiche evokes sympathy or abhorrence. To raise this question is to contemplate the viability of political revolution and to reconsider *Swellfoot*'s reception history, which was initially shaped by a bourgeois perspective that failed to negotiate between the visceral elements and the excessive artifice of Shelley's pastiche (Morton, 284–5). Shelley's letters from Italy during this period reveal his revulsion with the lower classes. Having already drafted *A Proposal for Putting Reform to the Vote throughout the Kingdom*, Shelley understood how his attitudes compromised his ability to support reform.[47]

This mimicry shifts registers once Swellfoot identifies these grunts as emanating from the 'very beasts [. . .] offered at [Famine's] altar/With blood and groans, salt-cake, and fat, and inwards [sic]' (*Swellfoot*, I, i, 20–22), and when he questions if these 'beasts' are those

> who grub
> With filthy snouts my red potatoes up
> In Allan's rushy bog? Who eat the oats
> Up, from my cavalry in the Hebrides?
> Who swill the hog-wash soup my cooks digest
> From bones, and rags, and scraps of shoe-leather [. . .].
> *Swellfoot*, I, i, 23–8

With the references to 'Allan's rushy bog', the 'Hebrides' and 'my cavalry', Swellfoot characterizes the anonymous mass of swine as the colonized Scots and Irish.

These swine consume critical resources that feed rebellion and the subsequent British military occupations of Scotland and Ireland. Patterns of imitation have devolved into patterns of consumption that once again prove cannibalistic. The swine's remains on Famine's altar suggest a sacrifice, but the blood, the groans, the salt-cake, fat and innards exist only as remnants and markers of what has been almost wholly consumed by power. Any sense of ritualized sacredness is subsumed by the disturbing cannibalism whereby the rebels eat the food designated for the troops and are in turn processed into swill to feed soldiers.

Swellfoot's speech reiterates what Homi Bhabha refers to as 'the discourse of post-Enlightenment English colonialism'.[48] Identifying the Scots and Irish by their diet of red potatoes and oats and by particular geographic locales – Alan's rushy bog and the Hebrides – the text alludes to the 1798 Irish rebellion, which led to the complete loss of Ireland's independence with the forced Act of Union in 1800, and the more recent working-class revolt in Scotland's western Lowlands in 1820. British forces responded to both events with exceptional brutality and force. These political protests exposed the disintegrated state of political relations between classes and between 'nations' within the imperial construct of the United Kingdom. Whether Scots, Irish or the working classes of England, imperial ambitions in the aftermath of the Napoleonic wars left very few people with any hope or any recourse to justice. Shelley's façade of Tory classicism in the Advertisement falls away here, unveiling a ruthless empire more than capable of consuming itself to feed its global ambitions. Making a farce of tragedy, this scene demonstrates how when 'colonialism takes power in the name of history, it repeatedly exercises its authority through the figures of farce' (Bhabha, 113–4).

Shelley then distinguishes two swine from the collective chorus:

> *First Sow.* My Pigs, 'tis in vain to tug.
> *Second Sow.* I could almost eat my litter.
> *First Pig.* I suck, but no milk will come from the dug.
> *Second Pig.* Our skin and our bones would be bitter.
> *Swellfoot*, I, i, 49–52

The anonymous but distinct voices function as witness testimony. Each pig/sow testifies to the untenable conditions that have brought the pigs to such an obviously revolting state. On the brink of revolution, the 'swinish multitude' constitutes a repulsive and monstrous mass. In a productive agrarian society – one with a 'Farmer King' (George III's sobriquet) or one reflecting Shelley's or Spence's agrarian vision – swine do not prey upon one another. Familial bonds have deteriorated to the point where a mother pleads with her children to find sustenance elsewhere and where another mother threatens to eat her litter despite the bitterness of cannibalizing 'our skin and our bones'.

The harrowing situation worsens. The Chorus pleads for an explanation of this oppressive exploitation. Desperate and conditioned to look to the Bible for meaning, the swine compare their situation with those of the Gadarean swine in the Gospels:

> Happier Swine were they than we,
> Drowned in the Gadarean sea –
> I wish that pity would drive out the devils,
> Which in your royal bosom hold their revels,
> And sink us in the waves of thy compassion!
> To bind your mortar with, or fill our colons
> With rich blood, or make brawn out of our gristles,
> In policy – ask else your royal Solons –
> You ought to give us hog–wash and clean straw,
> And sties well thatched; besides it is the law!
> *Swellfoot*, I, i, 55–66

The story of the Gadarean swine is told three times in the Gospels and in each case, men have broken their chains, escaped their captors and are living as exiles amongst the tombs. Demons possess these banished men. When confronted by Jesus, the demons ask to be cast out into a nearby herd of swine, which subsequently run down the hill into the sea.[49] In the context of Shelley's drama, the deaths of the 'swinish multitude' could be interpreted as a return to the sacrifices of the Hebrew Bible, significantly contrary to the promise of love and salvation offered by the New Testament. The swine in *Swellfoot* believe that religious sacrifice can render their deaths meaningful. While willing to condone this line of reasoning – something Shelley turns on its head in his essay, 'On the Devil and Devils' – the swine also reason that the devil exists within the monarch and that they have no rights, despite the presence of a legal guarantees of their liberty; they are no better than the outcasts who live among the dead in the Gospels. An element often overlooked in commentaries about this story is the fact that the locals invoke the law to chastise those like Jesus who attempt to ameliorate the sordid conditions and the violent oppression endured by the demonized outcasts. Showing more concern for the devils than the swine in his commentary in 'On the Devil and Devils',[50] Shelley depicts the Gadarean swine as 'a set of hypochondriacal and high-minded swine, very unlike any others of which we have authentic record; they disdained to live, if they must live in so intimate a society with devils as that which was imposed on them, and the pig-drivers were no doubt confounded at so unusual a resolution' (*Shelley's Prose*, 271). He later queries the fate of the devils after the pigs' deaths, suggesting that they returned to society through fish eaters or perhaps through desperate Jews who gathered up the dead swine and brought them to sell in the marketplace. In line with *Swellfoot*, Shelley indicates that fish eaters – Christians – recreate the devil through the habitual or ritualized consumption of fish or Christian doctrine. Alternatively, economic necessity coupled with ethnic and religious intolerance create a class of people who become the social and political scapegoats when anything bad happens. Devils exist because people consume religious doctrine indiscriminately and because they also gratuitously produce consumer goods for the sole purpose of making money.

To make this last point more clearly poignant in *Swellfoot*, Shelley foregrounds the grotesque bodily excesses – especially blood – in these scenes. In this, he reproduces Burke's rhetoric in his *Reflections on the Revolution in France* during the early Regency crisis. For Burke, it is in the blood. A cooling sentimental rhetoric can do as much as inflammatory remarks to produce social reform. Blood signifies aristocratic election, monarchical supremacy and the insignificance of the so-called lower orders.[51] Burke's articulation of an English national identity in *Reflections* relies upon these types of bodily figuration. His polemics are full of racial invectives, especially, as David Simpson observes, anti-Semitism.[52] Throughout his *Reflections* Burke makes scapegoats of religious dissenters, lawyers and financial speculators and he insists that they – and not the King or his ministers – control French political life. His hostility towards 'jew-brokers', and 'money-jobbers, usurers, and Jews' (*Reflections*, 204–5) calls to mind Swellfoot's summoning of the Jews, 'Solomon the court porkman [the lawyer],/Moses the sow-gelder [the embodiment of civil law,] and Zephaniah/The hog-butcher' [the tradesmen who work with the state to provide sustenance for the troops] (*Swellfoot*, I, i, 69–70) to drive away the bitterly incompliant swine who insist upon their lawful right to 'hog–wash and clean straw,/And sties well thatched' (*Swellfoot*, I, i, 65–70).

Shelley reproduces Burke's rhetoric for the purposes of satire and stages Burke's ethnocentric vision of civil society as ultimately leading to mass sterilization and wholesale slaughter. Swellfoot orders Moses to 'spay those Sows/ That load the earth with Pigs', emphasizing the need to 'cut close and deep' because every possible means of population control has failed. Moral restraint, starvation, typhus, war, prison and even the availability of prostitutes and the example of Swellfoot's immorality have failed to curb the swine's sexual appetites. Michael Scrivener reads Shelley's drama as satirizing Malthusian ideas about population and social control.[53] Yes, but there is also a more relevant point that can be made about how this performance of 'blood' and ethnic difference gives way to cannibalistic genocide. Moses attempts to warn Swellfoot of some imminent danger, but he is interrupted by Swellfoot's command to Zephaniah to cut the throat of an 'overfed' and seemingly 'Seditious hunk' that cries out for grain. When Zephaniah explains to Swellfoot that the pig has the dropsy and that there is not 'half an inch of wholesome fat/Upon his carious ribs' (*Swellfoot*, I, i, 85–6), Swellfoot responds,

'Tis all the same,
He'll serve instead of riot money, when
Our murmuring troops bivouac in Thebes' streets;
And January winds, after a day
Of butchering, will make them relish carrion.

Swellfoot, I, i, 86–90

Swellfoot relies upon the Jews to subordinate the swinish multitude by destroying normative social bonds through financial and legal means. If framed correctly, Swellfoot believes the populace will associate this perverse madness and misdirected ambition with the Jews – Zephaniah, Moses and Solomon – all of whom threaten the 'natural' order of society by engaging in gruesome and bloody acts. The scene satirizes Malthusian ideas about population control, while also – and I think with more cunning – exposing how politicians undermine political reform by invoking race and ethnicity. The Jews – like the Irish and the Scots – will be scapegoats and as such they will redirect the blame away from the government and the monarch. The Jews, the Irish and the Scots can be blamed for any rebellious act and can be forced to stand accused for all perpetrated crimes against the people. Shelley parodies and criticizes Burke in his racialization of political conflict. This scene satirizes the lethal political schisms between parties, classes and the 'kingdoms' throughout the United Kingdom. It exposes how racial and ethnic violence destabilizes local and national communities. Shelley's parody critiques both the lack of political acumen among the general population and this internecine legacy of 'blood', which has drenched the whole social order in unsightly gore, shed constantly and unnecessarily in the name of political necessity.

The focus shifts when Purganax enters with Mammon proclaiming disaster:

> The future looks as black as death, a cloud,
> Dark as the frown of Hell, hangs over it –
> The troops grow mutinous – the revenue fails –
> *There's something rotten in us* – for the level
> Of the State slopes, its very bases topple,
> The boldest turn their backs upon themselves!
>   my emphasis, *Swellfoot* I, i, 96–101

Mammon, the Arch-Priest and Purganax, the Chief of the Council of Wizards, represent Shelley's caricatures of Lord Castlereagh, the Foreign Secretary and Lord Liverpool, the Prime Minister. Although Mammon dismisses the possibility of imminent disaster, telling Purganax to decimate the mutinous regiments and 'coin paper/Till gold be at a discount' (*Swellfoot*, I, i, 104–5), he misses the point Purganax makes. Purganax identifies political revolution as symptomatic of an identity crisis. This does not suggest that political upheaval is merely a figment of the collective imagination. Alluding to *Hamlet*, Purganax refers to the persistent ghostly presence that those placed as guardians either fail to see or fail to interpret in a meaningful way. The body-politic does not know itself and has been allowed to rot unseen until the stench forces the issue, but at this juncture even the 'boldest turn their backs upon themselves'. Purganax's revolutionary apparition that takes form for him as the future represents what Slavoj Žižek, writing in a different context, refers to as a 'kernel' of reality. This spectre cannot assume a definitive bodily shape and so incarnates itself as a haunting spirit.[54] The spectres feared by Swellfoot, Purganax and Mammon are those the people will embrace. Each, as Žižek writes, will function as a 'dreamlike illusion [built] to escape insupportable reality' and as a 'fantasy-construction', which underpins and structures our social relations and 'reality' (*Sublime Object*, 45).

Two ghostly apparitions haunt the play and its characters: the oracle and Liberty. The oracle appears first as the play's epigraph:

> Choose Reform or Civil War,
> When through thy streets, instead of hare with dogs,
> A CONSORT–QUEEN shall hunt a KING with hogs,
> Riding on the IONIAN MINOTAUR.

A commonplace in classical tragedy, the oracle functions as the play's 'kernel' in structuring its plot and each character's actions. It wields a mysterious power that appears to embody the inevitability of fate, the sovereign power of the gods and the teleology of history as it progresses toward some unknowable end. Purganax first mentions the oracle when he attempts to explain to Mammon how dire the situation is: 'Oh, would that this were all! The oracle!!' (*Swellfoot*, I, i, 108). Mammon once again dismisses Purganax's histrionics and insists the oracle was spoken by him. He does not recall if he was inspired or dead drunk and he cannot remember what he said. Purganax repeats the oracle for Mammon but he changes the first line to read, 'Boeotia, choose Reform or Civil War!' Adding the word Boeotia to the oracle, Purganax refers to the region surrounding the city of Thebes *and* to the proverbial site of stupid citizens (*OED*). This alternative geographical reference takes us into the realm of satirical romance. Countering Purganax's authority, Mammon asserts that he, as a priest, knows about oracles. But his compendium of knowledge reduces to this formula: oracles either come to pass or they do not; they are either true or false; most importantly, the point is to take control of the prophecy once it is public:

> For prophecies, when once they get abroad,
> Like liars who tell the truth to serve their ends,
> Or hypocrites who, from assuming virtue,
> Do the same actions that the virtuous do,
> Contrive their own fulfillment.
> *Swellfoot*, I, i, 131–5

Mammon contends the oracle *per se* is insignificant, but he also understands that oracles can be appropriated and deployed to produce 'truths' that serve the purposes of liars and hypocrites. The question is who will be adept enough to act first and/or most effectively: the government or the people? Who has the power to reproduce the oracle as a spectacle, thereby, creating a fantasy-reality of ideology?

Shelley was skeptical about the political impact of the Queen Caroline affair. Would it lead to reform or to revolution? No one knew, but the political instability of the situation required action. From a historical perspective, the British government's Milan Commission – represented in Shelley's drama by the Leech, the Gadfly and the Rat – was charged by the Ministry to gather evidence regarding the

Queen's adulterous behaviour for the sole purpose of strengthening the Regent's case for divorce. The Commission however failed to prevent the Queen's return and, once she settled in London, the Regent and his ministers resorted to legal proceedings. As noted earlier in this chapter, the public campaign organized by reformers exposed the controversial and contentious nature of the trial and its use the notorious Green Bag. Subsequently, the Lords dropped the Regent's case, which deflated the movement's momentum. The government's ability to redirect the energy of public demonstrations toward the national and imperial spectacle of the King's coronation allowed it to undermine the reform movement's unexpected successes.

In *Swellfoot* the oracle offers a choice between reform and civil war, but as the play progresses and the violence escalates, the certainty of civil war becomes apparent. The 'Swellfoot system' (*Swellfoot*, II, i, 27), as Purganax refers to the government in his speech to the Assembly of Boars, has bankrupted the nation; the government acts under the rubric of 'state-necessity' (*Swellfoot*, II, i, 24) and conspires to manipulate the judicial system through the Green Bag, which Mammon has replenished recently with poison and calumny 'worse than death' (*Swellfoot*, I, i, 351). Its contents, Mammon assures Purganax and Swellfoot, 'Turn innocence to guilt, and gentlest looks/To savage, foul, and fierce deformity' (*Swellfoot*, I, i, 372–3). The monarch and his ministers believe Queen Iona's[55] trial is in the bag, quite literally; the 'perilous liquor' cannot fail to transform her into 'a ghastly caricature/Of what was human!' (*Swellfoot*, I, i, 377; I, i, 373–4).

Mammon proposes staging the Queen's trial as a public spectacle to undo 'all that has been done' (*Swellfoot*, I, i, 384). First, the government must entice the Queen 'away from the sty' and convince the 'pigs' that the trial is merely an opportunity for her to demonstrate her innocence, which will be marked by her transfiguration into an angel. However, the poison-filled Green Bag guarantees the transformation of the Queen's alleged innocence into a palpable scene of guilt. Guy Debord reminds us that spectacles such as this are complex cultural constructions, which at once allow for the masking and the revelation of power. Spectacles dramatize the instability of socio-political relationships and unexpectedly contravene the false proclamations for justice and unity.[56] Given the trial's inherent volatility and Purganax's insistence that 'it cannot fail' (*Swellfoot*, II, i, 74), it is not surprising when in the midst of this show, the Queen snatches the Green Bag 'with a loud laugh of triumph' (Scene Directions, 408) and dumps the 'Dews of Apotheosis' (*Swellfoot*, I, i, 110) onto Swellfoot and his Court, exposing them as they magically transform into 'filthy and ugly animals, and rush out of the Temple' (Scene Directions, 408).

With this Act the play breaks free of tragedy and fully engages the harlequinade storyline, where the magical transformation of characters enables the 'good' forces to triumph over 'evil'. Shelley also initiates the stage machinery audiences would have been familiar with in hippodrama, which features horses, elephants and even bulls charging across the stage. Invoking the novelty and the innovation of the illegitimate theatre and the carnivalesque atmosphere of the circus and the country fair, hippodrama proved an apt vehicle for conveying social mayhem and cultural conflict, especially war.[57] After this spectacle, the scene directions describe how Famine rises out of the floor with a tremendous sound. Here, Shelley reproduces popular scenes from Thomas Shadwell's *The Libertine* (1676) and George Colman the Younger's *Bluebeard; or, Female Curiosity!* (Drury Lane, 1798) where statues rise out of and disappear into the stage. The pigs begin scrambling for loaves of bread in the midst of this tumult, tripping over skulls in frenzied furor. Pigs that eat the loaves transform into bulls and afterwards line up quietly behind the altar like a jury in a court of law. Famine then sinks into a chasm in the earth, and a Minotaur rises up to replace her as a 'new' political icon. The speaking Minotaur declares himself the 'mightiest/Of all Europa's taurine progeny – /I am the old traditional Man-Bull' (*Swellfoot*, II, i, 103–5).[58] Another stage favourite, John Bull – the caricatured embodiment of English benevolence – exhibits a sharp severity as a Minotaur. The Minotaur features in Ovid's *Metamorphosis* and Homer's epics, where the tyrants, Zeus and Minos wreak havoc on the world. King Minos confines the Minotaur in a labyrinth built by Daedalus and feeds it human flesh. In this story the Minotaur represents a legacy of terror, tyranny and taboo bestiality, which is interrupted when Theseus, the legendary hero from Athens, kills the monster. But Theseus unwittingly preserves this tyrannous legacy when he kills his son, Hippolytus, in an act of misdirected revenge. The appearance of the Minotaur in Shelley's drama marks the tragic restoration of the conservative classicism associated with tragedy and its heroes. The offspring of Pasiphae – the Minotaur – embodies poetic justice. Shelley's final scene and Hazlitt remarks in his 'Review of *Coriolanus*' portray poetic justice as nothing more than a 'royal hunt, in which what is sport to the few is death to the many, and in which the spectators halloo and encourage the strong to set upon the weak, and cry havoc in the chase, though they do not share in the spoil' (*SWWH*, 3. 182). Poetic justice provides audiences with a happy ending, but the game itself – a hunt – has not changed.

In the midst of this action Liberty makes a brief stage appearance. As Iona Taurina (the Queen) stands in preparation for her ordeal, the stage directions describe Liberty – a graceful figure in a semi-transparent veil – walking unnoticed across the stage. In accordance with the traditions of the pantomime, where words were not spoken but written on placards for the audience to read, the word liberty is seen written on a banner that is covered by a sheer veil. The grunting pigs and the business of the trial on stage attract the audience's attention more than the figure, but she continues to move and, in the midst of this chaos, she kneels on the steps of Famine's altar and, breaking with the conventions of pantomime, she begins to speak in a voice that is initially faint but becomes increasingly louder. Like Swellfoot in the opening scene she directs her speech to Famine, the 'Mighty Empress! Death's white wife!/Ghastly mother-in-law of life!' (*Swellfoot*, II, ii, 84–5). Kenneth Neill Cameron and Jones have pointed out that the scene is indebted to Coleridge's 'LETTER from LIBERTY to Her Dear Friend FAMINE' and other essays in *Consciones ad Populum* (1795).[59] Coleridge addressed his pamphlet to the British public in these terms: 'O degenerate People, and bloated with the emptiness of recollected Liberty! SYLLA [sic] may resign the Dictatorship – but alas! he will have given a tempting proof to CAESAR, how much ye can endure' (*Consciones*, 52). Coleridge is suspicious of the allegorical figure of Liberty. So alluring, she makes easy work of the radical or the reformer who wants political change but cannot navigate effectively the cultural subtleties that differentiate spoofs from fiction or blatant propaganda. Portraying Liberty as he does Shelley once again alludes to the work of a vital figure in the revolutionary debates of the 1790s. *Swellfoot* stages Coleridge's allegorized appeal to Famine, where Liberty advocates for the impoverished and disenfranchised people while declaiming the blindness of the ignorant masses, including those in power who manipulate public opinion and 'become voluntary slaves to [. . .] bloody fanatics' (*Consciones*, 64).

Undoubtedly, Shelley found much to admire in *Consciones ad Populum*; he readily adapts Coleridge's fierce criticism of the 'Bigots of Despotism' (*Consciones*, 61) and his references to Burke's 'declamatory invectives' (*Consciones*, 53). *Swellfoot* also reproduces Coleridge's iconography of temples and sacrifices. For both writers the threatening face of Famine represents a composite image of impaired national faith, weakened social confidence and a perilous breach of liberties (*Consciones*, 68). However, as Jones observes, Shelley stages *Consciones* with a twist. Shelley 'manipulates and complicates the relationship between [Famine and Liberty]', as Jones suggests (*Shelley's Satire*, 141), but in both texts, this relationship is strained and adversarial. Shelley takes the additional step of charging the Whigs, radicals and even members of the Lake School with making the critical error of unwittingly appealing to Famine, Freedom's 'eternal foe' (*Swellfoot*, II, ii, 97). This alliance can yield nothing more than a hollow truce, and the sad result will be the continued oppression of radicals and reformers in the post-Napoleonic period and the eventual the restoration of monarchs throughout the Europe and the world.

Shelley's drama concludes with Iona Taurina mounting the Minotaur. As she does so she and the chorus cry out, 'Tallyho tallyho!' as they begin to hunt down the badgers, foxes, otters, hares, wolves and 'these anything but men' (*Swellfoot*, II, ii, 118). The opposition between Iona Taurina and Swellfoot is as nominal as that which exists between Liberty and Famine. To replace one monarch with another changes the regime, but it neither effectively changes nor dissolves the monarchy. For Shelley, the King and Queen existed as a Janus figure. The Queen might have a more appealing visage as does Liberty when compared to Famine but Britain needed more than to change the face of the monarchy, it needed to abolish it as an institution of governance. Classical tragedies with their heroes and their tyrants were too familiar and had been staged repeatedly for popular audiences as tragedies and romances. The British people needed a new form of drama with radically different characters and a new plot. Shelley did not compose *Swellfoot* with the same intent as *Prometheus Unbound*. As a satire, a parody and a farce it recreates the closed world of tragedy in an alternative form more resonant with popular dramas where role reversal and physical transformation feint toward subversion but do not enact it. The scenery shifts from the sty and Famine's temple to the more obvious realm of romance – the forest – but the laws (those of the government and of tragedy and revenge) still displace real justice with the more illusory poetic justice. Like the Queen Caroline affair, *Swellfoot* offers audiences little more than a brief and humorous respite from the unending series of social and political crises. The Queen Caroline affair and the spectacle of Liberty reproduced sovereign power as yet another simulacrum of destructive and violent power: the Minotaur and the 'royal hunt'.

A mere plaything of the imagination

Shelley's depiction of Liberty in *Swellfoot* highlights the contentious debates that took place in the 1790s, particularly in Burke's *Reflections* and Coleridge's *Consciones*. *Swellfoot* dramatizes the failures of reform and revolution and invites readers to rethink Liberty's 'circumvolving destiny' (*Swellfoot*, II, i, 52) that unites Liberty and Famine – *Laon and Cythna*'s the snake and the eagle – in an internecine struggle. *Swellfoot* portrays Liberty as no more capable than the monarchy of liberating her devotees. Liberty and Famine can 'wake the multitude', but in the end they only inspire their followers to tread the well-worn 'paths of blood' (*Swellfoot*, II, i, 90–91). *Swellfoot* dramatizes this effectively, but this was not Shelley's sole purpose in composing this drama.

Throughout this chapter I have suggested that Shelley situated the drama within the context of ongoing cultural debates about the political value of the drama – both in its classical form and in its contemporary manifestations. Keenly aware of the debate's twists and turns within pages of *The Examiner* and in *Blackwood's*, Shelley firmly aligned his work with Leigh Hunt, Keats and Byron – albeit always adopting strategies to expose and transform the '*poetry* of politics'. I suspect Shelley appreciated Lockhart's interest in classical literature and ancient Greek culture and was undoubtedly intrigued by *Blackwood's* promotion of a Schillerian conception of 'aesthetic education' where the theatre – at least in its Greek incarnation – could be considered 'a temple for the purification of the national manners' (*Blackwood's*, 1. 39). While Shelley obviously did not adhere to some of the values espoused by Tory classicism because he clearly derides them in his Advertisement to *Swellfoot*, he also advocates for the 'connexion of poetry and social good' in *A Defence of Poetry*, where he insisted that the nation's drama marked its social excellence as well as its 'corruption of manners, and [the] extinction of the energies which sustain the soul of social life' (*SPP*, 521).

Swellfoot criticizes the questionable cultural values formulated and promoted on stage, in the streets and within periodical reviews. Shelley, Hazlitt, Hunt and even Lockhart worked to reformulate cultural production for political purposes. The Hunt circle remained suspicious of the spurious classism and the bardolatry that played to aristocratic complacency and middle-class moralism and actively countered traditional classicism with their Cockney classicism.[60] The Shelley circle was keenly aware that John Philip Kemble had used the stage to orchestrate public displays of monarchical authority and that these performances encouraged the populace to succumb to 'the language of power' wielded by 'the strongest party' (*SWWH*, 3. 180–181). Appropriating the witty tactics employed by *Blackwood's* and other periodicals, Shelley produces a Cockney classic[61] that also incorporates the radical elements of satire, caricature and pantomime.

In his two-part essay, 'On Pantomime', Hunt announces that pantomime offers its audiences 'something *real*' (*SWLH*, 2. 84). Written two months after Hazlitt's 'Review of *Coriolanus*', Hunt's essay concedes to critical opinion that comedy, tragedy and even farce had degenerated into incoherence and that these conventional performances were staging nothing new. Acting practices and theatre management were producing comedy and tragedy as laboured and artificial productions. The pantomime, however, flourished as a theatrical form and as a commercial venture and it marked a groundswell of innovation that supported the efforts of talented actors like Edmund Kean and Mr Grimaldi. Kean eventually usurped Kemble's staid classicism and transformed Shakespearean performances from a series of stilted 'points' or discrete moments to productions filled with quick movements and exaggerated gestures.[62] Kean's characters emanated a corporeal intensity that reflected his dramatic apprenticeship as a performer in pantomime and melodrama. His acting style elevated bodily movement to the revered status of language, giving his characters, as Jane Moody notes, a 'poetic intensity'.[63] Energized by physical movement and human corporeality, the pantomime, Hunt argued, allowed actors to better imitate bullies and coxcombs. It rejuvenated the national and 'legitimate' drama being performed at the government-licensed patent theatres. And its biting satire staged the real-life dullards and tyrants as well as the savagery and the more benign and playful eroticism of humanity. Pantomime could also offset what Hazlitt would have identified as the suspect nature of romance and tragedy, where the aristocratic hero restores order either through his death or through magic, which belied the real difficulties of securing liberty and social order.

Shelley adapted satiric tactics in *Swellfoot* that were readily visible in journals like *Blackwood's* and *The Black Dwarf*. These periodicals presented their readers with highly dramatized narrative performances and like the pantomime, their success could be measured in terms of how well they could transform the tragedies of real life into some form of comic relief. Spoofs proved to be a popular means of satire because they disarmed audiences with their humour and their supposed transparency. Satire relies upon the audience's savvy and their ability to negotiate the subtleties that distinguish reality from fiction. As a story developed over multiple issues the tenuous connection produced a more sensational story that captivated audiences and encouraged them to quite literally buy into the illusion: purchasing a novel or subscribing to a journal. These literary strategies proved indispensible in an era when commercial success was tied indelibly to the shifting valence of political discussion.

The central concern of this chapter has been to examine how Shelley deployed demotic satire, Cockney classicism and the frameworks of plagiarism to expose the cultural performances that empower obvious contrivances like the Green Bag. Shelley's *Swellfoot* brings together an extended archive of techniques and cultural narratives that constituted Britain's liberation fantasy and undermined efforts to create the conditions for real freedom. Often dismissed as a 'plaything of the imagination', *Swellfoot* explores how society produces seemingly harmless 'plaything[s] of the imagination' that deny people their right to a fair trial and obscure historical realities initially by depicting them as tragedy and then later as parody or farce. The significance of Mary Shelley's seemingly offhand remark becomes clearer when we turn to Lockhart's *Peter's Letters to His Kinfolk*, an extended satire he published in 1819. The book is a series of fictional letters that construct a Tory cultural politics by lampooning Scottish public figures and institutions. It traces the ideological formation of a national culture by reproducing Scotland's romance with its national culture. In letter XIII, 'Peter' criticizes the Scottish university curriculum and insists that history is

> the only study which presents to all our endeavours and aspirations after higher intellectual cultivation, a fast middle-point, and grappling-place [. . .]. Without the knowledge of this great and mighty *past*, the philosophy of life, with whatever wit she may enchant, with whatever eloquence she may charm us, can never effectually lift our view from the ground on which our feet tread – *the present* – from the narrow and limited circle of our own customs, and those of our immediate neighbours an[d] contemporaries.[64]

The speaker discourages provincialism and suggests that history functions as romance in that it 'seizes and expands before us [. . .] a true and entire philosophy, intelligible in all things, and sure in all things' (*Peter's Letters*, 1. 160). Reading history potentially liberates people from the confines of their national consciousness. The question is what displaces this nationalism? Imperialism? Is one enchanting fiction merely taking the place of another? Can history 'furnish us with a fair and quiet point of view from which to survey the *present*' (*Peter's Letters*, 1. 161)?

History and 'the fine arts' connect audiences with 'the actual experience of man' and these cultural productions transport readers and viewers 'into the air and spirit of the times in which they were produced [. . .]' (*Peter's Letters*, 1. 160). Everything else is 'an empty sport, a mere plaything of the imagination' (*Peter's Letters*, 1. 160). It is impossible to say if Mary Shelley or others in the Shelley circle were aware of Lockhart's satire, but the resonances are suggestive and shed light on the possibility that Mary Shelley may very well have been quoting Lockhart in an attempt to direct her more erudite readers to read *Swellfoot* in light of the larger debates about cultural politics and nationalism, which often adapted the form of transparent hoaxes.

Shelley's *Swellfoot* is playful yet poignantly satirical drama that portrays the Caroline affair as one of many familiar national tragedies, as a sordid romance and ultimately as a thought-provoking pantomime that could potentially – at least according to Leigh Hunt – break the mind-forged manacles of ideology and provide audiences with 'something *real*' (*SWLH*, 2. 84). Adapting the satiric practices of periodical editors too, *Swellfoot* lampoons those cultural productions that idolized Liberty and which Hazlitt perceived as portraying the 'history of mankind [as] a romance, a mask, [and] a tragedy constructed upon the principles of *poetical justice'* (*SWWH*, 3.182). Reproducing what audiences 'delight to read in books' (*SWWH*, 3.183) as a transparent hoax, Shelley followed Hazlitt in encouraging his readers to 'understand their own interest[s]' as opposed to those who governed them ('Review of Robert Owen's *A New View of Society'* (*SWWH* 4.96–7).

Notes

1 William Keach, *Arbitrary Power: Romanticism, Language, Politics* (Princeton, 2004), p. 151. See also Keach's more extensive analysis of the poem, pp. 151–8.

2 Mary Shelley makes this point in her 'Note on Oedipus Tyrannus', *Poetical Works*, 410. Because of its availability I am referencing the copy of Shelley's *Oedipus Tyrannus; or, Swellfoot the Tyrant* that is available in *The Complete Poetical Works of Shelley,* referred to throughout as *Poetical Works*.

3 *SPP*, p. 312, fn.4. G.M. Matthews, 'A Volcano's Voice' in Shelley, *English Literary History* 24.3 (September 1957): pp. 191–228; edited and reprinted in *SPP*, pp. 550–570. Also, Cian Duffy in his *Shelley and the Revolutionary Sublime* (Cambridge, 2005) writes that 'Shelley's mature political poetics found its most powerful – and most problematic – expression in his response to Europe's other famous example of the death-dealing mountain sublime: Vesuvius' (150).

4 Slavoj Žižek, *Tarrying with the Negative: Kant, Hegel, and the Critique of Ideology* (Durham, 1993), p. 89. In his *Seeing Through Race* (Cambridge, MA, 2012), W.J.T. Mitchell employs this notion of precariousness to describe the perception of race (pp. 16–17). Judith Butler's discussion of this topic is more obviously centred on the work of Emmanuel Levinas in her *Precarious Lives: The Powers of Mourning and Violence* (New York, 2004).

5 Mary Favret, *War at a Distance: Romanticism and the Making of Modern Wartime* (Princeton, 2010).

6 Michael Scrivener, *Radical Shelley: The Philosophical Anarchism and Utopian Thought of Percy Bysshe Shelley* (Princeton, 1982), p. 92, p. 120.

7 Timothy Morton's 'Porcine Poetics: Shelley's *Swellfoot the Tyrant'*, in Alan M. Weinberg and Timothy Webb (eds), *The Unfamiliar Shelley* (Farnham, 2009), pp. 279–95, p. 282.

8 Morton's most recent contribution is 'Porcine Poetics' but he also comments on the play in his earlier studies of Shelley, including, *Shelley and the Revolution in Taste: The Body and the Natural World* (Cambridge and New York, 1994). Steven Jones's work includes *Shelley's Satire: Violence, Exhortation, and Authority* (DeKalb, 1994), ' "Choose Reform or Civil War": Shelley, the English Revolution, and the Problem of Succession', *Wordsworth Circle* (Summer 1994): pp. 145–9. Samuel Gladden, 'Shelley's Agenda Writ Large: Reconsidering *Oedipus Tyrannus; or, Swellfoot the Tyrant'*, in 'Reading Shelley's Interventionist Poetry, 1819–1820', Michael Scrivener (ed.), a special edition of *Romantic Praxis*. Available at http://www.rc.umd.edu/praxis/interventionist/gladden/gladden.html Also, Gladden's *Shelley's Textual Seductions: Plotting Utopia in the Erotic and Political Works* (New York and London, 2002).

9 See J. Anne Hone's discussion of the early 1819 parliamentary sessions in *For the Cause of Truth: Radicalism in London 1796–1821* (Oxford, 1982), pp. 270–319, specifically, pp. 292–5.

10 In *Shelley and the Revolution in Taste*, pp. 195–202, Timothy Morton discusses *Swellfoot* in these terms. More recently, he has developed these ideas in 'Porcine Poetics', p. 284.

11 Mary Dorothy George, *Catalogue of Political and Personal Satires*, 9 vols. VII–X (1942–52): vol. IX (1949): p. 914, nos 13252, 13253 and 13254. The first two

caricatures depict a metamorphic relationship between animals and humans. The third, significantly, features a character who threatens, 'You had better take you flight or there will be a *Hunt*, after you, and I can swear they'll make *game* of you' (915).

12 Edmund Burke, *Reflections on the Revolution in France: A Critical Edition*, ed. J.C.D. Clark (Stanford, 2001), p. 242. As the editor to this edition notes, Burke's Biblical allusion to Matthew 7.6 was familiar, but Burke's detractors made this reference, often changing the article from a to the, to working-class radicals notorious through their parodies: for example, Thomas Spence entitled his radical journal *Pig's Meat* and Daniel Isaac Eaton's journal, Politics for the People was subtitled *A Salmagundy for Swine*.

13 Anne Hone writes, 'While Peterloo can be regarded as a massive ideological victory for the radicals, disappointment and frustration followed their first efforts to call to account those deemed responsible for the "massacre"' (341). I discuss the Spenceans in Chapter 1, fn. 12.

14 'State Trials', *The Examiner*, XIII, 30 April 1820, p. 273. This essay is one in a series that includes 'Alleged Conspirators in Cato-Street', *The Examiner*, XIII, 5 March 1820, pp. 145–7 (reprinted in *SWLH*, 2. 242–8), 19 March 1820, pp. 177–8; 7 May 1820, pp. 289–91 and 'Execution of the Conspirators', 7 May 1820, pp. 289–91 (*SWLH*, 2. 252–6).

15 T.J. Wooler's STATE THEATRICALS, sometimes referred to as THEATRICALS EXTRAORDINARY conflate the acts of dramatic composition, dramatic criticism and political critique; these works are, as Wooler writes in his Prospectus, a 'survey of the DRAMA', whereby he refers to the unfolding dramas, involving radicals like William Cobbett, whose Potley Theatre (referring to Cobbett's residence and a site for 'legitimate political drama' [176]) closes early in 1817, when he flees to the United States in fear of further prosecution for his radical writing (No. 11, Wednesday, 9 April 1817, p. 176). Another example is his recasting of Richard Brinsley Sheridan's 1777 *School for Scandal* (No. 34, Wednesday, 16 April 1817, p. 574) where he assures readers that 'Messrs. Oliver, Castles, Richmond, Reynolds, and several other professional gentlemen will shortly appear in *first-rate* characters, before the new-drop-curtain is withdrawn' (574). William Oliver and John Castle, like George Edwards were known spies for the government. This is part of an ongoing critique of government spies and *agents provocateurs*.

16 Jane Moody, *Illegitimate Theatre in London, 1770–1840* (Cambridge, 2000), pp. 74–8, p. 74.

17 Jane Martineau (ed.) provides a brief discussion of Harlow's painting in *Shakespeare in Art* (London, 2003), pp. 148–9.

18 Moody, *Illegitimate Theatre*, pp. 228–36.

19 E.A. Smith discusses this in *A Queen on Trial: The Affair of Queen Caroline* (Dover, 1993), p. 187.

20 See Ann Clark's 'Queen Caroline and the Sexual Politics of Popular Culture in London, 1820', *Representations* 31 (Summer 1990): pp. 47–68.

21 William Cobbett, *William Cobbett: Selected Writings*, ed. Leonora Nattrass, consulting editor, James Epstein, volume 4 of the series entitled *Popular Politics and Power 1817–1826* (6 vols, London, 1998), 4. 304. Burke, *Reflections*, p. 238.

22 David Duff discusses Burke's scene in *Romance and Revolution: Shelley and the Politics of Genre* (Cambridge, 1996), pp. 19–21. Burke, *Reflections on the Revolution in France*, pp. 237–8.

23 Thomas Paine, *The Rights of Man* in *Paine: Political Writings*, ed. Bruce Kuklick (Cambridge, 1989), p. 63.

24 David Duff in *Romance and Revolution* provides an erudite commentary on the politics of romance in chapter 1. See also, Ian Duncan's *Modern Romance and Transformations of the Novel: the Gothic, Scott, Dickens* (Cambridge, 1992).

25 Jones in *Shelley's Satire* refers to Bakhtin and the clown figure in his discussion of *Swellfoot*, pp. 131 and 134. See also, Mikhail Bakhtin, *The Dialogic Imagination: Four*

Essays by M.M. Bakhtin, eds and trans. Caryl Emerson and Michael Holquist (Austin, 1981), p. 163. The full quote is instructive insofar as it reveals the underlying theatrical nature of satire:

'They grant the right *not* to understand, the right to confuse, to tease, to hyperbolize life; the right to parody others while talking, the right not to be taken literally, not "to be oneself"; the right to live a life in the chronotope of the entr'acte, the chronotope of theatrical space, the right to act life as a comedy and to treat others as actors, the right to rip off masks, the right to rage at others [. . .] and finally, the right to betray to the public a personal life, down to its most private and prurient little secrets'.

26 John Barrell, *Exhibition Extraordinary!! Radical Broadsides of the Mid 1790s* (Nottingham, 2001), pp. xiii–xiv.

27 Jean I. Marsden, 'Sex, Politics, and She-Tragedy: Reconfiguring Lady Jane Grey', *Studies in English Literature 1500–1900* 42.3 (Summer 2002): pp. 501–22.

28 One duel between John Scott, editor of the *London Magazine* and Thomas Christie, acting for Lockhart, occurred on 16 February 1821 at Chalk Farm, near London and resulted in Scott's death. For accounts of this event, see *The Times*, Friday, 13 April 1821; Andrew Lang, *The Life and Letters of John Gibson Lockhart* (2 vols, London, 1897), 1. 250–282; and Marion Lochhead, *John Gibson Lockhart* (London, 1954), pp. 82–5. Lockhart's quarrel with Scott testifies to the virulent underpinnings of these cultural debates.

29 Lockhart launched his first attack, signed Z, against the Cockney School in *Blackwood's Edinburgh Review Magazine* 2.7 (October 1817): pp. 38–41.

30 For a more detailed account of the politics of Scottish journals, see Ian Duncan's *Scott's Shadow: The Novel in romantic Edinburgh* (Princeton, 2007). See also the Introduction to *SWLH*, volume 1, Periodical Essays, 1805–14, specifically, pp. xxix–xxxiii.

31 James Hogg, *The Private Memoirs and Confession of a Justified Sinner*, ed. Adrian Hunter (Peterborough, 2001), p. 226.

32 There are several suggestive essays written about Inchbald's drama: Betsy Bolton, 'Farce, Romance and Empire: Elizabeth Inchbald and the Colonial Discourse', *The Eighteenth Century* 39.1(Spring 1998): pp. 3–24; Daniel O'Quinn, 'Elizabeth Inchbald's *The Massacre*: Tragedy, Violence and the Network of Political Fantasy', *British Women Playwrights around 1800*, 1 June 1999, 8 pars. http://www.etang.umontreal.ca/bwp1800/essays/oquinn_massacre.html; and his 'Scissors and Needles: Inchbald's *Wives as They Were, Maids as They Are* and the Governance of Sexual Exchange', *Theatre Journal* 51 (1999): pp. 105–25; Vita M. Mastrosilvestri, 'Elizabeth Inchbald: Translation as Mediation and Re-writing', in Maria Crisafulli and Keir Elam (eds), *Women's Romantic Theatre and Drama*, pp. 159–68.

33 O'Quinn, 'Elizabeth Inchbald's', paragraph 4.

34 Jones links *Swellfoot* and 'Rough Festivals' in *Shelley's Satire*, pp. 124–48.

35 For a more extensive discussion of this reference to *King Lear*, see Hugh Robert's 'The Communicative Strategies of Shelley's Prefaces', in *The Unfamiliar Shelley*, pp. 183–98, p. 192.

36 I'm referring to the composite text of Shakespeare's *King Lear* in the Norton edition.

37 Michael Erkelenz makes this point in his 'The Genre and Politics of Shelley's *Swellfoot the Tyrant*', *Review of English Studies* (November, 1996): pp. 500–520, p. 524.

38 Both of these articles appeared in the first volume of *Blackwood's Edinburgh Magazine*, which was initially published as *Edinburgh Monthly Magazine* prior to its transformation into *Blackwood's* (April 1817): pp. 9–16, pp. 39–42.

39 'On the Sculpture of the Greeks', *Blackwood's*, p. 39. In the September issue of *Blackwood's Edinburgh Magazine* (September 1817): pp. 579–82, there is also a rather indulgent and cerebral letter to the editor entitled 'On the Symbolical Uses of Salt' which might explain Shelley's reference to *Attic Salt*. Notably, the article – perhaps a hoax to advertise the Miscellany – traces customary uses of salt through Scottish texts – *The Tales of my Landlord* – the Bible, Pliny, Cicero and the *Iliad*, and insists on its relevance in

sacred rites, including divination and establishing covenants of friendship. Also, as the correspondence collected by Walter Sidney Scott suggests, Shelley and his circle at Marlow considered themselves as Athenians. See *The Athenians: Being a Correspondence between Thomas Jefferson Hogg, and his Friends Thomas Love Peacock, Leigh Hunt, Percy Bysshe Shelley, and Others* (London, 1943).

40 Jeffrey N. Cox, *Poetry and Politics in the Cockney School: Keats, Shelley, Hunt and their Circle* (Cambridge, 1998), pp. 146–86.

41 Tilar J. Mazzeo, *Plagiarism and Literary Property in the Romantic Period* (Philadelphia, 2007), p. 1.

42 Benedict Anderson, *Imagined Communities: Reflections on the Origin and Spread of Nationalism* (London, 1991).

43 This is the key phrase in Steven E. Jones edited collection of essays, *The Satiric Eye: Forms of Satire in the Romantic Period* (New York, 2003).

44 In his discussion of Cockney classicism, Jeffrey N. Cox identifies Romantic classicism as an aesthetic doctrine, a functional or utilitarian art (pottery) and a political project. He adopts Walter Benjamin's vocabulary in 'The Work of Art in the Age of Mechanical Reproduction' to distinguish the more conventional classicism from Cockney classicism, p. 146. Benjamin's essay is available in *Illuminations*, Hannah Arendt (ed.) and Harry Zohn (trans) (New York, 1968).

45 Duncan discusses this process in a different context in *Scott's Shadow*, specifically chapters one and nine. Once again, Benjamin's 'The Work of Art in the Age of Mechanical Reproduction' is relevant insofar as the innumerable reproductions of the monarch's image undermined it cultural authority.

46 Timothy Morton, 'Porcine Poetics', p. 284.

47 One instance of this occurs in Shelley's letter to Thomas Love Peacock (20 April 1818; *Letters* 2. 9): 'The people here, though inoffensive enough, seem both in both & soul a miserable race. The men are hardly men, they look like a tribe of stupid & shriveled slaves, & I do not think I have seen a gleam of intelligence in the countenance of man since I passed the Alps. The women in enslaved countries are always better than the men; but [with] a mixture of coquette & the prude that reminds me of one of the worst characteristics of English women'.

48 Homi Bhabha, 'Of Mimicry and Man: The Ambivalence of Colonial Discourse', in Philomena Essed and David Theo Goldberg (eds), *Race Critical Theories* (Malden, 2000), pp. 113–22, p. 114.

49 In the RSV translation of the Bible, the story of the Gadarean swine is told in the gospels of Matthew (1.28–34), Mark (5.1–20), and Luke (8.26–39).

50 Shelley discusses the episode of the Gadarean swine in 'On the Devil and Devils', *Shelley's Prose*, pp. 264–75. pp. 271–2.

51 Daniel O'Quinn discusses this and the rhetorical devices employed by Burke and Fox in his article, 'Fox's Tears: The Staging of Liquid Politics', in Alexander Dick and Angela Esterhammer (eds) *Spheres of Action: Speech and Performance in Romantic Culture* (Toronto, 2009), pp. 194–221, especially, p. 198 ff.

52 David Simpson, *Romanticism, Nationalism, and the Revolt against Theory* (Chicago, 1993), p. 57.

53 Michael Scrivener, *Radical Shelley: The Philosophical Anarchism and Utopian thought of Percy Bysshe Shelley* (Princeton, 1982), pp. 261–7. While I believe Shelley responds directly to Malthus, I don't agree with Scrivener that Shelley 'takes the Queen Caroline affair as the plot material which he transforms to an argument against Malthus and in favor of libertarian reform' (262).

54 Slavoj Žižek, *The Sublime Object of Ideology* (New York, 1989), p. 45. Also, Jacques Derrida deals with this phenomenon in *Specters of Marx: The State of Debt, the work of Mourning, and the New International*, trans. Peggy Kamuf (New York, 1994), p. 6. Derrida and Žižek describe a similar concept – a spectral presence – that underlies ideology.

55 Queen Iona is the name Shelley gives Queen Caroline. Significantly, the name, which refers to an island in the Hebrides reinforces the Scottish and Irish associations within the play: the island hosted a monastery that was central to Irish monasticism.

56 Guy Debord, *The Society of the Spectacle*, trans. Donald Nicholson-Smith (New York, 1995), p. 46. Specifically, I'm thinking of these observations made by Debord:

'Whatever lays claim to permanence in the spectacle is founded on change, and must change as that foundation changes. The spectacle, though quintessentially dogmatic, can yet produce no solid dogma. Nothing is stable for it: this is its natural state, albeit the state most at odds with natural inclination'.

and

'The unreal unity the spectacle proclaims masks the class division on which the real unity of the capitalist mode of production is based. What obliges the producers to participate in the construction of the world is also what separates them from it. What brings together men liberated from local and national limitations is also what keeps them apart. What pushes for greater rationality is also what nourishes the irrationality of hierarchical exploitation and repression. What creates society's abstract power also creates its concrete unfreedom'.

57 Michael Gamer writes on hippodrama in 'A Matter of Turf: Romanticism, Hippodrama, and Satire', *Nineteenth-Century Contexts*, 28.4 (December 2006): pp. 305–34.

58 George Colman the Younger also wrote *John Bull; or, The Englishman's Fireside* (Covent Garden, 1803); along with Colman's *Bluebeard* and his *Inkle and Yariko* (Haymarket, 1787), these were some of the most popular theatrical dramas in the period.

59 Samuel Taylor Coleridge, *Consciones ad Populum* (New York, 1992); Kenneth Neill Cameron, *Shelley: The Golden Years* (Cambridge, MA, 1974), pp. 361–2, 629–30, n. 43; Steven Jones, *Shelley's Satire*, pp. 140–142.

60 Hazlitt's 'Review of *Coriolanus*' first appeared in *The Examiner* (15 December 1816). For earlier comments on classicism made by writers for *The Examiner*, see the editions dated 3 June 1810, p. 344 and 19 December 1813, p. 810. See also, Jane Moody's astute discussion of 'Illegitimate Shakespeare's' in *Illegitimate Theatre in London, 1770–1840* (Cambridge, 2000), pp. 118–47.

61 Jeffrey N. Cox, *Poetry and Politics*, pp. 146–86.

62 Lisa A. Freeman discusses 'points' in *Character's Theater: Genre and Identity on the Eighteenth-Century English Stage* (Philadelphia, 2002), pp. 31–6. See also, Joseph R. Roach's *The Player's Passion: Studies in the Science of Acting* (1985; Rpt. Ann Arbor, 1993).

63 Moody, *Illegitimate Theatre in London*, p. 232.

64 John Gibson Lockhart, *Peter's Letters to His Kinsfolk* (3 vols, Edinburgh, 1819), pp. 1. 158, 159.

3 'Titleless nothing', 'lifeless idol' and 'enchanted phantom'

Reconfiguring the King's image and the politics of memory

Nature rejects the monarch, not the man;
The subject, not the citizen: for kings
And subjects, mutual foes, for ever play
A losing game into each other's hands,
Whose stakes are vice and misery.
                    —*Queen Mab*, II. 170–174.

Shelley sketched the framework for 'Charles the First' between 1817 and 1822. Following Thomas Medwin, who described this fragment as 'an inextricable web of difficulties',[1] critics have tended to ignore this interlined and interworded text. More recently, it has emerged 'as a far more conceptualized piece than it has hitherto appeared to be', and Nora Crook enjoins us to believe it 'will appear increasingly so as all the material connected to it is collated' (*BSM* XII, xiiv). The title of Shelley's fragment marks it more clearly than *The Cenci* or *Swellfoot the Tyrant* as a national tragedy: one that I believe Shelley would have reformulated into a liberating historical drama if he had finished his project. Charles I ascended the throne in 1625, and his reign proved to be contentious, when he attempted multiple times to rule without Parliament. A series of legal battles ensued between the Court and Parliament and this contest eventually devolved into civil war. The debate centred on the extent of the King's prerogatives and whether Parliament had the constitutional right to limit his power. The colonial upheavals in Scotland and Ireland seemed to merge into England's first Civil War, which lasted from 1642 until 1647. After the Scots captured Charles I and turned him over to Parliamentary forces, the King escaped to the Isle of Wight, where he encouraged the Scots to invade England. The Second Civil War was over within a year. Claiming the need to bring Charles I to account, Parliament charged him with treason and brought him to trial. Throughout the trial Charles I refused to play his assigned role. He never acknowledged the court's legitimacy; he never entered a plea, and Parliament found him guilty. Charles I was executed by order of the English Parliament on 30 January 1649. The King's execution brought the violent contest between the monarchy and Parliament to a conclusive end. The English Commonwealth rose out of the ashes of this regicide and civil strife, but it too was haunted by political, religious and cultural turmoil. Two documents exemplify this clash between the Commonwealth and the royalists: *Eikon Basilike; The Pourtraiture* [sic] *of His Sacred Majestie in his Solitudes and Sufferings* (London, 1648) and John Milton's response, *Eikonoklastes* (1649).

Both titles feature the Latinate form of icon, and this word in addition to iconology and iconography represent the operative vocabulary in the cultural and political debates addressed in this chapter. The performative masques produced in the Tudor, Stuart and Caroline courts had married ideology to iconography in support of monarchical power, but this competition over the future conception of the kingdom gave birth to a semiotic web of coded and conventional signs and interpretable objects that linked the seventeenth century to the Romantic period. Shelley's 'Charles the First' represents a comparative and inter-textual study of the iconology of the King's portrait and the various attempts to reconstruct or to eradicate that image. Despite its status as an unfinished fragment, Shelley's drama invites early nineteenth-century audiences to shift their radical or royalist perspective of the English monarchy and to consider how the interplay between the verbal, visual and dramatic arts can reveal the ideological register of different mediums and what values they serve when they adhere to and/or transgress text, image and performance boundaries. 'Charles the First' focuses our attention on how genres and modes individually and collectively produce and disseminate cultural icons. Very much alive after more than 175 years, the cultural memories that circulated around the image of Charles I reproduced the long-standing political divisions between royalists and radicals. 'Charles the First' marks Shelley's attempt to reconfigure these cultural memories of the British monarchy and Charles I into a politics of forgiveness[2] grounded in the collective experiences of vulnerability, grief and hope.[3]

Shelley both follows and breaks with convention in his composition of 'Charles the First'. Like William Havard in his popular production of *Charles the First: An Historical Tragedy. Written in Imitation of Shakespeare* (1737), Shelley adopts the Renaissance practice of the classical *imitatio*, a critical and creative principle of writing that allowed writers to recreate or translate the *auctors* – cultural authorities – of the past in a way that would be relevant to the present. *Imitatio* creates an inter-texual situation by encouraging dialogue and comparison but it also destabilizes the relationship between texts and between the past and the present. It is in this sense that Shelley imitates Shakespeare in 'Charles the First'. Many of the play's critical scenes need to be read through the lens of Shakespearean dramas: particularly, *Coriolanus*, *The Tempest* and *King Lear*. But Shelley also breaks with his predecessor insofar as he writes a history play not a historical tragedy. Like Shakespeare's *Richard II*, this drama features a character that must resign himself to the loss of his power and title and acknowledge his own humanity. Shelley's history play dramatizes an account of how the royalists as well as the radicals and the reformers failed the nation and how that failure was one of the collective imagination. Like *The Cenci*, 'Charles the First' is both a character study and a palimpsest of historical and literary references, all of which Shelley reworks so as to reformulate the static and paralysing iconography associated with theatrical and political displays of power. A theatrical performance that challenges the monumental and stately tragedy of Charles I, Shelley's drama adapts what would have been a very familiar story to British audiences, staging contesting ideologies that inhibited reform in the early nineteenth century.

Most scholars agree that the seed for 'Charles the First' was planted while Shelley resided at Marlow in 1817, where he discussed Republican history – and specifically the Ship-Money litigation case of 1637–38 – with his friend, Thomas Love Peacock.[4] Perhaps William Godwin roused Shelley in 1818 when he suggested that Mary Shelley write something on the English Civil War and the Glorious Revolution. But it is in an 1820 letter to Medwin that Shelley announces his intention to 'write a play, in the spirit of nature, without prejudice or passion, entitled "Charles the First"' (20 July 1820; *Letters* 2. 219–20). What we have of the play are four scenes in draft; most obviously, the final two scenes are incomplete.[5] As a history play 'Charles the First' reconstructs and challenges the image of the British monarch as a national icon. It does so by depicting a period of contention between the Charles I and London barristers, which culminated in an attempt on behalf of the London Inns of Court to speak to the King through the performance of James Shirley's 1634 masque, *The Triumph of Peace*. This series of events represents a critical historical juncture for Shelley. If the monarch had been able to read aright the masque presented to him by the Inns of Court, he might have inaugurated reforms, changed the course of history and saved his life.

Shelley's drama breaks with convention and does not represent Charles I as a tragic hero. In fact there is no evidence to suggest that his play would have concluded with the monarch's execution. As it stands, the play examines the possibilities for resuscitating charged cultural memories through theatrical performance.[6] While it is tempting to speculate about Shelley's intentions for his drama – effectively, attempting to imaginatively complete it – I focus on situating Shelley's text within the larger historical and cultural contexts of republican and royalist iconography. Ultimately 'Charles the First' represents a play of shifting cultural lenses wherein Shelley combines a radical and demotic iconography with the more elevated and 'legitimate' forms of iconography associated with the court masque and Shakespearean drama. Steven Jones has noted that Shelley 'produced some of his [. . .] most "overtly political" poetry [. . .] intended for a popular audience reeling from the implications of Peterloo, the Six Acts, and the Queen Caroline Affair' while working on 'Charles the First'.[7] And critics, including Jones, Stuart Curran and Michael Scrivener have commented extensively on Shelley's use of popular iconography in *Swellfoot the Tyrant*, *The Mask of Anarchy* (1819) and 'England in 1819'.[8] In these works Shelley adapts the ribald humour, the poignant satire and the visceral theatrics commonly associated with the *Punch and Judy* puppet show, holiday pantomime theatrics and sensational melodramas. He also clearly engages the print politics and the radical iconoclastic and iconographic practices promulgated by George Cruikshank, William Hone and T.J. Wooler. Appropriating radical traditions and simultaneously very aware of the tumultuous play of radical and reactionary icons in the contemporary moment, Shelley understood, as did Milton and Francis Bacon, that many of the most popular icons were fictions designed to maintain the power of the monarchy, and as such, represented 'idols of the mind' and spectacles of power that needed to be dismantled if there were to be real reform. With a full awareness of the changes in theatrical and print practices that had transpired since the seventeenth century, Shelley deploys iconographic allusions to represent his vision of the past, his approach to contemporary dilemmas and his hopes for the future.

'Medusa's Art': souvenirs, icons and the politics of memory

Shelley's translation of the Walpurgis Night section of Goethe's *Faust* provides us with some sense of how he might have viewed the volatility of icons as encounters with idols and phantoms. In this passage Mephistopheles warns Faust to beware of a vision that appears to be Gretchen:

> Let it be – pass on –
> No good can come of it – it is not well
> To meet it – it is an enchanted phantom,
> A lifeless idol; with its numbing look
> It freezes up the blood of man; and they
> Who meet its ghastly stare are turned to stone,
> Like those who saw Medusa.[9]

Walpurgis Night represents a fantasy construction. Reality and illusion merge into a timeless space where the past collapses into the present. Arguably, this phantom epitomizes how Faust has always seen Gretchen: an abstraction of love or femininity, but regardless, Faust at this juncture is incapable of acknowledging her humanity. An 'enchanted phantom' and a 'lifeless idol', Gretchen is not Gretchen but more like the mythic gorgon, Medusa, who had the power to petrify innocent bystanders and heroic adventurers curious or brave enough to look at her. The myth conveys a story about both a physical and a 'visual assault' and the subsequent prohibition to look at Medusa, whose beauty or monstrosity strikes terror into onlookers.[10] The myth is replete with a play of mirrors, shields and looks. Medusa's death at the hand of Perseus and his attachment of her severed head to Minerva's shield or breastplate can be regarded as a tale of decapitation and resuscitation. Although Medusa's head is severed from her body, her visage retains its power to paralyse onlookers. Athena/Minerva initially transforms Medusa into a monster: in an act of anger and so that Medusa can protect herself. But Athena also reappropriates the power she bestowed upon Medusa once Perseus kills her. Medusa's power as a living, breathing body resolves into a reflection of itself and then transforms into a powerful representation that merges with a material object: the shield with Medusa's head attached. Medusa dies in an act of self-petrification. At this moment, the material reality slips into its simulacrum and the linear movement of time appears to become fixed in the immobility of an icon.

Icons, idols and phantoms embody this critical ambiguity that shifts almost restlessly between the material and the ephemeral: the representation, the image and the thing itself. As Shelley's translation suggests, the iconicity of a person undermines and effaces the emotional attachments between people and, more significantly, supplants human encounters – human sympathy and even human grief – with a material exchange of objects: objects that people infuse with life and transform into powerful political and cultural icons. In contrast with Shelley's translation, John Prudhoe's version foregrounds the erotic and emotional charge of this image of Gretchen as 'every lover's dream'.[11] This makes clearer Shelley's decision to downplay the emotional charge in order to emphasize the dangers of what Prudhoe refers to as 'Medusa's art'. This phrase, like 'enchanted phantom' and 'lifeless idol', delineates the icon's art and its power as inhuman and monstrous. 'Medusa's art' transforms living history into a performance of iconographic images that can extract the life force from viewers who are frozen by fear and as such remain blind to their own interests and invulnerable to love and devoid of human sympathy. Shelley amongst others in his circle was concerned about the pervasive cultural malaise that enveloped the aristocracy and paralysed the middle class while artisans and the working classes were on the verge of revolution.[12] Shelley's *Faust* translation underscores how icons posed a disabling threat to society and the politics of reform.

Shelley formulates an alternative iconographic praxis in many of his dramas, and particularly in 'Charles the First', a story where the polarized iconography that exists in *Eikon Basilike* and *Eikonoklastes* exacerbates political conflict and misunderstanding. 'Charles the First' stages historical scenes where misinterpretation aggravated and inflamed conflict into enmity. Taking a cue from *The Cenci*, Shelley revolutionizes the staid and inflexible portrait of Charles I by representing him as

> something like an actor on the historical stage, a presence or character endowed with legendary status, a history that parallels and participates in the stories we tell ourselves about our own evolution from creatures 'made in the image' of a creator, to creatures who make themselves in their world in their own image.[13]

As W.J.T. Mitchell points out, iconoclastic polemics do not alter the fact that images exist and circulate culturally and historically. Nor does it help to try and isolate or confine images within particular institutionalized discourses. Images and icons embody a fluidity and the performative quality of actors who bring characters to life when they walk on stage. They exist in a network of social and cultural practices 'and in a history fundamental to our understanding not only of what images are but of what human nature is or might become'.[14] For icons and images to survive they must be culturally mobile and as such they are reformulated in accordance with ongoing historical processes: reconstructing the past and molding the future. Far from being solid or monolithic, their malleability makes it possible for them to crisscross historic and generic boundaries and take different forms that cannot be eradicated by an iconoclastic impulse.

As actors, it becomes clearer how Charles I, Beatrice Cenci or even the mythic character of Prometheus can be remade to reflect the conjunction of cultural values in the present moment and the perceived cultural needs for the future. Directing attention to the cultural frameworks that structure and promulgate historical memories, Shelley's dramas encourage audiences to be more critical and self-aware of the performative nature of icons. Images are a kind of language that helps us make sense of the world. They are, to adapt a phrase from Michel Foucault, 'figures of knowledge'[15] that traverse the cultural landscape. When images no longer help us make meaning they disappear.

Henry VIII, more clearly than other English monarchs, combined the energies of iconoclasm and iconography to reconfigure the English monarchy in the sixteenth century. With the radical and iconoclastic dissolution of the Catholic Church – appropriating its lands and dismantling its religious authority throughout England – Henry VIII produced an image of the King that merged both religious symbolism with political power and the creative force of iconography with iconoclasm. His daughter, Elizabeth I, further solidified the iconography of the English monarchy through her calculated deployment of court pageantry and the masque, where we see the cultural negotiation of a mythic spectacle of power that integrates iconic and iconoclastic energies – seen in the masque and antimasque – into one performance. James I (James VI of Scotland) translated these court performances into a political doctrine in *The True Law of Free Monarchies* (1598) and *Basilikon Doran* (1599), which he composed before taking the English throne in 1603. The Caroline masques resuscitated and memorialized these cultural and political traditions until the critical moment in 1649, when Parliament's act of regicide severed the King's head from his body, materially dismantling the English monarchy as a national icon.

In her account of Charles I's execution in *Cultural Aesthetics*, Patricia Fumerton describes how on his final day, the King delivered all his remaining wealth in the form of diamonds and jewels to his children, gave his keeper, Colonel Hacker, a silver clock and ' "bade him keep it in memory of him"',[16] and appeared on the scaffold with the same demeanor he had often adopted on masque-nights. After his death, she writes, 'Mementos proliferated [. . .]. Bits of hair as well as of blood-stained sand and cloth were often inserted in lockets and rings bearing commemorative mottoes'.[17] The death of Charles I produced a litany of responses. Private and public memorials, history books and theatrical performances repeatedly reanimated the King's body, producing a seemingly endless series of spectacles that excited cultural debates about sovereignty and iconography for the next 200 years. Printed and distributed within hours of Charles I's death, *Eikon Basilike* represents the first attempt to reconstruct the King's image for the historical record. Ascribed to Charles I, but purportedly composed by John Gauden (1605–62), the Bishop of Exeter, who had been given the King's notes, *Eikon Basilike*, with its famous frontispiece designed by William Marshall (Figure 3.1), was marketed as the monarch's spiritual autobiography. The text and its accompanying frontispiece identify the King as a saint, a martyr and a tragic hero who had withstood the turbulent upheavals of civil war and imprisonment. As pictured in Marshall's design, the book's emblematic iconography is distinctly theatrical. The colonnade divides the pictorial set into a doubled scene representing interior

Figure 3.1 William Marshall, Frontispiece of *Eikon Basilike*, 1649

contemplation on the right and, on the left, a more symbolic depiction of the King's strength and perseverance.

The emblematic iconography of Marshall's design places Charles I in a Roman basilica. The cultural and political resonances of the Roman basilica reflect Britain's imperial ambitions as well as the King's inclination to preserve the Catholic lineaments of the Anglican service. The open basilica on the right partially encircles Charles kneeling at the altar. The architectural framework represents the Church and the monarchy as the nation's figurative and institutional foundations insofar as both are integral to the nation's legal system and its spiritual life. Marshall also depicts three crowns in a vertical line. Initially, this seems to contravene our expectations for a pictorial representation of the King's two bodies. The King's two bodies were defined by Edmund Plowden in the sixteenth century as 'a Body natural' and a 'Body politic [. . .] consisting of Policy and Government, and constituted for the Direction of the People, and the Management of the public weal'.[18] Charles I holds the crown of thorns and, in his mind's eye, he perceives the eternal crown of glory. He has discarded the third crown, the splendid crown of vanity, which represents his sacrifice of earthly wealth and personal self-regard. The crown of thorns vividly portrays the physical body and its capacity for suffering, while the other crown is eternal and assures viewers that the King embodies a divine power. To the left, Marshall replicates this scene of patient endurance with a series of allegorical images. At the top left, a rock withstands the raging waters of the sea, and below, a palm tree is laden with weights. The imagery on both sides of the divide identifies the monarch as a martyr to his people. He has endured the revolutionary violence with a strength (the weights) and a constancy (the rock) indicative of his divine right and sovereign power. The symbolic emphasis on Charles I's patient suffering casts the scene as a tragedy. David Loewenstein attests to Gauden and Marshall's success by counting to no fewer than 35 English editions of *Eikon Basilike* printed in 1649, and if one counts those printed on the Continent, the number rises to 40.[19]

Milton responded to this reappearance of the 'King's Image' with *Eikonoklastes*, which was published in early October 1649. Insisting that *Eikon Basilike* contains 'little els but the common grounds of tyranny and popery, drest up, the better to deceiv, in a new Protestant guise',[20] Milton recasts Marshall's 'conceited portraiture' as a 'drawn out [. . .] Masking scene [. . .] sett there to catch fools and silly gazers'.[21] Its 'quaint Emblems and devices', he insists, are 'begg'd from the old Pageantry of some Twelf–nights entertainment at *Whitehall*, [and] will doe but ill to make a Saint or Martyr'.[22] Milton downplays Marshall's frontispiece as nothing other than an expensive, fanciful illustration designed like the masque to convey the monarch's power and his identity as a martyr. Moreover, in an attempt to dismantle the 'tragick scaffold'[23] erected by Gauden and other royalists, Milton reminds his audience that the King's adherents 'never lov'd him, never honour'd either him or his cause, but as they took him to set a face upon thir own malignant designes'.[24] Gauden may have represented Charles I as a heroic tragic martyr in the pages of *Eikon Basilike*, but for Milton, the dead monarch is a volatile cultural memory that it were best to lay to rest. Dismissing him as nothing more than a dramatic figure in a masque, a mere actor, Milton insists that the dead King, as in his life, does not speak for himself but as another and for others. Milton's radical iconoclasm attempts to subvert the tragic paradigm that sustains royalist ideology by withdrawing the curtain and exposing the monarch as a masked figure, a mere puppet controlled by others. But as Mitchell's description of the icon as an actor suggests, Milton's counterattack is misdirected and will prove ineffective except insofar as it further polarizes the cultural imagery that distinguishes royalists from radicals and reformers.

As celebrating the King's death as an act of martyrdom became more fashionable during the Restoration (1660), throughout the eighteenth century and even into the early nineteenth century, these texts, including Plowden's, and other 'remembrances' appeared everywhere, reproducing a material connection between the past and the present. There existed a distinct resonance, Timothy Morton and Nigel Smith observe in their Introduction to *Radicalism in British Literary Culture*, between the mid-seventeenth century and the Romantic period. '[A]ll of the surviving artifacts from the 1640s and 1650s', they write, represent 'potentially powerful agents in a revival of revolutionary energy in the 1790s, or warnings against those energies'.[25] Morton and Smith's essay collection affirms the cultural, historical and political connection between the two revolutions: the English Civil War and the French Revolution. Throughout the Romantic period both conservatives and radicals collected and circulated mementos and souvenirs, marking the different veins of Britain's revolutionary and reactionary history. These cultural and historical artifacts – including paintings, translations, poems, essays, jewellery, dishes, locks of hair and plaster busts – entwined opposing political traditions, as Morton and Smith write, 'in the marketplace of bourgeois art-collecting'.[26] This material chronicle reconstituted itself as a formidable politics of memory: mirroring the acrimony that effectively sustained the oppositional divide between royalists and the radical reform movement.

Shelley's wrote his dramatic fragment in response to the circulation of cultural objects, artifacts and souvenirs from the mid-seventeenth century. Shelley had even requested that a box of materials be sent to him in Italy and when it was lost at sea, he exclaimed in a letter to John and Maria Gisborne, 'My unfortunate Box! it contained a chaos of the elements of Charles the first' (5 June 1811; *Letters*, 2.294). The material nature of Shelley's project is striking when one considers how scholars have repeatedly emphasized the abstract and philosophical character of his work. Shelley's historical project encompassed Bacon's *Great Instauration* (1620), *Eikon Basilike*, Milton's *Eikonoklastes* and Bulstrode Whitelocke's *Memorials of the English Affairs* (1682). It also responded to the proliferation of popular iconography that sustained the pamphlet wars of the 1790s and the culture wars of the early nineteenth century, all of which informed written histories, portraits and theatrical productions, including Shakespearean drama. Variant iconographic practices developed throughout the period. Byron's 'Windsor Poetics', Keats's early poems, Leigh Hunt's essays and his reworking of the masque in *The Descent of Liberty* (1815) represent some of the experimental works that shifted the ideological valences of iconographic practices. These interventions, like Shelley's fragment and William Godwin's *Essay on Sepulchres: or, A Proposal for Erecting some Memorial of the Illustrious Dead in all Ages on the Spot where their Remains have been Interred* (1809) attempted to reconfigure and mediate the popular iconographies that animated and defused reactionary and radical politics in the period.

The 'antic disposition' of Charles I

After his death in 1649, Charles I made his first stage appearance in Havard's 1737 production of *Charles the First*. Havard portrays the history and the tragedy of Charles I's execution through the lens of Shakespearean drama and, like many of the pamphlets written during the Restoration period, he represents him as a tragic hero and a martyr.[27] First performed at the Theatre-Royal in Lincoln's Inn Fields, this drama held its place in the English repertoire throughout the eighteenth century and was reprinted on the order of 10 editions in the period from 1737 to 1810. John Philip Kemble, the actor-manager, who Jane Moody notes, 'designed his Shakespeare productions as the quintessential defence of monarchical legitimacy',[28] made his debut in the play. John Bell reprinted the tragedy in volume 19 of his 1797 edition of *Bell's British Theatre*. Printed in the aftermath of Louis XVI's execution in France on 21 January 1793, Bell's anthology amplifies the historical resonance between the theatrical performance and the historical event, which occurred almost 150 years after the debut of Havard's tragedy. Responding to the crisis brought about by revolutionary events in France, Bell reasserts the aesthetic and political importance of the martyred Charles I as a requisite cultural icon to be kept 'perpetually presented to Englishman' so as to steel the populace 'against the wiles and impositions of modern regicides'.[29] Bell's remarks and the drama's production history affirm its emblematic status as the King's portrait and the perceived political necessity of its reproduction, especially during periods of intense political controversy and social upheaval.

With a very different political charge, Charles I appears in 'Windsor Poetics', where the speaker in Byron's poem discovers 'headless Charles' next to 'heartless Henry'. '[C]omposed', Byron writes, 'on the occasion of his royal highness the Prince Regent [crowned George IV in 1820] being seen standing between the coffins of Henry VIII and Charles I, in the royal vault at Windsor' (*CPW*, 3. 86), 'Windsor Poetics' unveils the mystery of royalist iconography as nothing more than a fetishized commodity whose material value no longer reflects a real social relationship between people but rather what Marx refers to as 'a fantastic form': a 'magical' relationship between things.[30] Byron subverts the monarchy's legitimacy by exposing the marvellous and the wonderful as sensational, surreal and grotesque. Setting the scene in the royal crypt, Byron's satiric history of the British monarchy unfolds as a vampire tale:

> FAMED for contemptuous breach of sacred ties
> By headless Charles see heartless Henry lies;
> Between them stands another Sceptred thing –
> It moves, it reigns, in all but name – a King:
> Charles to his People, Henry to his Wife,
> – In him the double Tyrant starts to Life:
> Justice and Death have mixed their dust in vain,
> Each Royal Vampyre wakes to life again;
> Ah! what can tombs avail – since these disgorge
> The blood and dust of both – – to mold a G[eor]ge.[31]

Referring to the Prince Regent as 'another Sceptred thing', Byron depicts the cultural and the figural materiality of an inanimate object that has been infused repeatedly with life and power. The Regent, an amalgamation of Charles I and Henry VIII, 'starts to Life' like Mary Shelley's doppelgänger figure of the modern Prometheus, Frankenstein's monster. This imagery resonates with Shelley's 'lifeless idol' and 'enchanted phantom' in his translation of *Faust* and it casts the British monarchy as 'Royal Vampyre' that 'wakes to life', disgorging 'blood and dust [. . .] to mold' the most current manifestation of sovereign power, 'a G[eor]ge'. A satiric gothic tale of regeneration, Byron's poem bears a resemblance to Marx's critique of capitalism. In one word, 'G[eor]ge', it reduces the glorious imperial British monarchy to a coin, which was first minted to celebrate the slave trade and the Georgian era (George I–IV [1714–1830]). The guinea or sovereign appeared initially in 1663,[32] marking the Restoration and Britain's expansive financial and cultural investments in the slave trade; it was withdrawn from circulation in 1814 at a critical moment in the Napoleonic wars and after successive currency crises and devaluations. Byron's poem, like the title of Milton's 1649 pamphlet, questions the tenure of kings and magistrates by displacing and conflating the conventions of royal iconography; it also suggests that the G[eor]ge – the Prince Regent and the coin – might soon be forced out of circulation. Byron's satire transfigures the monarchy into a caricature of parasitical and oppressive economy on the verge of collapse.

Shelley's drama and Byron's poem radicalize iconographic praxis. Byron grounds his image of the monarchy in a capitalist economy, where the terrifying realities of slavery and war accompanied a ballooning culture industry[33] that included Shakespeare and vampire fiction. Byron conflates economic and cultural forms of currency to satirize the Prince Regent and criticize the British monarchy. Shelley is less concerned with satirizing the monarchy in 'Charles the First' than he was in *Swellfoot the Tyrant*. Even so, like Bryon's 'Windsor Poetics', Shelley's drama brings to life one of Britain's most powerful and contentious iconographic figures in an act of *imitatio*, which challenges the static iconography that sustains the 'ideal of every restoration culture': namely, 'to abolish the irreversibility of history and render the past everlasting'.[34] This play weaves Shakespearean allusions into an inter-textual framework that highlights the deliberate nature of this performance. Charles I will not emerge as a tutelary spirit of tragic heroism, but as one misdirected actor amongst other actors playing a part and improvising as necessary but also making serious errors in judgement. This dramatic praxis revises the traditional iconography associated with *Eikon Basilike*, the courtly masque and divine right and casts Charles I as all too human in his ruthless ambition and his willingness to betray his own people. Shelley thus anticipates Mitchell and takes a cue from Milton in creating a performative iconography wherein actors bring to life characters moving across historical and theatrical stages.

The cultural archeology of scene 1

Informed by David Hume's conventional account of mid-seventeenth-century events in his *History of England* (1754–62), Catherine Macaulay's eight-volume republican *History of England* (1763–83), and Whitelocke's *Memorials*, Shelley, according to Crook, began formally drafting scenes of the play in January 1822, after he had completed *Hellas* (*BSM* XVI, xxx–xxxi).[35] Many of these historians, Crook notes, expressed pity for Charles while condemning him. Cromwell too was criticized as a hypocrite and a tyrant.[36] The question for someone like Shelley was one of how to frame these historical figures and the accompanying events without condemning the Commonwealth as a failed experiment or elevating Charles I as a tragic martyr. In the first scene Shelley keeps these charged figures at the edge of his audience's cognitive and visual periphery. The scene depicts the pageant that preceded the 1634 performance of Shirley and Inigo Jones's masque, *The Triumph of Peace*. The backstory for Shelley's drama can be found in Whitelocke's text, where he describes a series of legal cases that exacerbated the friction between the Court and the nation's legal system during the years Charles I reigned without Parliament (1629–40). One of the most striking of these cases involved William Prynne, a barrister in Lincoln's Inn who was tried twice (1633 and 1637) in the Star Chamber for sedition. Initially, William Noy – the Attorney General from 1631 until 1634 who also orchestrated the extension of the ship money tax to inland counties and other cash-generating schemes – charged Prynne with seditious libel after the publication of his anti-theatrical tract, *Histrio-Mastix; The players scourge, or, actors tragaedie* (1632). Noy specifically denounced the section of Prynne's pamphlet entitled 'Women-actors notorious Whores' as a criticism of Queen Henrietta Maria, who frequently participated in court entertainments and had recently performed a speaking role in Walter Montagu and Inigo Jones's *The Shepherd's Paradise*. Additional charges were levelled against Prynne for his insinuating comparison of Charles I with the infamously cruel Roman emperor, Nero (*DNB*). Prynne denied these allegations, and his lawyer insisted his 'greatest Cryme [. . .] was that he did not bethinke himselfe what interpretation there might be made of his writing'.[37] As Whitelocke and others have pointed out, Prynne could not have been guilty of the main charge because he published his pamphlet six weeks before the Queen's performance. The Star Chamber disregarded this information and found Prynne guilty. The court imposed harsh punitive measures, which included a fine, disbarment, being pilloried and having his ears cropped. Four years later the Star Chamber summoned Prynne, and again he was accused and found guilty of sedition. This time the court sentenced him to life imprisonment and ordered that he be even more brutally disfigured: his ears were severed completely from his head, his nose slit and the letters S.L. (Seditious Libeller) were branded into his cheeks (*DNB*). Prynne has never been lauded as a great legal mind or a particularly effective radical, but after his second trail his body became a visual testament to the government's tyranny. News of Prynne's treatment transformed his homecoming in 1640 into a public spectacle; he further capitalized on this in his 1641 tract, *A New Discovery of the Prelates Tyranny* (*DNB*).

According to Whitelocke's history, members of the Inns of Court were gravely concerned about how Prynne's trial and punishment would affect them and their relationship with the King. In an attempt to speak to Charles I, they retained the services of Jones, the famous set designer and architect, and Shirley and bank-rolled one of the most magnificent Caroline festivals. Spending over £21,000, the Inns of Court financed *The Triumph of Peace*, a courtly masque performed on 3 February 1634, four days before Pyrnne's trial, and again, by royal command at the Merchant Taylor's Hall on 13 February. This performance about the relationship between power and law, as Martin Butler notes, made visible 'a territory that would become [in succeeding years] bitterly contestable'.[38]

Whitelocke's account[39] of Shirley's masque begins with a description of how the evening began with a winding cavalcade down Chancery Lane to Whitehall in Westminster. This pageant, an adaptation of a Roman triumph, drew hundreds, maybe thousands of spectators into London's streets. One of the most splendid spectacles of the period, it featured footmen, 100 mounted gentlemen, antimasquers, music, chariots, singers, and then four more chariots carrying the principle masquers, all of which was followed by a procession of 200 halberdiers. A lavish accompaniment of barristers, law students, horsemen, musicians, dancers and actors, intermittently animated by a number of antimasques, rounded out the street performance. Staged for the general populace rather than the courtiers at Whitehall, this public display integrated performances that criticized court policies with courtly triumphs and imperial iconography. Symbolically, the street procession represented the barristers' public appeal to the monarch and the people; potentially, this assembled citizenry also radically recast the conventional iconography of the monarch by displacing the stolid and singular figure of power with a larger and more diverse political community. This pageant, Butler notes, opened the door, which admittedly was quickly closed, to a highly charged and very public dialogue between the Crown, court advisors, legal counsellors and the people.[40]

Shelley's drama opens to this street scene in 1634. The conversation between the anonymous citizens identifies this event as the tipping point in the reign of Charles I. According to the *Second Citizen*, 'This Charles the First/Rose like the equinoctial sun, . . . /By vapours, through whose threatening ominous veil/Darting his altered influence he has gained/This height of noon' (i,46–50;489). In the coming years, 'he must decline/Amid the darkness of conflicting storms,/To dank extinction and to latest night' (i,50–52; 489). The questions raised by these observers focus on how to interpret this 'stage-scene' (i,35; 489). The metadramatic and metatheatrical nature of 'Charles the First' draws attention to the material nature of the stage and its players. For the *Youth*, the scene '"tis like the bright procession/ Of skiey visions in a solemn dream/From which men wake as from a Paradise,/ And draw new strength to tread the thorns of life' (i,17–20; 489). The *Youth*, like Ferdinand in Shakespeare's *The Tempest*, is a little naïve in his appreciation of this masque. This allusion creates a parallel between Prospero and Charles I as well as between the not-quite deserted island upon which Prospero and Miranda settle and Great Britain and its more remote island-continent colonial possessions, North America and India. These lines inflect romance into the tragic and historical make-up of the play. They also set the groundwork for a later scene in 'Charles the First' where the republican rebels verbalize their romance with the New World as they debate whether to flee England. The Youth's blindness, like Ferdinand's, provides a reflective interlude; he is one of the few characters who engage actively with the romance of the scene unfolding before him. His view thus represents a viable alternative to what others read as an inevitable and inescapable tragedy. The youth's ability to envision a 'Paradise' in a 'barren world' also marks him as possibly incapable of effecting change because he remains oblivious to the cycles of violence and retribution that structure power in the world he inhabits. Similar to Shelley's other protagonists, Prometheus in the first Act of *Prometheus Unbound* and Beatrice Cenci, the Youth's vision of humanity's liberation must survive the ordeal of history; if it cannot, he will be condemned like Beatrice Cenci to commit the sins of his fathers, but there is also the possibility that his visionary glimpse of freedom is enough to sustain him through the trying times ahead, as is the case with Prometheus.

The *Youth*'s speech also splits the performance into imaginative and visual fields, which mark the parallel planes of cultural and political awareness. The *Second Citizen* is reminiscent of an ancient seer or prophet who employs a similar language of contrasts:

> How young art thou in this old age of time!
> How green in this gray world? Canst thou discern
> The signs of seasons, yet perceive no hint
> Of change in that stage–scene in which thou art
> Not a spectator but an actor? or
> Art thou a puppet moved by [enginery]?
> The day that dawns in fire will die in storms,
> Even though the noon be calm.
> 'Charles the First', i,31–9; 489

Accusatory in his tone, the *Second Citizen* suggests these performances – on stage, in the theatre and in the street – are about distinguishing between players and spectators. This character invites us to consider the question of voice: as the power of speech and as indicative of having the right and/or the privilege of speaking. Amongst the players, who are the actors? Who are those capable of controlling themselves and impacting others and who are those merely playing a part? Either as a puppet-master or the puppet? The interweaving of historical events with theatrical performances makes this task of distinguishing players from actors a formidable one. The discussion entwines the Youth's 'green' idealism and hope into the citizenry's 'gray' worldview ('Charles the First', i,33; 489); the play's historical realities are punctuated by Alexander Leighton's cameo appearance in the middle of the scene. Shelley's citizens perceive the pageant as both an entertainment and a political spectacle. Their remarks constitute a political debate about royal prerogatives and the political influence held by William Laud, Archbishop of Canterbury (1573–1645) and Thomas Wentworth, Earl of Strafford (1593–1641).

Shelley's first scene alludes to Shakespeare's *Coriolanus*, where a group of anonymous citizens fill the stage debating the fate of Caius Martius, identified as 'a chief enemy to the people' (*Coriolanus*, I,i,5). One can immediately see the parallel between Charles I and Coriolanus. Set in a period of Roman history, some 500 years before the Roman Republic emerged as the Roman Empire, *Coriolanus* features the power struggles between citizens, Tribunes and an oligarchy tied to the military. The opening scene functions effectively as a threatening but ultimately meaningless show trial. Class tensions have been escalated by corn riots, which Plutarch in his *Parallel Lives*[41] cites as the source of the people's grievance. By the time Shelley began writing his play, corn riots were a commonplace in English history. England had regulated the price of corn since the seventeenth century. The corn riots in Oxfordshire (1557) and in the Midlands (1607), which were largely due to enclosures, are often cited in discussions of Shakespeare's drama. The Corn Laws passed in 1815 instigated an era of public, sometimes violent protest, including the Spa Fields riots (1816). These laws forbade the foreign import of corn and created food shortages in metropolitan areas where the increasingly industrialized landscape made it impossible for people to grow their own food. Real food shortages compounded with cases of hording and high food prices fuelled public agitation for reform. Most importantly, the scene features a debate about the power of the citizenry and what role they play within the larger state. It is fairly obvious that the Patricians – despite their protests to the contrary – have no real interest in caring for the people, but can or will the citizenry claim the right to speak and act for themselves? How do Menenius's speech and Coriolanus's actions curb their effectiveness and make them into the Tribunes' puppets? These were critical questions for nineteenth-century audiences.

Shelley's dramaturgy embeds history into the familiar theatrical performances of Shakespeare. This evocative and economic formulation produces uncanny doublings and repetitions that resonate like a parody but they also infuse this play with an emotion of belatedness and loss. The structural allusion to *Coriolanus* and Shakespeare's antecedent, Plutarch's *Lives* reinforces the scene's discordant tone while also drawing parallels between the birth of the English republic and the slow rise of the Roman republic. The kaleidoscope of literary and historical allusions would have struck at the core of several cultural debates in the early nineteenth century. Throughout the Regency (1811–20), the British monarchy appeared vulnerable, even precarious. George III's illness was compounded by his son's profligacy. The actor and manager, John Philip Kemble, responded to this situation, one exacerbated further by Napoleon's successes on the global battlefield and by a reignited conflict with the United States in 1812. He created at Covent Garden a 'theatrical monarchy which shored up', in Moody's words, 'the kingship of an incapacitated George III'.[42] Kemble's performances as King Lear, Prospero and Coriolanus skilfully orchestrated and defined the visual character of monarchical authority, showcasing the characteristics of dignity and solemn venerability in the face of emotional and political duress. The spectre of Charles I haunted Kemble's audiences, which were only too eager to buy into the theatrical illusions produced at Covent Garden and other patent-holding venues. These performances mollified those in power by creating a diverting spectacle for the populace, but, as Moody notes, 'the authority and decorum of Kemble's Shakespearean monarchs irritated' reviewers at *The Examiner*.[43] While appreciative of the efforts taken at Covent Garden to stage Shakespeare, reviewers at *The Examiner* were also critical of how these productions promoted a stultifying morality and political complacency. In reviews dating from 1813, Thomas Barnes – who took over theatre reviews for Leigh Hunt while he was in prison for libelling the Prince Regent – and William Hazlitt (Hunt joined them after being released from prison) mounted a collective and sustained critique of Kemble's portentous and statuesque performances.

Shakespeare's *Coriolanus* is set in the early years of Rome: a period of political strife, marked by food shortages, civil riots and military campaigns. Sent to the battlefield as a child, Coriolanus knows nothing other than conflict and bloodshed. His life has been directed by his mother's patriotism and the State's perceived need to protect itself from invaders and civil strife. He is dutiful, faithful, brave and loyal, but when peace is declared, he needs to adapt and redefine himself. Many in Kemble's audiences were as battle-scarred as Coriolanus. If they had not seen action in his majesty's forces, they had suffered at home: facing the twinned traumas of poverty and personal loss. Kemble's productions famously expanded the part of Volumnia, Coriolanus's mother. This emphasis on the role of women and the family shifts the play toward melodrama and simultaneously away from being an exploration of class and politics or the ideals and problems of self-made men on the battlefield who cannot find a place in their own country once they return from the wars. In Shakespeare's drama, the elite attempt to reform Coriolanus into a politician, but Coriolanus refuses to follow the script for his newly assigned role. He alienates the Tribunes and the common people. Once exiled he turns to his rival, Tellus Aufidius, general of the Volscian army and the sworn enemy of the Roman republic, and drives his army relentlessly toward Rome. Now a traitor rather than a hero, Coriolanus forbids 'all names', all titles and becomes 'a kind of nothing' (*Coriolanus*, V,i,12–13).[44] Would a nineteenth-century British audience have condemned Coriolanus at this moment as they did Jeremiah Brandreth or other radicals for treason? Before his exile, Coriolanus has titles and, like the early Napoleon Bonaparte, he appeared to be the rising star in the fledgling empire. Like Napoleon and other military figures in the period from Tipu in India to the Duke of Wellington, he also manifests ruthless cruelty, intolerance and insensitivity. Coriolanus is a man of action, but we discover he lacks a voice, a critical necessity for a politician, who, like the people's Tribunes, Sicinius and Brutus, speaks for others and in turn directs the people to speak for them. As a split character Coriolanus represents different characters for different audiences. He can be one of the many thousands of demobilized British soldiers coming home from war. Or he can be the cloistered and managed George III. Or the fierce Napoleon or some other heroic military figure.

Thomas Lawrence's portrait of Kemble as Coriolanus (Figure 3.2) captures what most British audiences were being directed to see. This painting portrays the actor as a statuesque Roman figure. The viewer glimpses the warrior's breastplate, where the black drape falls away, but a cloak of dignity and power overlays this mostly internalized military code of honour. Reflecting on Kemble's performances as Coriolanus, Barnes, in his 19 December 1813 review of the play, contested how the actor, William Conway – who was standing in for Kemble that night but also following precisely Kemble's interpretation of Coriolanus – drew the audience's attention to his character's 'conjugal fondness' and his 'filial obedience',[45] effectively vindicating his arrogance and his disdain for the people. Barnes unmasks the politics of the patent theatres, and how their actors and their theatrical productions legitimized the monarchy and the government's oppressive tactics in the midst of wars being fought on too many fronts. Like Havard's portrayal of

Figure 3.2 Thomas Lawrence, *John Philip Kemble as Coriolanus in* Coriolanus *by William Shakespeare*, c.1798, oil on canvas, 29.5 × 18 in., © Victoria and Albert Museum, London

Charles I, Kemble infuses his character with humanity by highlighting the scenes where he is a good husband and a faithful son. With few exceptions – Barnes, among others – Kemble's audiences did not see the ruthlessness of Napoleon or Wellington, for that matter, nor did they see the oppressive political tyranny of the government officials who manipulated the people for their own purposes. They saw Kemble playing Coriolanus.

Hazlitt's 1816 review expresses concern about the complacency of actors and audiences. Like Shelley in the opening scene of 'Charles the First', Hazlitt directs his readers toward a metatheatrical awareness of the play. Hazlitt recounts how audiences feel 'some concern for the poor citizens of Rome' until 'Coriolanus comes in and, with blows and big words, drives this set of "poor rats", this rascal scum, to their homes and beggary, before him'. Kemble's acting resolves the psychological tension in the scene by converting 'our admiration of [Coriolanus's] prowess [. . .] into contempt for [the citizen's] pusillanimity' (*SWWH*, 3. 181). Hazlitt insists repeatedly that reality cannot compete with theatre. Poverty cannot and should not be portrayed as noble or attractive. But Hazlitt points out that the theatre is not as magical as it appears. Its actors are real people who get sick, who have bad habits and who sometimes play the wrong part. Ultimately, performances must be reviewed and characters will be unveiled as either good or bad actors whose '*fleshiness*' or 'supercilious airs' bring the audience back to a crude human physicality that can be both gross and funny (*SWWH*, 3. 183). The theatre reproduces the King's image as national icon, but it does so at a price that exposes that icon as a commercial and political venture. Edmund Kean's performance in Robert Elliston's revival of *Coriolanus* at Drury Lane in 1820 challenged Kemble's staid acting style. Staged days before George III's death, Kean, in Hazlitt's words, failed to convey Coriolanus's 'inordinate self-opinion, and haughty elevation of soul, that aspire above competition or control'.[46] '[I]nstead of "keeping his state", instead of remaining fixed and immovable [. . .] on his pedestal of pride', Kean 'seemed impatient of his mock dignity, this *still-life* assumption of superiority' and 'burst [. . .] from the trammels of precedent, and the *routine* of etiquette, which should have confined him'.[47] Kean's acting style coupled the oppositional psychology featured in melodrama[48] with the physical intensity of the pantomime. Mixing elements of legitimate and illegitimate theatrical praxes, Kean's radical interpretations of Shakespeare's most popular characters and his iconoclastic performances paved the way for what Moody has termed 'Illegitimate Shakespeares',[49] a practice, I suggest, Shelley was aware of and engaging in his 'Charles the First'.

In the midst of this inter-textual play of cultural allusions, Alexander Leighton (c.1560–1649) steps on stage, bringing the audience back to the material realities of history. He appears at a central moment in the scene, entering, as if on cue, in the middle of a discussion about 'martyred saints' ('Charles the First', i.84; 490). Leighton evokes the barrister, Prynne. A physician rather than a lawyer, Leighton was prosecuted by the Star Chamber for publishing *An Appeale to the Parliament, or Sions Plea Against the Prelacy* (1628). This pamphlet urged Charles I and members of Parliament to assume the leadership in Europe's Protestant

Reformation by abolishing the English episcopate and seizing its wealth. Obviously Leighton was an enthusiastic admirer of Henry VIII. The government failed to appreciate Leighton's plea and had him fined, pilloried, defrocked, both of his ears cut off and his face branded with 'S.S.' (Sower of Sedition). The only named character in the scene, Leighton represents the disfigured body politic and exposes the brutal physical violence that constitutes and sustains sovereign power as threatened and undermined by rebellion. Leighton's body is an image of radical disfigurement: one representing what Shelley might well have equated with the disturbing elements of religious fundamentalism and one that clearly reveals why the government and the monarchy could not be supported if it continued to impose such ruthless punishments on its citizens. His body makes visible humanity's physical vulnerability and its fundamental mortality; it also identifies this scene as an antimasque, which as the Youth blithely tells another character, 'serves as discords do' (i.175; 492). Leighton's stage presence contrasts with the appearance of Charles I in the next scene. The opposition and the incongruity of these images – both iconic in different ways – provides Shelley with a means of criticizing the political policies and aesthetic practices that represent cultural debates in reductive, oppositional terms.

Steven Jones suggests the play's first scene is filled with moral ambiguity, 'and we would do well to attend to [its] dialogic (or skeptically dialectical) implications [. . .], not to mention its potential ironies'.[50] What Jones identifies as moral ambiguity is perhaps better viewed in terms of the indeterminacy of historical narratives. Foucault used archaeology and genealogy to convey the significance of these often amorphous elements.[51] Gilles Deleuze and Félix Guattari build upon Foucault's work in their discussion of the rhizome in *A Thousand Plateaus*, where, like Godwin in his *Essay on Sepulchres*, they consider history as interconnective rather than as a linear progressive movement.[52] Shelley represents history and historical characters in his dramas in terms of a cultural archaeology of historical and theatrical performances that extends from Shakespeare through the early nineteenth century. In this light, the first scene presents distinct yet interconnected sedimentary strata, revealing not the 'face' of history but rather the various elements that are over time divided, distributed, ordered and arranged so as to create the illusion of a totalized and coherent visage of history.[53] Shelley's scene thus offers audiences a means of accessing and exposing the complex iconography that sustained the saga and the character of Charles I in history books, on stage, and within the deep vestiges of Britain's cultural memory.

This scene captures a moment of cultural reflection, staging how the politics of memory played to a multivalent iconography that both challenged and sustained the monarchy. Shelley's deployment of these cultural reference points does not, like the Jacobean and Caroline masques, hold time in abeyance and thereby extend the moment wherein the monarch reveals his divinity.[54] It does not, in the words of Guy Debord, create a *'false consciousness of time'*,[55] creating the illusion of a synchronous – interminable and indisputable – ideology. Conventional histories relied on the spectacle of the King's image to organize the narrative, effectively captivating the reader or viewer and suspending the acts of memory in an illusory timelessness. From the perspective of reform politics, the problem with this formulation is that the icon – the monarch, the actor, Shakespeare – appears to be clothed in the diachronic movement of history but is masked by a stultifying synchronicity. Shelley's dramaturgy contested this static iconography by recreating a networked genealogy of historical reference points whose interplay emphasizes connectivity and access rather than privilege or hierarchy.

Masques and masks of violence

The formal masque began once the pageant arrived at Whitehall. Maintaining iconographic traditions, Charles I and Henrietta Maria embody the ordering principles of Jove (Divine Power) and Themis (Divine Law). The other main characters are Peace, Law and Justice: corresponding to the Greek goddesses, Irene, Eunomia and Dike. These figures mediate between the barristers as the masquers and the King and Queen, creating a dialogic allegory that proves complimentary to the monarchy while allowing for critique. The scenic backdrop featured the Piazza of Peace, which displaced the classical and imperial Roman motifs that defined the street performance. This more republican set coupled with the increased number of antimasques reflects the escalating tension between the court and the country's legal profession. Historically, the performance began with a series of dances introducing two groups of presenters, reflecting the dissonance between the cosmopolitan and rakish courtiers (led by Confidence, Fancy, Jollity and Laughter) and the less refined but increasingly more vocal gentry (represented by Opinion, Novelty and Admiration). The antimasques depict the social and political disorders that disturbed the peace. Several scenes take place in front of a tavern, and feature gamesters, wenches, beggars and thieves. These episodes, Butler points out, allude to 'the Book of Orders, and its criminalization of vagrancy, idleness, and insobriety' and playfully highlight the issues of 'social and moral regulation'.[56] The ongoing commentary is poignant yet humorous; the action is distracting and moves quickly forward to the next scene. Other antimasques focus on the abuses of law enforcement in the provinces and on the issue of monopolies. Like Swift's *Gulliver's Travels*, they also satirize the promotion of dubious and fraudulent enterprises, including a submarine suit. The action gets more complex when Peace – presumably because it is disorderly – is chased off stage by the Law, but a dialogue between Peace and Law is still maintained, suggesting that real peace can only be secured through law and justice.

With its large number of antimasques and its unconventional placement of them, even erupting in the masque's final revels to expose the carpenters, tailors and painters, whose behind-the-scenes work created the masque, Shirley's *The Triumph of Peace* exposes the material realities that underlay the transcendent iconography of the monarchy. Moreover, it provided a release valve to those 'quotidian pressures'[57] that increasingly threatened to unravel the masque's pre-eminent fiction of divinely sanctioned order. Stressing the interdependence of the court and the magistracy, Shirley's masque addressed the policies that threatened to undermine the Crown's political and legal credibility. Most critics agree that

Charles I was delighted with this performance.[58] From his perspective, the masque did what masques do: 'stage the court's idealized picture of itself'.[59] The allegory mirrored the formal interplay between order and disorder within the masque and allowed for multiple – even contradictory – readings of its multiple episodes. While the iconography associated with the Court and the monarchy might have been occasionally 'emptied of its imperial resonance',[60] the masque's devices and its iconography were always fully in play.

Whitelocke's description of these events acknowledges the marvellous spectacle of this performance, however, in contrast with Charles I's response, it concludes on a note of resignation. Shirley's masque rivalled those performed at Court; it also mirrored them too well and effectively masked the entertainment's real purpose: namely, to speak to the Court and to make visible the necessity of restraining royal prerogative within the bounds of the law. Although England in 1634 was not yet polarized along the lines that would divide the nation during the Civil Wars, there existed a need to stake common ground and build alliances that would allow for necessary legal reforms. Whitelocke believed the masque failed to emplot either its message or its critique of the monarchy effectively.

Shelley's drama reformulates the traditional masque through which the Stuart and Carolingian courts constructed the early performative iconography of sovereign power. The traditional masque isolates the monarch at one end of the room, aligning him with the Divine, Aristotle's unmoved mover. The King's stationary body represents the fixed point within an elaborate visual display where other participants – a mix of actors and courtly personages – move and engage in the interplay between order and disorder.[61] As Butler observes throughout his Introduction, the performance visually organizes a nebulous constellation of political power into a state-sanctioned spectacle, where the dance of exclusion and incorporation proves integral to shifting the monarch's and/or the court's perspective of national and local interests and the larger stages of international politics and cosmopolitan concerns. Conventional masques elevated the emblematic potential of the King's 'mysterious sovereign body' and, through the rituals and performance of narrativized festive dances, it reaffirmed the King's place 'as the symbolic, structural, and emotional centre of the [. . .] state'.[62] Prior to Charles I's death the masque effectively deployed the King's image within the Court and amongst those with enough power to mount a significant challenge to the state.

Functioning as a disruptive antimasque – and here Shelley follows his friend Leigh Hunt's experiments with the masque form in his 1815 *The Descent of Liberty* – the first scene with its palimpsest of literary and historical allusions, sets up the second scene, a more obvious engagement with the masque. The action moves off the street and into the Court. This progression between scenes creates an illusion of fluidity that accompanies modal shifts throughout its four extant scenes. Shelley does this in many of his plays, most clearly in *Prometheus Unbound*, which as I discuss in Chapter 5, produces as a cascade of moving genres, which transform as characters move through different landscapes. Following Whitelocke's narrative, the King and Queen enter the scene, along with Lord Strafford, Archbishop Laud and others, to receive the representatives from the Inns of Court. The monarch's appearance on stage marks the shift to the formal masque. Queen Henrietta animates the stilled and statuesque iconography of the masque by speaking about her father's French court. The implicit comparison between the English and French Courts reveals Charles I's deficiencies as a monarch. Lord Strafford's and Archbishop Laud's speeches imitate the King's speech and thereby appropriate his power for themselves. Shelley does not give Charles I the stateliness of Kemble's characters. Charles I is distracted and keenly aware of how others perceive him. Acting more like Kean than Kemble, he expresses impatience and distrust. Once again we see the metatheatrical nature of Shelley's performance. Shelley's masque parodies the form and reveals the scene as a masquerade. The parody destabilizes the static iconography and allows for the critique that Shirley, Jones and the barristers failed to make visible. It also demonstrates Shelley's perspective of how icons worked culturally. Charles I exists as a multifaceted image that others mimic for their own purposes. The icon reproduces itself as an illusion of power and it allows others to simulate power. The iconicity of the King's image is inherently iconoclastic and divests him of his authority and his voice. Throughout the scene he will be isolated and will find it impossible to hear the good counsel offered by Lord Cottington and his fool, Archy.

The opening speeches resuscitate an icon of power and they effectively derail the barristers' attempt to advocate for judicial reforms. According to Whitelocke the formal exchange of pleasantries masked the deep disappointment felt by the delegation sent by the Inns of Court. Despite the barristers' efforts and the expense of the enterprise, Charles I remained oblivious to their critique of his appropriation of the law for his own purposes and financial gain. Shelley portrays this collective disappointment through the character of St John, historically Sir John Finch, the spokesperson for the Inns of Court. Jacqueline Mulhallen identifies Finch as a royalist, whom Shelley described in his reading notes as 'a mean rascally lawyer'.[63] Displacing Finch with St John, Shelley creates a more historically nuanced and radical reading of the scene. The barristers, Oliver St John and Robert Holborne represented John Hampden (1595–1643), a relatively moderate parliamentarian who opposed Charles I's policies, especially ship money – a military expedient in times of war that dealt with the government's appropriation of coastal vessels to fight at sea – that had been redeployed by Noy as a national tax. Hampden refused to pay and subsequently stood trial in 1637–38. Although he lost the case, Hampden's trial aroused national interest and made him into a national hero (*DNB*).

In contrast with Finch, St John parries with the Queen, countering her wistful yearning for her father's court with a blunt reminder that she now resides in England. The scene's tension becomes palpable when St John exits and Charles I comments bitterly, 'Mark you what spirit sits in St. John's eyes?/Methinks he is too saucy for this presence' ('Charles the First', ii.34–5; 493). This statement shatters any hope for reconciliation and it undermines the image of monarchical benevolence. The scene thus exposes the royal masque as little more than a masquerade of power. The celebratory performance has become a prelude to tragedy.

As a tragic figure, the King becomes more visible; he now wears a 'rugged mood' and is as 'stiff' as the Scots who refuse to submit to the Anglican yoke;

even Henrietta Maria declares, 'My dearest lord,/I see the new-born courage in your eye/Armed to strike dead the Spirit of Time,/Which spurs to rage the many-headed beast' (ii.64, 68, 113–15; 494–5). The mythic dimensions of the Queen's description of her husband briefly displace the historical narrative, bringing to light how myth, prejudice and opinion – Bacon's 'idols of the mind' – blind people to the Crown's obvious failures. Only Archy, the King's fool, 'whose owl-eyes are tempered to the error of his age', sees Charles I and his ministers as they are and understands the dire circumstances that define this historic moment. A mirror of King Lear's fool, Archy refuses to succumb to the spectacle of monarchical power and his ability to counter these self-destructive delusions calls to mind how 'Medusa's art' – iconography – blinds characters and audiences with vague 'promises' and 'protestations' and, in Archy's words, lets the 'wise and godly slit each other's noses and ears (having no need of any sense of discernment in their craft)' and entreats 'madmen to [. . .] manage the state of England' (ii,43–62; 493–4). Archy's observations allude to Leighton and Prynne but they also loosely equate these radicals with Stratford, Laud and even the King. All of these characters are puppets and madmen.

Another way of reading this scene is through the allusion to *King Lear*. Consider the possibility that Shelley consciously structured the scene as a mirror to the divestiture scene in *King Lear*. Replace Goneril and Regan with Laud and Strafford. Just as Lear is moved to give all he has to his daughters in accordance with their *shows* of love, so too Charles I, cajoled and manipulated by Laud's fervent religious enthusiasm, Strafford's perfidious ambition and the Queen's desire for power, eventually surrenders his crown and forfeits his life. Although the scene alludes to Lear's madness, it focuses more on how Charles I, like Lear is stripped of his power and authority and how he plunges himself and his country into the chaos of civil war.

In the following speech, the Queen chides her husband for contemplating political alternatives to the current financial and political crises:

> To a parliament?
> Is this firmness? and thou wilt preside
> Over a knot of   censurers,
> To the unswearing of thy best resolves,
> And choose the worst, when the worst comes too soon?
> Plight not the worst before the worse must come.
> Oh, wilt thou smile whilst our ribald foes,
> Dressed in their own usurped authority,
> Sharpen their tongues on Henrietta's fame?
> It is enough! Thou lovest me no more!
> > 'Charles the First', ii, 206–25; 500

The icon of an *absolute* monarch, with which the scene opened, is falling into disarray. The masque is shifting into tragedy and moving quickly toward farce as Henrietta, in a vein similar to Shakespeare's Cleopatra, imagines her 'ribald foes [. . .]/Dressed in [. . .] usurped authority', sharpening 'their tongues on [her] fame').[64] Both characters express a certain horror of seeing themselves through the eyes of the people, specifically in the terms of a vulgar parody. Laud's and Strafford's speeches are similarly sensational. Instead of fear, they convey their sadistic pleasure in their ability to inflict terror upon the state and its citizens. Laud envisions an army quenching the heresies of the Scottish church 'in fire and blood,/and tears and terror' (ii,331–2; 500). Strafford argues that 'the game [may still be] won' if his troops arrive from Ireland (ii,347; 500). In the midst of this hysteria, Lord Cottington checks the Court's many illusions and fears. The reality is that there is no more money to finance these fantasies of terror and without money Charles I will have to reconvene Parliament (ii,326–36; 500).

The scene closes with the King's order to detain the rebels – John Pym (1595–1643), Hampden, Arthur Hazlerig (1601–61), Sir Henry Vane (1613–62), Oliver Cromwell (1599–1658) and others – who attempt to flee to North America. Far from keeping 'the fierce spirit of the hour at bay,/Till time, and its coming generation,/Of nights and days unborn, bring some one chance' (ii,165–7; 496), this commission – as does this scene – reveals the arbitrary power and the volatility of iconography. The 'tragick scaffold', as Andrew Marvell refers to it in his 'Horatian Ode upon Cromwell's Return from Ireland', is visibly collapsing under this pressure. What remains in the two final scenes are the remnants of a royalist farce and a republican romance. The King's warrant for the arrest of these men will spark the Civil War, an event that defines Charles I as no other act he committed in his life. There will remain two roles for the King to play: the tyrant or the martyr. The iconography for either role engages what Archy deftly identifies as the 'New devil's politics' (ii,360–64; 501). Archy's closing references to literary utopias, including Gonzalo's in *The Tempest* and Lucifer's in *Paradise Lost*, direct the play's action toward romance.

The third scene (Rossetti and Hutchinson's fourth scene) turns away from the Court and the masque and opens with a dialogue between Hampden and Vane. Charles I has made his move, now they must choose to either 'sit steady' (iii/iv,7; 505) or to flee and try to create their 'inheritance of freedom' (iii/iv,4; 505) in the New World. Hampden explains how his fellow countrymen have pawned their inheritance of freedom for a 'despoiler's smile' (iii/iv,6; 505) and how in the New World they will find

> floating Edens cradled in the glimmer
> Of sunset [. . .] lone regions,
> Where Power's poor dupes and victims yet have never
> Propitiated the savage fear of kings
> With purest blood of noblest hearts; whose dew
> Is yet unstained with tears of those who wake
> To weep each day the wrongs on which it dawns;
> Whose sacred silent air owns yet no echo
> Of formal blasphemies; nor impious rites

Wrest man's free worship, from the God who loves,
To the poor worm who envies us His love!
'Charles the First', iii/iv, 23034; 505–6

Hampden creates the republican romance with the New World. He envisions an isolated paradise; an Edenic island where the people are noble and pure of heart, where even the air has not yet been polluted with the sounds of 'blasphemies' or 'impious rites'. But the repetition of 'yet' suggests that it will only be a matter of time before this new world becomes a mirror image of the old world. The Hutchinson text at this juncture is unclear. It appears that Hampden is still speaking, but Crook suggests that the lines under the asterisks are Vane's and allude to Milton's *Areopagitica*.[65] Reading these lines as Vane's, his position becomes clearer. Fleeing England and travelling to the New World will not change anything. Freedom and the conditions for its sustainability must be created. The person who is enslaved will be so everywhere. There is in these lines something reminiscent of Shelley's 'Mont Blanc': the sublime and revolutionary power that will not be denied. But the references to tempests and storms and Hampden's romance also allude to Shakespeare's *The Tempest*: to Gonzalo's ideal commonwealth that sustains the contradiction of sovereignty, albeit not without being roundly criticized by Antonio and Sebastian, who are in fact conspiring to take Alonzo's crown. This play of allusions points to the real difficulties of imagining and realizing a republican ideal. How does drama and particularly historical drama not simply hold a mirror up to nature? To the rivalry, the strife and the violence of human conflict? How does the dramatist reproduce the past without succumbing to its oppressive ideologies? Shelley was not without answers to these questions. As is clear in his other dramas – *Swellfoot the Tyrant*, *Hellas* and *Prometheus Unbound* – Shelley was adept at creating a cognitive movement through genre shifts and it appears that he was planning to use that strategy here as well. But Shelley is also experimenting with *imitatio* in 'Charles the First' and this calls upon the need to develop alternative strategies and specifically a new form of iconology that can both make it real and, adopting Ezra Pounds famous phrase, 'make it new'.

Writing in a slightly different context, Nigel Smith notes that republican iconography generated an idea of the English republic as 'the apogee of civic virtue' and its 'negative counterpart [. . .] as a place of conspiracy, deceit and ruthless ambition'.[66] This complex interplay of texts and contexts reflects the difficult balancing act Shelley sustains between his desire to advocate for republican reforms and republican heroes like Vane and his attempt to complicate the conventions of cultural iconography, whether radical or reactionary. Shelley subverts the power of iconography and allegory but he does so by complicating the audience's responses to what would have been familiar literary, theatrical and historical scenes.

Shelley sets the fourth scene in the Star Chamber, the court that tried cases deemed relevant to the Crown. This scene takes us to 1638 and resuscitates the haunting spectre of Leighton's body in the first scene. Laud, Strafford and Bishop Buxon stand in judgement against Prynne, John Bastwick (1593–1654) and John

Williams (1582–1650), the Lord Bishop of Lincoln and a long-term litigant in the Star Chamber who struggled repeatedly to retain his lands and position. This scene is another formulation of the antimasque. Instead of enacting sovereignty, this performance mobilizes the politics of allegory into an iconoclastic masquerade. This judicial court is a torture chamber; its judges do not pursue truth and justice; they inflict punishments designed to mortify and terrorize both victims and spectators. The distinction between loyalty and treason is radically destabilized in this scene where Laud's and Strafford's appropriation of the monarch's power produces an assemblage of mutilated bodies. This show of power reveals how the court masque masks the violent fantasy that structures the political realities of Charles I's reign. The iconography of power is iconoclastic: it erodes the effectiveness of the judicial body and will erase – if only momentarily – the King's image. In this scene Bishop Juxon – Charles I's confessor prior to his execution – is the only voice of reason as he makes an urgent appeal for mercy when Laud's demand for more torture becomes clearly excessive:

> Stop!
> Forbear, my lord! The tongue, which now can speak
> No terror, would interpret, being dumb,
> Heaven's thunder to our harm; [sic]
> And hands, which now write only their own shame,
> With bleeding stumps might sign our blood away.
> 'Charles the First', iv/iii,35-40; 504

The Star Chamber's sentences were written indelibly on the bodies of puritan dissidents, and this language condemned those in power as much if not more than those against whom the court acted. Juxon is no republican, obviously he sits as a judge in the Star Chamber, but he understands that Laud's brutality and his sadistic corporal punishments will turn the people against the government and will eventually lead to more radical and revolutionary violence. But just as Charles I cannot see or read the masque as a critique of his power, so too neither Laud nor Strafford will acknowledge Juxon's warning.

It is impossible to say how 'Charles the First' would have evolved as a dramatic composition or if Shelley would have ever finished it given more time. But with its abundant Shakespearean allusions, the drama affirms both 'the centrality of theatre to national life'[67] and how the theatre reified the country's national icons and reiterated Britain's national tragedies. Crook argues that Shelley intended for Act II to end with Parliament's reassertion of its control and with the execution of Strafford for treason in 1641. She also believes that, if completed, 'Charles the First' would span a period of 15 years, closing with the King's execution[68] and that Shelley wished to provide his audiences with an alternative republican icon in the form of Henry Vane. Cromwell might have been considered by the radicals as preferable to the Stuarts, but he was still a tyrant and a dictator who had destroyed the Commonwealth.[69] Shelley's iconology throughout 'Charles the First', his remarks in *A Defence of Poetry* about Homer's Achilles, his comments in his

Preface to *The Cenci* about actors and genre and his observations in his essay 'On Love' about sympathy, suggest that Shelley considered Charles I more as an actor and a human being than a fixed image of monarchical power. Developing an alternative iconography and a corresponding experimental dramaturgy, Shelley's dramatic fragment reformulates the monarchy and other characters as more fraught and complex. Not fixed and statuesque like the actor John Philip Kemble, but more like Edmund Kean, these characters appear physically and emotionally animated. It is difficult to condemn or apotheosize these Kean-like characters. Situating the British monarch within a dramatic framework that encourages readers and viewers to sequentially reimagine these events through the shifting lenses of different genres, including history, tragedy, the masque and romance, Shelley constantly shifts the valence of the King's image and redirects the audience's attention to other figures and other elements in this history.

Shelley lived in a culture of circulating images, which reproduced semblances of the King with a regularity of theatrical performances and the printing press. Theatre and drama negotiated between the word and the image, between the verbal and the visual, and, in the best scenarios, this inter-textual interplay alerted people to the power of images and made audiences more aware of how the changing modes of representation were altering and structuring human experience. Shelley's drama recreates the history of Charles I for the purposes of revolutionizing the nation's politics of memory. Against this backdrop of civil strife and civil war, which loomed larger than friendship or the everyday material realities people experienced, the idea of forgiveness might have appeared laughable. But the country needed a politics of forgiveness to come to terms with its violent past and its spectral icons that threatened at every moment to manifest fully into violent revolution and civil war. The fragments we have of Shelley's drama represent a cluster of concerns about remembrance, the need for public apologies and a social and political obligation to confront a tumultuous history of personal and national violence. Forgiveness displaces antagonism and most importantly it opens the door to public discussions and political solutions to the *agon* of enmity and hate that arises from regicide or the threats of treason as well as reactionary and oppressive laws.

If finished, 'Charles the First' might have provided audiences with a theatrical version of what Godwin had proposed in his 1809 *Essay on Sepulchres*. Godwin's essay marks his attempt to produce a more radical historiographical model that shifted the traditional focus on idolized and monumental figures to an alternative 'habit of seeing with the intellectual eye things not visible to the eye of sense'.[70] Godwin considered history to be a narrative comprised of cultural memories. The act of recollecting history brought literary and historical figures to life, which otherwise exist only as what Bacon referred to as 'idols of the mind'.[71] Influenced by Godwin, Shelley had learned from reading Bacon that

> Every human mind has [. . .] its *idola specus*, peculiar images which resided in the inner cave of thought. These constitute the essential and distinctive character of every human being, to which every action and every word bears intimate relations, and by which in depicturing a character the genuineness

and meaning of those words and actions are to be determined. Every fanatic or enemy of virtue is not at liberty to misrepresent the greatest geniuses and the most heroic defenders of all that is valuable in this mortal world. His story to gain any credit must contain some truth, and that truth shall thus be made a sufficient indication of his prejudice and his deceit.

(*Essay on Christianity*, *Shelley's Prose*, 199)

Inexorable and multivalent, these idols and figurative icons embody the intellectual biases and the socio-political prejudices that are reified in public opinion.[72] While skeptical about public opinion, Godwin and Shelley also considered that the debates about the revolutionary upheaval of the French Revolution had affected a corrective skepticism that made wholesale idolization less pervasive. Truths existed alongside prejudices and deceit, and the problem was one of locating and distinguishing them. History existed for Godwin, as Rowland Weston observes, 'as a perennially available resource for the appropriation of moral knowledge and the exercise of political action'.[73] Godwin's proposal to mark the burial sites of Britain's cultural heroes with a simple wooden plaque constitutes an act of memorialization and as such reflects on a historiographical crisis, perhaps represented by those occasional 'plot[s] [. . .] to abolish the memory of the things that had been, and to begin the affairs of the human species afresh'.[74] In contrast with acts of reading history, where the reader becomes 'idle and unimpassioned', Godwin encouraged readers to take their books outside and like the fictionalized Byron in *Childe Harold's Pilgrimage* to 'wander among the scenes of ancient Greece and Rome [. . .] and feel [. . .] surrounded with the spirits of Fabricius, and Regulus, and Gracchus, and Scipio, and Cicero, and Brutus'.[75] Acknowledging the fact that 'poetical scenes affect us in somewhat the same manner as historical', Godwin suggests we visit the graves of historical figures, writers and even 'the spot where Cervantes imagined Don Quixote to be buried, or the fabulous tomb of Clarissa Harlowe'.[76] Godwin encourages a psychological associationism with dead and fictional characters, ostensibly through the interconnective gateways that link the living with the dead or the material with the intangible: graves, historical sites and material artifacts.[77] Godwin's and Shelley's attempts to revive the past creates what Carlson refers to as 'temporal ambiguities', which challenge 'the deadness of the past' and scrutinize 'our desires to fix or affix it'.[78] One of the issues with the dramatization of history is that convention forces the dramatist to employ dramatic modes such as the masque, tragedy, romance and comedy. The masque and tragedy tend to still images in a historical framework whereas romance and history plays signify both the pastness of history and contemporary designs on the future. The issue here is that there is an inevitable doubling that occurs that devolves into iconic figures like Henry V or Richard III. Hal and Hotspur in *1 Henry IV* and Falstaff and the Lord Chief Justice in *2 Henry IV* merge to produce the national icon of Henry V. In romance magic and art intervene to preserve the narrative of social and political order. The many and complex elements in all of these plays are directed toward one final image through the play of genres and modes.

Shelley wrote in an era where the oppositional formulas of melodrama dominated the boards and where the performance of Shakespearean drama attested to the 'genuine conflict of cultural values'.[79] Writing a play about Charles I, Shelley engaged a culturally volatile topic. Years later Mary Mitford (1787–1855) discovered just how much controversy a seventeenth-century monarch could generate when, encouraged by Charles Kemble and William Macready, she wrote *Charles the First: An Historical Tragedy in Five Acts* (1825). Submitting the play to George Colman the Younger, the licenser for the Lord Chamberlain's office, Mitford was undoubtedly surprised when he refused to license her play on the grounds of its title and subject. Havard's play had been a mainstay in the theatrical repertoire for generations so why did Mitford have to wait nine years and require the intervention of William Cavendish, Sixth Duke of Devonshire, to stage her play at the Royal Victoria Theatre in 1834?

Throughout the eighteenth and nineteenth centuries, Havards's and Mitford's dramas – both as texts and theatrical performances – persistently resuscitated and restored Charles I to his throne just prior to the moment of his execution and the historical dissolution of the British monarchy. Both dramatists employed a Shakespearean tragic framework for their plays, ostensibly building the tragic scaffold that supported the British monarchy throughout the crises and political turmoil of the eighteenth and nineteenth centuries. These dramas reproduce the tragedy of a martyred king who dies with the full realization of the wrongs done to him and his family, but who nonetheless adopts the Christ-like role of forgiving those who know not what they do. These dramas reproduce the iconography and the politics of memory that developed in the immediate aftermath of Charles I's execution and alter the historical record to include his wife and children (most of whom had fled to France) in order to stage scenes depicting Charles I as a loving father and a doting husband. Both writers contrast Oliver Cromwell and Charles I, setting up Cromwell as a foil who obviously does not embody the charisma or the sovereign authority of the King. Charles I spends very little time on stage in these tragedies because the there exists no need to develop his character. The cultural iconography has done the dramatist's work. When the audience finally sees him on stage, it is the intention of both writers they should *see* the icon of kingship, martyrdom and tragic heroism.

These recurrent productions constituted one of many sedimented layers of iconographic representation that Shelley hoped to unsettle with his drama. Developing an alternative iconography through a corresponding experimental dramaturgy, Shelley's dramatic fragment reformulates how the audience perceives the monarchy. More fraught and complex like the actor, Edmund Kean, who was physically and emotionally alive on stage, Shelley's character subverts the efforts of earlier actors who sought instead to depict the monarchy as fixed and statuesque. Situating Charles I within a dramatic framework that encourages audiences neither to condemn nor apotheosize him, Shelley's play invites audiences to sequentially reimagine the monarchy through the shifting lenses of different genres and thus divests the King's image of its iconic status as either a tyrant or a martyr. The play reviews the historical record for the purposes of rediscovering the drama of human sympathy that could reunite a divided nation that was once again on the verge of civil war.

Conclusion

Franco Moretti identifies the 'ideal of every restorative culture' as the ability to 'abolish the irreversibility of history and render the past everlasting'. 'Social relations', he adds, 'are reformulated in transparent and spatial – that is, static – form'.[80] Tragedy, the masque even romance can be deployed to sustain and restore sovereign power. Prior to the execution of Charles I, the masque effectively stabilized and fortified the King's image against the threats of political upheaval. After his death, tragedy displaced the masque as the means of preserving the cultural memory of sovereignty. In *Eikonoklastes* Milton attempted to undermine this powerful emplotment with his radical iconoclasm, but this did not stop royalists from employing the 'tragick scaffold' to reconstruct royal prerogative. *The Famous Tragedie of Charles I. Basely Butchered* (1649) provided a model for a political pamphlet drama that rejected the tragic-comic mode of most royalist drama during the Civil War.[81] According to Smith's study of mid-seventeenth-century dramas, royalists tended to rely on vindictive satire and romance early on in the period, but as it became more apparent that a restoration of the Stuarts might occur, tragedy held greater sway. Moreover, as Smith observes, the idea and the presence of 'kingship [n]ever disappear[ed], as the attempt to make Cromwell king showed'.[82] This suggests the pervasive rhetorical power of traditional forms such as the masque and tragedy and their ability to evoke cultural icons – whether republican or royal – and how, more often than not, these icons and their embodiment in tragedy or the masque remained slippery despite the user's intentions.

Taking a moment to consider how Shelley might have concluded his drama, it seems probable that he would have focused on Charles I's desperate betrayal of Strafford rather than adhering to the more conventional staging of the King's trial and execution. While Shelley had no interest in propping up the British monarchy, he was also critical of Cromwell's theocratic Commonwealth. Both governing bodies exercised tyranny and justified their actions in the name of God.[83] Reading through the various accounts of his trial, it is worth noting that the Charles I laments this deed; he does not apologize for waging war against Parliament's forces – even when pressed by the prosecution – nor does he accede to having ever acted as a tyrant. When the court rules against him, he does not grieve for himself, but he does mourn Strafford's death, and it is this expression of human grief that transforms the monarch into a person who laments his complicity in another's death. This is all speculation, of course, because it is impossible to know if Shelley would have followed his notes to the letter or if he would have made some considerable editorial adjustments that would have redefined the scope and the purpose of his drama.

It is notable that in William Hazlitt's review of Mary Shelley's 1824 edition of *Posthumous Poems* he signals his disappoint about 'the unfinished scenes of *Charles I.*, (a drama on which Mr Shelley was employed at his death)'.[84] In this fragment, he writes, 'the *radical* humor of the author breaks forth, but "in good set terms" and specious oratory. We regret that his premature fate has intercepted this addition to our historical drama'. These sentiments have pervaded studies of 'Charles the First' and have inspired scholars to search for clues about how Shelley might have concluded his work. But at present, the material archive is limited to dramatic fragments, notes and a few references made in his correspondence. My study of 'Charles the First' has been more attentive to the performance genealogies that would have been relevant to Shelley while composing his drama. I have identified 'Charles the First' as a performance of counter-memories that appears alert to the discrepancies and the overlap 'between history as it is discursively transmitted and memory as it is publicly enacted by the bodies that bear its consequences'.[85] In all of his dramas, Shelley reveals a concern with how societies remember and how memories and histories are amassed in theatrical and dramatic performances. The theatre still effectively functions as a place or site where historical scripts are reproduced and transmitted through actors as living, embodied memories. What is perhaps unique about drama is its ability to hold the collective memory, to still the movement of history in iconic moments and restorative gestures, within a space that exists as essentially improvisatorial and transformative. 'Charles the First' represents an inventive displacement of early nineteenth-century iconographic practices and the cultural iconography then available to anyone, including actors, dramatists, stage managers and historians. As it stands, 'Charles the First' offers readers the opportunity to reflect on Shelley's attempt to further disrupt the iconic stasis that tended to define royalists and republican histories of Charles I. In ways that resonate with Godwin's discussion of historical markers in his *Essay on Sepulchres*, Shelley approaches history in 'Charles the First' through an act of *imatatio*, where, quoting Joseph Roach, 'memory operates as both quotation and invention, an improvisation on borrowed themes, with claims on the future as well as the past'.[86]

Notes

1 Thomas Medwin, *The Life of Percy Bysshe Shelley* (Oxford, 1913), p. 341.
2 Jacques Derrida, *On Cosmopolitanism and Forgiveness*, trans. Mark Dooley and Michael Hughes (New York, 2004). See also, Michael Janover's 'The Limits of Forgiveness and the Ends of Politics', *Journal of Intercultural Studies* 26.3 (August 2005): pp. 221–35.
3 See Judith Butler's *Precarious Life: The Powers of Mourning and Violence* (New York, 2004). The power of mourning has often been directed toward violence, particularly acts of martyrdom or revenge, but she insists that these feelings can also be produce opportunities to reconceive the human condition. See also Jeffrey N. Cox, 'Staging Hope: Genre, Myth, and Ideology in the Dramas of the Hunt Circle', *Texas Studies in Language and Literature* 38:3/4 (Fall/Winter 1996): pp. 245–64.
4 Michael Rossington in 'Shelley's republics', in Heather Glen and Paul Hamilton (eds), *Repossessing the Romantic Past* (Cambridge, 2007), pp. 63–79.
5 Nora Crook in 'Calumniated Republicans and the Hero of Shelley's "Charles the First"', *KSJ* 56 (2007), pp. 155–72, points out that the W.M. Rossetti edition, upon which the play text in *Poetical Works* is based, is wrong about the placement of the third and fourth scenes. Hutchinson and Matthews also include a fragmentary fifth

scene, which I will not take up because it is so problematical. The third and fourth scenes nonetheless should be reversed; I will follow Crook's lead in my discussion of the drama since forthcoming editions from Johns Hopkins and Longman will probably make this adjustment. However, I will use the Hutchinson edition to make textual references since it is still the most widely available text. The references will take the format of act, scene; page number.

6 Nora Crooke in 'Shelley's Late Fragmentary Plays: "Charles the First"' and the "Unfinished Drama"', in Alan M. Weinberg and Timothy Webb (eds), *The Unfamiliar Shelley* (Farnham, 2009), pp. 297–311, observes that 'Shelley told Trelawny that "Charles the First" was intended for the stage, adding, "It is affectation to say we write a play for any other purpose"' (298). See Edward Trelawny's *Recollections of the Last Days of Shelley and Bryon* (London, 2000), p. 53.

7 Steven Jones, '"Choose Reform or Civil War": Shelley, the English Revolution, and the Problem of Succession', *Wordsworth Circle* 25.3 (Summer 1994): pp. 145–9.

8 Stuart Curran in *Shelley's Annus Mirabilis: The Maturing of an Epic Vision* (Pasadena, 1975), pp. 186 ff, Steven E. Jones in *Shelley's Satire: Violence, Exhortation, and Authority* (DeKalb, 1994), and Michael Scrivener in *Radical Shelley: The Philosophical Anarchism and Utopian Thought of Percy Bysshe Shelley* (Princeton, 1982) focus their analyses on Shelley's deployment of popular iconography, particularly in the aftermath of Peterloo in 1819.

9 'Scenes from the Faust of Goethe' first appeared in part (scene ii) in *The Liberal*, No. 1 (1822); Mary Shelley prints Shelley's more complete translation in *Posthumous Poems* (London, 1824). I have taken these lines as they have been reprinted in *Poetical Works*, ll. 383–9.

10 Sophie Thomas, *Romanticism and Visuality: Fragments, History, Spectacle* (New York, 2008), p. 153. Thomas provides a more extensive account of the myth of Medusa, drawing on Bacon's account in 'Perseus, or War'.

11 Goethe, *Faust, Part One*, trans. John Prudhoe (Manchester, 1974), p. 141.

12 For example, consider Shelley's post-Peterloo letter to Peacock, 24 August 1819; *Letters*, 2.115, where he asks, 'What is to be done?' See also Hunt's post-Waterloo articles in *The Examiner*: 'Victory of Waterloo – Bonaparte's Abdication' (*SWLH* 2. 32–5) and 'Gloomy State of Things in France' (*SWLH* 2. 36–9).

13 W.J.T. Mitchell, *Iconology: Image, Text, Ideology* (Chicago, 1986), p. 9.

14 Mitchell, *Iconology*, p. 9.

15 Michel Foucault, *The Order of Things: An Archaeology of the Human Sciences* (New York, 1973), p. 17.

16 Patricia Fumerton, *Cultural Aesthetics: Renaissance Literature and the Practice of Social Ornament* (Chicago, 1991), pp. 4–5. Fumerton is quoting from Sir Thomas Herbert's *Memoirs of the Martyr King: Being a Detailed Record of the Last Two Years of the reign of His Most Sacred Majesty King Charles the First (1646–1648–9)*, Allan Fea (ed.) (London, 1905), p. 143.

17 Fumerton, *Cultural Aesthetics*, p. 9.

18 Significantly, *The Commentaries, or Reports of Edmund Plowden* [1548–79] were reprinted in London 1816. Plowden was a law apprentice of the Middle Temple during Queen Elizabeth's reign. Marjorie Garber cites Plowden in *Shakespeare After All*, p. 250. See also, E.H. Kantorowicz, *The King's Two Bodies* (Princeton, 1957), p. 7.

19 David Loewenstein, *Milton and the Drama of History: Historical Vision, Iconoclasm, and the Literary Imagination* (Cambridge, 1990), p. 53 and 164, n. 3. Loewenstein also provides a more detailed analysis of Marshall's frontispiece and it relationship to Milton's *Eikonoklastes*.

20 John Milton, *Eikonoklastes* in Merritt Y. Hughes (ed.), *The Complete Prose Works of John Milton* (8 vols, New Haven, 1962), 3. 339.

21 Milton, *Eikonoklastes*, 3. 342.

22 Milton, *Eikonoklastes*, 3. 342–3.

23 This phrase is from Andrew Marvell's 1650 'An Horatian Ode upon Cromwell's Return from Ireland'.

24 Milton, *Eikonoklastes*, 3. 345.

25 Timothy Morton and Nigel Smith, 'Introduction', *Radicalism in British Literary Culture, 1650–1830: From Revolution to Revolution*, Timothy Morton and Nigel Smith (eds) (Cambridge, 2002), p. 5.

26 Morton and Smith, 'Introduction', *Radicalism in British Literary Culture*, p. 5.

27 For examples, see *The trial and execution of King Charles I*. Also, Walter Benjamin discusses martyr drama at length in *The Origin of German Tragic Drama*, John Osborne (trans) (New York, 1998). Jeffrey N. Cox employs Benjamin's concept and that of liberatory drama to situate his analysis of this play in 'The Dramatist', in Timothy Morton (ed.), *The Cambridge Companion to Shelley* (Cambridge, 2006), pp. 65–84.

28 Jane Moody, *Illegitimate Theatre in London, 1770–1840* (Cambridge, 2000), p. 122.

29 John Bell, *Bell's British Theatre, consisting of the most esteemed plays* (34 vols, London, 1797), 19. 312.

30 Marx, Karl. *Capital: A Critique of Political Economy*. Vol. 1. trans. Ben Fowkes (New York, 1990), p. 165.

31 Lord Byron, 'Windsor Poetics', in *CPW*, 3. 86. McGann provides three versions of this poem.

32 Joanna Lipking touches on this topic in her essay, 'The New World of Slavery – An Introduction', in her edition of Aphra Behn's *Oroonoko*, ed. Joanna Lipking (New York, 1997), pp. 75–89, p. 80.

33 This term was coined by Theodor Adorno and Max Horkheimer in *Dialectic of Enlightenment*, trans. John Cumming (New York, 1993), specifically in the chapter entitled 'The Culture Industry: Enlightenment as Mass Deception', pp. 120–167. See also Adorno's *The Culture Industry: Selected Essays on Mass Culture* (New York, 2002).

34 Franco Moretti, '"A Huge Eclipse": Tragic Form and the Deconsecration of Sovereignty', trans. D.A. Miller, in Stephen Greenblatt (ed.), *The Power of Forms in the English Renaissance* (Norman, Oklahoma, 1982), pp. 7–40, p. 23.

35 See also Nora Crooke's 'Shelley's Late Fragmentary Plays', p. 299.

36 Crook, 'Shelley's Late Fragmentary Plays', p. 300.

37 Huntington Library, HM 80, 'Documents relating to the prosecution of William Prynne', *The Proceeding in the Starrchamber against Mr Prinn for Writing a Booke intitled Histrio Mastix 15 die February: Ano Caroli Regis nono 1633*, f. 7v. Also cited in Lauren Shohet's *Reading Masques: The English Masque and Public Culture in the Seventeenth Century* (Oxford University Press, 2010), p. 1.

38 Martin Butler, *The Stuart Court Masque and Political Culture* (Cambridge, 2008), p. 301.

39 Bulsrode Whitelocke, *Memorials of the English affairs: or, an historical account of what passed from the beginning of the reign of King Charles the First, to King Charles the Second his happy restauration. . . . with the private consultations and secrets of the cabinet. A new edition: with many additions never before printed* (London, 1732), pp. 20–21. Retrieved from *ECCO*.

40 Butler, *The Stuart Court Masque* p. 302.

41 In Mary Shelley's 1818 *Frankenstein; or, The Modern Prometheus* (ed.) Marilyn Butler (Oxford, 1993), p. 103, the monster finds a bag of books, which includes Milton's *Paradise Lost* (1667), Plutarch's *Lives* (c.100 CE), and Goethe's *Sorrows of Young Werther* (1774). Arguably, these texts represented a revolutionary literary canon.

42 Moody, *Illegitimate Theatre*, p. 123. See also her essay, 'Romantic Shakespeare', in Stanley Wells and Sarah Stanton (eds), *The Cambridge Companion to Shakespeare on Stage* (Cambridge, 2002), pp. 37–57.

43 Moody, *Illegitimate Theatre*, p. 123.

44 In this analysis of *Coriolanus* I am indebted to more detailed studies of the play: Katherine Eisaman Maus's introduction to *Coriolanus* in *The Norton Shakespeare*,

pp. 2785–92; Paul Cantor's 'Part One: *Coriolanus*', in *Shakespeare's Rome: Republic and Empire* (Ithaca, NY, 1976), pp. 55–124; Annabel Patterson's *Shakespeare and the Popular Voice* (Cambridge, 1989).

45 *The Examiner*, VI, 19 December 1813, pp. 810–811.

46 William Hazlitt, 'Mr Kean as Coriolanus', *London Magazine*, No. II, February, 1820. Reprinted in *Hazlitt on Theatre*, William Archer and Robert Lowe (eds) (New York, 1957), pp. 186–8, p. 186.

47 Hazlitt, 'Mr Kean as Coriolanus', *Hazlitt on Theatre*, p. 186.

48 Peter Brooks in *The Melodramatic Imagination: Balzac, Henry James, Melodrama, and the Mode of Excess* (1976; New Haven, 1985) describes melodrama in terms of its Manichean psychology.

49 See Chapter 4 in *Illegitimate Theatre in London*; also, 'Romantic Shakespeare', pp. 37–57.

50 Jones, ' "Choose Reform or Civil War": Shelley, the English Revolution, and the Problem of Succession', p. 146.

51 Michel Foucault, *The Archeology of Knowledge*, trans. A.M. Sheridan Smith (New York, 1972).

52 Gilles Deleuze and Félix Guattari, *A Thousand Plateaus: Capitalism and Schizophrenia*, trans. Brian Massumi (Minneapolis, 1987). See also Tilottama Rajan's 'Uncertain Futures: History and Genealogy in William Godwin's *The Lives of Edward and John Philips, Nephews and Pupils of Milton*', *Milton Quarterly* 32 (October, 1998): pp. 75–86, pp. 77–8 and Rowland Weston, 'History, Memory, and Moral Knowledge: William Godwin's *Essay on Sepulchres 1809*', *The European Legacy* 14.6: pp. 651–65, pp. 660–62.

53 Foucault, *The Archaeology of Knowledge*, p. 9 and p. 6.

54 Steven Orgel provides an extensive and illuminating discussion of the Caroline and Jacobean masque in *The Illusion of Power: Political Theater in the English Renaissance* (Berkeley, 1975).

55 Guy Debord, *Society of the Spectacle*, trans. Donald Nicholson-Smith (1994; New York, 1999), p. 144.

56 Butler, *The Stuart Court Masque*, p. 303.

57 Butler, *The Stuart Court Masque*, p. 307.

58 Butler, *The Stuart Court Masque*, p. 308; Stephen Orgel and Roy Strong, *Inigo Jones: The Theatre of the Stuart Court* (2 vols, Berkeley, 1973), 2. 538.

59 Shohet *Reading Masques*, p. 2.

60 Butler, *The Stuart Court Masque*, p. 308.

61 This conception of the masque is consonant with the work of Jonathan Goldberg in *James I and the Politics of Literature: Jonson, Shakespeare, Donne, and their Contemporaries* (Baltimore, 1983) and Stephen Orgel's *The Illusion of Power*. More contemporary studies include Martin Butler's *The Stuart Court Masque and Political Culture* and Lauren Shohet's *Reading Masques*.

62 Butler, *The Stuart Court Masque*, p. 124.

63 Jacqueline Mulhallen, *The Theatre of Shelley* (Cambridge, 2010), p. 136. Mulhallen cites Crook and *BSM* XVI, pp. 226–7.

64 See *Antony and Cleopatra*, V,ii,207–17.

65 Crook, 'Shelley's Late Fragmentary Plays', pp. 301–2.

66 Nigel Smith, *Literature and Revolution in England, 1640–1660* (1994; New Haven, 1997), p. 84.

67 Crook, 'Shelley's Late Fragmentary Plays', pp. 305–6.

68 Crook, 'Shelley's Late Fragmentary Plays', p. 299. Crook cites HM 2111 fol. *4r (*MYR* VII: 326–7).

69 Michael Scrivener, 'John Thelwall and the Revolution of 1649', in Timothy Morton and Nigel Smith (eds), *Radicalism in British Literary Culture*, p. 126. Crook makes a similar observation in 'Shelley's Fragmentary Plays', p. 300.

70 William Godwin, *Essay on Sepulchres: A Proposal for Erecting some Memorial of the Illustrious Dead in all Ages on the Spot where their Remains have been Interred*, in Mark Philp (ed.), *Poltical and Philosophical Writings of William Godwin* (7 vols, London, 1993), pp. 5–30, p. 6.

71 William Godwin, *Essay on Sepulchres*, p. 12. See also Francis Bacon, *The Great Instauration* in Rose-Mary Sargent (ed.), *Francis Bacon: Selected Philosophical Works* (Indianapolis, 1999).

72 Bacon phrases this idea in these terms: '[p]hilosophy and the intellectual sciences stand like statues, worshipped and celebrated, but not moved or advanced' (*The Great Instauration*, 70).

73 Rowland Weston, 'History, Memory, and Moral Knowledge: William Godwin's *Essay on Sepulchres* (1809)', *The European Legacy* 14.6 (2009): pp. 651–65, p. 661.

74 Godwin, *Essay on Sepulchres*, p. 16.

75 Godwin, *Essay on Sepulchres*, p. 19.

76 Godwin, *Essay on Sepulchres*, p. 24.

77 Mark Salber Phillips, *Society and Sentiment: Genres of Historical Writing in Britain, 1740–1820* (Princeton, 2000), pp. 322–7. See also Rowland Weston's 'History, Memory, and Moral Knowledge'.

78 Julie Carlson, 'Fancy's History', *European Romantic Review* 14.2 (2003): pp. 163–76, p. 165, p. 166.

79 Moody, *Illegitimate Theatre*, p. 129.

80 Franco Moretti, '"A huge Eclipse": Tragic Form and the Deconstruction of Sovereignty', p. 23.

81 Smith discusses this drama and others in *Literature & Revolution*, pp. 81–92.

82 Smith, *Literature and Revolution*, p. 113.

83 Accounts of the King's trial are available as a collection of pamphlets in *The trial and execution of King Charles I; facsimiles of the contemporary official accounts contained in The charge of the Commons of England against Charl Stuart; King Charls, his tryal [and] King Charles, his speech made upon the scaffold* (Leeds, 1966).

84 Hazlitt, Review of *Posthumous Poems* (1824), *Edinburgh Review*, July 1824, xi, 494–514. Rpt. in *Shelley: The Critical Heritage*, ed. James E. Barcus (New York and London, 1975), p. 344.

85 Joseph Roach, *Cities of the Dead: Circum-Atlantic Performance* (New York, 1996), p. 26.

86 Roach, *Cities of the Dead*, p. 33.

Part II

Epic stages of power and liberation

4 'O, write no more the tale of Troy'

Classical dramas now available in pictures and sound

Joseph Roach tells us that performance and memory operate 'as both quotation and invention, an improvisation on borrowed themes, with claims on the future as well as the past'.[1] Theatre, street performances, caricatures, portraits, icons and written histories dramatize cultural memories as well as the aesthetics and the politics of cultural memory. Shelley wrote *The Cenci*, *Swellfoot the Tyrant* and 'Charles the First' in an effort to locate memories that were tied to British tragedies produced – both on and offstage – throughout the Romantic period. *The Cenci* locates the taboos – incest, patricide and treason – of dramatic and historical tragedies in mute performances, which can be both complicitous and oppositional and are often both simultaneously. My discussion focuses on portraiture as a form of mute performance and how Shelley in his Preface attempts to direct his audiences away from casuistic interpretations that restlessly anatomize and condemn historic and literary figures. *The Cenci* portrays an untenable 'state' of domestic abuse and incestuous violence exacerbated by a corrupt government and a compromised judicial system. These characters and events parallel and mirror a contentious period in the early nineteenth century when the British government employed *agents provocateurs* – radicals turned government spies – to instigate acts of treason, which Leigh Hunt and others identified as British tragedies. *Swellfoot* identifies the allegorical figure of Liberty as a critical site for the production of British cultural memories. Reproduced in caricatures, reviews, theatrical and street performances, Liberty functions politically as little more than a ridiculous parody, a 'plaything of the imagination' in contemporary political affairs, in this case, the Queen Caroline affair of 1820, which arguably took the country to the brink of civil war. *Swellfoot the Tyrant* juxtaposes the absurdities of the Queen Caroline affair with the equally ludicrous and abhorrent oppression of the poor and disenfranchised perpetrated in the name of Liberty and an ethnocentric patriotism. 'Charles the First' links cultural memory to the material objects and the human bodies – actors – that animate the King's portrait: a site for creative iconography and the production of ideology as well as iconoclastic energies. 'Charles the First' takes the twinned tragedies of the King's execution in 1649 and the failed English republic (1640–60) and begins the process of recasting it as a history play and a politics of forgiveness. Shelley never completed this drama. Locating and reproducing the networks of tragic production in these plays,

Shelley portrays the 'sad realit[ies]' that haunted the British people and drama-tizes how these performances effectively locked the cultural gaze in performative frameworks of memory. These tragedies facilitated the construction of a national consciousness, a complex psychological and ideological figuration, which wove together an assemblage of violent transgressions that emblematically represented the British nation. Each of Shelley's dramas portray the too often repressed and resurrected traumas that shaped Britain's cultural and political dynamics through-out the period.

Hellas and *Prometheus Unbound* mark Shelley's engagement with a future-oriented perspective: one that locates and actively transforms the tragic cultural memories of war and slavery into liberating and cosmopolitan performances. These lyrical dramas have been read traditionally as poetry or, equally restrictive, as reflecting Shelley's formal investment in neoclassical and operatic perfor-mances. While these elements are certainly extant within these dramas, Shelley, as Stuart Curran and Jeffrey N. Cox note, stretched the parameters of conven-tion to produce dramas that 'appear to cast an eye to the past'[2] but which in fact, as Shelley writes in *A Defence of Poetry*, create 'mirrors of the gigantic shad-ows which futurity casts upon the present' (*SPP*, 535). *Hellas* and *Prometheus Unbound* encourage audiences to 'abandon'[3] the compelling but destructive ideologies that sustained the British Empire throughout the nineteenth century. Staging scenes of 'wild abandon' that stretch the reader's historical conscious-ness and their awareness of transnational and cross-cultural exchanges, *Hellas* and *Prometheus Unbound* produce epic stages of psychological and political transformation and suggest how the theatre might engage in different forms of cultural and ideological work that fosters liberation and promotes reform. Both plays are sweeping in their ability to encompass an expansive geo-historical landscape and they both radically reconceive the dramatic and the theatrical pos-sibilities of staging history and contesting slavery, war and empire. Ripostes to the sustained experience of wartime[4] in the post-Waterloo era, these dramas stand in opposition to the tragedies that perpetuated internecine violence and normal-ized atrocities like genocide and slavery.

I begin with Shelley's *Hellas*, his final drama composed in the first weeks of October 1821. *Hellas* is often read as Shelley's personal response to the Greek uprising against the Ottoman Turks, which erupted when Prince Ypsilanti (some-times, Hypsilantes), a high-ranking Russian officer of Greek descent, entered Wallachia with 10,000 men in the spring of 1821 and declared Greek indepen-dence. More than an enthusiastic philhellenic endorsement of the Greek uprising that establishes Greece as an ideal for contemporary republicanism,[5] Shelley's drama represents a complex rejoinder to these events by adopting and adapting contemporary dramatic practices to reconfigure conventional melodramas about war and empire. Critics condemned melodrama as a monstrous generic hybrid and yet it dominated the boards throughout the nineteenth century, despite continuous outcries like that made by Coleridge in his 'Critique of *Bertram*', first published anonymously in 1816 and later reprinted as chapter 23 in his *Biographia Lit-eraria*.[6] An atypical melodrama, *Hellas* builds upon the classical topography of

Aeschylus' *Persians*, transforming its tragedy into a more liberating tableau of the complex, multi-ethnic society of Europe and the Levant. Like Byron's *Childe Harold's Pilgrimage* (1812–18), *The Giaour* (1813), *The Corsair* (1814), *The Siege of Corinth* (1816), *Sardanapalus* (1821) and Joanna Baillie's *Constantine Paleologus; or, The Last of the Caesars* (1804), *Hellas* portrays Levantine conflicts and provides commentary on Britain's tenuous alliance with the Ottoman Empire that stretched back to the sixteenth century: the moment of England's emergence into the 'heterogeneous matrix of Mediterranean [. . .] trade'.[7] Historically, England worked through the auspices of the Levant Company (1592), which soon became the East India Company (1599), aligning itself with the Ottomans against its rivals, Spain and Holland. The English thus positioned themselves within the global marketplace and adapted culturally to its new-found economic and political roles through its dramatic productions that featured border-crossing figures who negotiated this new and changing relationship between England and the East. Sir Thomas Stukeley in George Peele's *The Battle of Alcazar* (c. 1590) and the Sherley brothers in the *Travels of the Three English Brothers* (1607), were, as Daniel Vitkus observes, among the characters created in this early period.[8] As England's and then Britain's relationship with the East evolved, its theatrical productions mirrored the rigid binaries employed to sustain an evolving Orientalism.[9] Throughout the nineteenth century melodrama provided the cultural framework for this globalized Manichaean vision.[10] Melodrama, like the pantomime, employed a corporeal dramaturgy that usurped the power of language. Its reliance on histrionic bodily expressiveness, as Jane Moody observes with regard to John Fawcett's 1800 production of *Obi; or Three-finger'd Jack*, transformed the terms of socio-political debates into 'a diagrammatic yet highly intense corporeal discourse' that sustained 'powerful ideological oppositions' rather than attempting to resolve them.[11]

Philhellenism, the Greek revolt against the Ottoman Empire and the 'polemic of Ottoman Greece', as Nigel Leask refers to the tendentious debate about Britain's interests in the Eastern Mediterranean, were exhibited in a multitude of textual formats: including Levantine travelogues, William Eton's 1798 *A Survey of the Turkish Empire*, Thomas Thornton's *The Present State of Turkey* (1807), Baillie's *Constantine Paleologus*, Byron's Eastern tales, and Shelley's final drama. In his notes to *Childe Harold*, Byron viewed many of these discursive cultural engagements as largely ineffective, producing little more than 'paradox on one side, and prejudice on the other' (*CPW*, 2. 203). A former British consul in Turkey, Eton regarded it as a necessity for Britain to align its political and cultural interests with those of the Greeks. Eton made no distinction between the ancient *and* contemporary Greeks, and he effectively idolized Greek culture as the cynosure of Western civilization. Thornton, a British Levantine merchant, held a more complex position that was, as Leask observes, 'pro-Ottoman and anti-Greek as well as philhellenic and "orientalist" in Said's specialized sense of that word'.[12] Byron's Giaour-like border-crossing figures, including Harold, correspond to the sixteenth-century dramatic characters who negotiated cultural and ideological discrepancies. Bryon's poetic and dramatic narratives mirrored the destabilized conjunction of political, historical and economic interests in the region. *The Giaour, Childe Harold, Sardanapalus, Hellas* and *Constantine Paleologus* contest tyranny while also portraying the cultural and political complexities that informed the fraught pan-European and philhellenic discussions regarding Greek independence. *Hellas* adapts melodramatic tactics, specifically, tableaux or lyric pictures to contest the popular wartime melodramas of the early nineteenth century. It also creates what I refer to as a newsreel history in its final scenes, wholly reforming the historical determinism embodied by Aeschylus' *Persians* in order to promote what Shelley referred to as 'the great drama of the revival of liberty' (*Hellas*, l. 1078).

Wartime melodrama

Throughout the Romantic period, British theatres staged re-enactments of contemporary and historic battles. These dramas were set throughout the globe – from Assyria and Bangalore to Constantinople and the Americas – and marked the rise and fall of empires, which spanned the whole of mythic, literary and recorded history. These performances recreated scenes from newspaper accounts as well as literary and historical sources. During the French Revolution and the Napoleonic wars (1789–1815), audiences clamoured to the theatres, eager to *see* revolutionary Gothic productions and, later, the more reactionary re-enactments of specific battles they had read accounts of in the newspapers. In 1804 Sadler's Wells attempted to make their productions more real by filling a tank with water from the New River; they even hired shipwrights from the Woolwich Dockyard to design scaled models for patriotic productions such as *The Battle of Trafalgar* (1806) and *The Battle of the Nile* (1815).[13] Theatres functioned as news venues for audiences eager to hear the latest news from abroad or to relive Britain's 'glorious' battles. As the war effort intensified throughout the early nineteenth century and even in the post-Waterloo era when patriotic feelings ran high, the theatre capitalized on wartime sensibilities: fear, terror, sorrow, grief, revenge and the relief and elation that accompanies the announcement of victory. The post-war years witnessed a decline in the numbers of these performances but still venues like Astley's Royal Amphitheatre and Sadler's Wells, Gillian Russell notes, 'survived by revisiting the war in the form of spectacular re–enactments of the battles of Trafalgar and Waterloo and by elaborating forms such as nautical melodrama'.[14]

Theatrical productions worked hand in hand with other media to create a wartime experience that defined the Romantic period. As the work of David A. Bell, Simon Bainbridge, Jeffrey N. Cox, Mary Favret and Philip Shaw reminds us, war was never completely out of sight and seldom, if ever, effectively erased from the collective imagination.[15] Wartime, according to Favret, represents an epistemic and affective means of registering the terrors of wars taking place abroad. Theatrical productions worked hand in hand with other media – novels, newspapers, dioramas and the panorama – to create a wartime experience during the Romantic period. These mediating performances, according to Favret, can effectively unmoor time and space and change how people perceive themselves as historical agents. The linear and progressive movement of history appears increasingly static and synchronous in wartime dramas. War emerges as a totalizing and perpetual conflict that engulfs the temporal and spatial coordinates of history. The idea of war as a singular event that was delineated in terms of its geographical scope and its duration appeared now as an ever-lasting continuum, almost a myth. As the cognitive boundaries dissolved into 'a melee of temporal synchronies and discontinuities',[16] the increasing variety of available media sources became more relevant to the construction of human experience and the transformation of war from a discrete incident into an inescapable condition of being.[17]

Gothic romances like John Dent's *The Bastille* (Royal Circus, 1789) depicted the cultural hopes of the Revolutionary era and the belief that the oppressive institutions would soon collapse under the pressure of this new era. Melodrama adapted the Gothic romances to what was ostensibly a tragic worldview. Hundreds of melodramas featured military and imperial plots.[18] Described by Moody as the 'theatre of physical peril, visual spectacle and ideological confrontation',[19] melodrama cast soldiers and sailors as adventuresome heroic figures and often concluded with huzzah-inspiring displays of the flag and the tune of *Rule, Britannia*. In many ways melodrama proved to be an ideal vehicle for British imperial ideology. While its plots revolved around topical issues and current events, melodrama relied upon repetition and striking contrasts. The core melodramatic plot is visible in Thomas Holcroft's *A Tale of Mystery* (Covent Garden, 1802), the first play in Britain to be labelled a *mélo-drame* (literally, musical drama). Like romance, melodrama is essentially a comic movement, peppered with tragic elements. Holcroft's drama portrays how the union of two lovers, Selina and Stephano, is blocked by an 'evil' character, Romaldi, who must in the end recant and reform.[20] Melodrama encodes cultural contradictions by means of its polarized characters and its well-orchestrated juxtapositions. But its repetitious scenarios coupled with its comic conclusions (reconciliation and weddings) impede the clear expression of radical positions. Melodramatic characters are often debilitated by guilt and self-recrimination.[21] Blinded by relentless 'self-anatomy', and here we might think of *The Cenci*,[22] these characters prove incapable of identifying 'with the beautiful which exists in thought, action, or person' (*SPP*, 517).

Shelley would have been critical of melodrama's conservative ideological register; however, melodramatic praxes, specifically its emphasis on music and vibrant imagery, resonated with his conception of poetry in *A Defence of Poetry*, where he praises Plato for 'the truth and splendour of his imagery and the melody of his language' (*SPP*, 514). 'The practise [sic]' of innovatively producing language accompanied by music, Shelley writes, 'is indeed convenient and popular, and to be preferred, especially in such composition as includes much form and action [. . .]' (*SPP*, 514). Shelley would have easily distinguished the conception of melodrama from its production. As Michael Erkelenz and others have argued, *Hellas* is not 'a genuine tragedy', but rather, an experimental hybrid, which, like the performances of one of the most famous *improvvisatore*, Tommaso Sgricci

(1789–1836), mixes lyric and dramatic forms, producing a performance more akin to melodrama than Aeschylus' tragedy.[23]

Shelley identified *Hellas* as a lyrical drama not a melodrama, and we should not conflate the two forms nor should we ignore the resonances between the two modes either. Lyrical drama evokes Coleridge and Wordsworth's experiments in *Lyrical Ballads*, first published anonymously in 1798. Shelley's generic tag also calls to mind the lyrical dramas of the seventeenth and eighteenth centuries.[24] William Mason's *Sappho, a Lyrical Drama*, published posthumously in 1796, looked back to its neoclassical forebears. *Dramma lirico* is an Italian term Shelley would have been familiar with as a description of the librettos in Verdi's and Puccini's operas.[25] The fact that Shelley was aware of these traditions does not negate the fact that he most probably wrote his dramas as 'a deliberate assault on the integrity of the tripartite generic division – epic, drama, lyric – inherited from Aristotle and Horace and reinforced through the eighteenth century by major arbiters of neoclassical criticism'.[26] *Hellas*, like Shelley's other dramas, represents a radical experiment that, in the words of Stuart Curran, is concerned 'with the very nature of the dramatic'.[27] Shelley's lyrical dramas adopt the many innovative stage practices that melodramas popularized while at the same time they challenge the oppressive theatrical machinery that reified the psychological state of wartime in British cultural productions.

Hellas is distinctive amongst Shelley's dramas for its lack of dramatic division into Acts and scenes. Composed of 1099 lines, *Hellas* is a hybrid of poetic and dramatic elements. Stephen Cheeke and Mark Kipperman have recognized this generic tension as an 'imaginative movement effected by the mixing of "antithetical" modes'.[28] Mixing lyric and dramatic elements, Shelley also integrates historical chronicle, dream vision, lyric pictures, news reports and Byronic border-figures – Ahasuerus and Mahmud – who signal 'a transition from one stage of consciousness to another'.[29] Imitating what we would today identify as cinematic transitions from one scene to the next, *Hellas* abandons one dramatic framework as it brings another into focus. The drama is rife with ideological paradox and dynamic tension. It challenges Britain's imperial and Eurocentric vision that emerged in post-war melodramatic performances that focused on war, revolution and slave revolts. *Hellas* produces the music, the explosions and the panoramic historical stages that defined melodrama while also creating a performance of imaginative abandon that opens up a profusion of imaginative possibilities.[30] *Hellas* and *Prometheus Unbound* thus encourage their audiences to abandon those cultural practices that promulgate the experience of wartime and oppressive ideologies.

Hellas portrays the tyrant Mahmud's struggle to come to terms with his sense of historical determinism and his belief in Ottoman and Islamic hegemony. Haunted by a nightmare, which is enacted by the opening choral movement, Mahmud slowly confronts the reality of Greek independence and the slow, inevitable collapse of the Ottoman Empire. Shelley begins *Hellas* with the strophe/antistrophe movement common to the ode and to the choral movements of Greek tragedy. Juxtaposing the anonymous choral voices comprised of a lone Indian woman and an assembly of Greek women, Shelley's multi-ethnic chorus recreates the violence of war in terms of the ethnocentric aggressions and religious intolerance that often gave way to genocidal brutality during the Ottoman/Greek conflict. Echoing the opening stanzas of Shelley's 'Ode to the West Wind', first published in the 1820 *Prometheus Unbound* volume, the chorus of Greek captive women strews opiate flowers on the Sultan's pillow, noting in their song that they have been '*stript* from Orient bowers' (my emphasis) by an 'Indian billow' (*Hellas*, ll.1–4). Here and in the 'Ode to the West Wind' Shelley depicts the changing and threatening physical environment as a production of social and political oppression.[31] Imperial violence is sexualized, naturalized and orientalized, and in accord with this formation, the violation comes from the East (the Indian billow) rather than the West. The disquieting song becomes increasingly menacing in the final lines when the chorus expresses their anger with Mahmud and their grief for their fallen soldiers when they chant: 'Be thy sleep/Calm and Deep,/Like theirs who feel, not ours who weep!' (*Hellas*, ll. 5–8). The choruses and the semi-choruses reiterate the sentiment of these lines in the stanzas that immediately follow, but the song of the Indian woman, who interposes her self as a shield to protect the sleeping Mahmud, checks the incipient violence of the overall choral movement. The Indian woman's love for Mahmud is never acknowledged outside the choral lyric because Shelley does not develop a romance between the two characters as does Bryon between Sardanapalus and Myrrha, the Greek slave in *Sardanapalus* (1821). The Indian woman's love for Mahmud is nonetheless apparent as she stands jealously over him and commands the other women who 'love not' to 'move not' (*Hellas*, ll. 110–11). She realizes their passion – their 'panting loud and fast' (*Hellas*, l. 112) – is hatred and their desire is for nothing more than revenge.

The chorus's song depicts Mahmud's dream, which contains the elements of a sexualized fantasy and a violent nightmare. The scene's visual language merges sights and sounds into an oppositional melodramatic plot that oscillates between the promise of a comic union and a threat of tragic proportions. At its core, melodrama tells the tale of two lovers blocked by either unseen and/or unspoken terrors. Family secrets must be discovered and rivalries must be resolved but not before the players and the audiences have experienced the heightened emotional intensity that accompanies scenes of entrapment and spectacular escapes.[32] The horrors of war and slavery are often interwoven into these plots, almost to the point of rendering them invisible.[33] The binary construction of this and other scenes in *Hellas* opens the door to the sexualized dynamics of romance that structure the autocratic relationships between master and slave, men and women and kings and subjects. Byron employs this template in *Sardanapalus*, where he casts Myrrha as a Greek slave. It is also developed as a staple in the period's slave dramas and slave narratives. The 'subconscious' violence that informs this scene is confined within the liminal space of Mahmud's dream. Bryon displays this cultural intrigue more clearly in *Sardanapalus* as a matrix of ensnaring passions and complicitous actions that subject women, the poor and the disenfranchised to the 'triple alliance' between man, master and the monarch[34]:

King, I am your subject!
Master, I am your slave! Man, I have loved you! –
Loved you, I know not by what fatal weakness,
Although a Greek, and born a foe to monarchs –
A slave, and hating fetters – an Ionian,
And, therefore, when I love a stranger, more
Degraded by that passion than by chains!

CPW, 6. I,ii,496–502

Myrrha is Sardanapalus' lover and his slave. Her self-awareness of her situation contrasts sharply with the typical melodramatic character that is moved along by a plot that appears to embody the relentless force of fate. Myrrha initially exemplifies a self-critical attitude and can only criticize what she identifies as her 'fatal weakness'. She wishes she could repress her love for Sardanapalus and that she could fully incarnate her patriotic sensibilities and her national identity as a Greek. She yearns to be a melodramatic character, but it is her love that transforms her into a tragic character: one who realizes the social and political consequences of their actions and still pursues their vision. Myrrha's heroic stance marks her as an exception to the rule. Her love for Sardanapalus proves greater than her patriotic nationalism. They embrace each other in an *auto-da-fé*, a secularized act of faith that will literally and figuratively set fire to the conventions that separate them. They will become one in a massive conflagration that marks the end of the Assyrian empire. Byron's tragedy, like Shelley's *Hellas* aspires 'to make mankind understand their own interests, and those who govern them care for any interest but their own' (William Hazlitt, 'Review of Robert Owen's *A New View of Society*; *SWWH*, 4. 96–7).

Shelley's opening scene puts melodrama's stage machinery and its plot dynamics into motion. While Byron uses the conventions of tragedy to liberate his characters, albeit to their deaths, it is difficult at this juncture to see how Shelley will liberate his audiences and his characters. In contrast with Myrrha and the Indian woman, the Greek chorus of women will pursue their plot of revenge against Mahmud. This scene of mutual hatred reflects the historical record of the Greek revolution, where ethnic tensions exploded into acts of genocidal violence. But the contrast between the Indian woman and the Greek women within the chorus also establishes the drama's dialogic tempo. Shelley refashions the traditional movement of the chorus – left and right – into a shifting consciousness between hope and doubt that synthesizes on occasion into what Shelley in his Preface refers to as a 'lyric picture' (*SPP*, 430). The play's first lyric picture comes into focus in the song of generation ('In the great Morning of the world' (ll. 46 ff), which conveys the story of liberty's emergence into a prelapsarian world. This mythic vision represents a version of history that is neither fully idealistic nor elegiac; it is simply a movement between 'glory or the grave' (*Hellas*, l. 93).

The ebb and flow of the choral lyric in this lyric picture suddenly takes dramatic form when Mahmud starts from his sleep, calls for the guard and orders the 'match' that would 'spark' the apocalypse of 'reconciling ruin' (*Hellas*, ll. 114–9).

At this point it becomes clearer that the chorus's song and the mythic history we have just 'seen' represent dream visions that haunt Mahmud. As the play unfolds, Mahmud will have to confront the cultural memories that are embedded into familiar performances of history and tragedy. Mahmud relies upon this cultural knowledge to navigate a series of political and personal crises. Only the audience is aware that Mahmud is caught in a rubric of wartime melodrama. The situation seems impossible and inevitably tragic.

When Mahmud awakes, he realizes his dream has left 'no *figure* upon memory's glass' (my emphasis, *Hellas*, 1.31). Mahmud's dream appears to lack a visual dimension that he considers necessary to interpretation. He does not yet realize that he must see both the figure and listen to the sounds and that this requires him to engage the amorphous plurality of anonymous figures that cannot be easily resolved into one distinct figure or interpretation. The scene presents Mahmud and the audience with an interpretive dilemma, which proves pivotal because it expresses the cultural longing for a melodramatic figure that is clearly identified as a heroic character because it stands in contrast to the villain. Mahmud's 'gloomy vision' lacks both a heroic figure and an intelligible interpretive framework. Faced with the unknown and with his own failure to formulate a judgement of the situation he now encounters, he summons Ahasuerus, 'A Jew, whose spirit is a chronicle/Of strange and secret and forgotten things' (*Hellas*, ll. 133–4). Mahmud's characterization of Ahasuerus as a 'chronicle' betrays his hope that this seer-prophet will help him recuperate a viable narrative that can situate the unfolding events into a cogent teleology that will legitimize his efforts to preserve his empire against revolutionaries who fight for their freedom. Mahmud's dream and later his vision of his ancestor, Mahomet II, mark his intellectual and cultural habit of turning inward for answers in times of crisis. This inward turn does not inspire reflection, as one might expect but rather it prompts a desire for didactic clarity that one expects when watching melodrama or reading an adage, an epigram or an allegory. The melodramatic action that structures *Hellas* will eventually redirect Mahmud's attention outward. His conversations with Hassan and Ahasuerus engage him in dialogic thinking but this, he discovers, will not provide him with the resolution he seeks. What *Hellas* ultimately reveals to Mahmud and its audiences is that teleology is an illusion. No definitive figure of Truth exists and history has no endpoint. The only real answer can be found by immersing oneself in the cacophony of voices and the endless movement of lyric pictures, where liberation becomes an act of sequentially abandoning one position after another in search of more liberating possibilities.

Hellas creates a metadramatic play of words, sounds and images that demonstrates the 'haphazard and improvised business'[35] of producing melodramas in the early nineteenth century. Mahmud wakes up, disoriented by a dream where language and meaning seem to dissolve into music and bodily movement. This experience epitomizes melodrama, which requires audiences to make meaning by integrating the play's disparate and incongruous elements that have led to 'irreconcilable clashes' between characters and 'unresolved dissonances'.[36] Interpreting melodrama poses audiences with formidable difficulties that require them to reconcile themselves subconsciously to illogical scenarios and irresolvable contradictions. Once Mahmud awakes, the choral lyrics are temporarily displaced by other dramatic components. The 'truth of day' brings Mahmud a torrent of reports detailing mutiny and revolt as well as the fascinating but 'treasonous' tales of Greek heroism. Even the loyal Hassan confesses that he speaks the 'words [of Freedom] I fear and hate;/Yet would I die for – ' (*Hellas*, ll. 457–8). Although Mahmud is conscious only of these incoming reports, the chorus continues to perform intermittently, building upon the puzzling and troubling images presented in the initial choral song/movement. The first of these lyrics is a variation of Milton's ode, 'On the Morning of Christ's Nativity'. Shelley's allusive lyric portrays the arrival of Christ and the subsequent departure of the Greek pantheon – Apollo, Pan, Love and even 'Olympian Jove' – from the world. Milton's pageantry presents a performance of evolving religious frameworks, beginning with Greek mythology and concluding Christian monotheism. Shelley's lyric depicts the fall into time from myth to linear historicism. Prior to the arrival of the 'Promethean Conqueror', as Shelley refers to Christ, 'Worlds on worlds are rolling ever/From creation to decay' (*Hellas*, ll. 197–8). Subject to the cycle of life and death, endless possibilities exist; 'New shapes' gave way to 'new Gods, [and] new Laws' (*Hellas*, ll. 197–208). Once the 'Power from an unknown God' (*Hellas*, l. 211) arrives, the oracles go silent and a rigid teleology is constructed from a vision of 'Hell, Sin, and Slavery' (*Hellas*, l. 218) that erases 'the radiant shapes of sleep/From [those] whose dreams are Paradise' (*Hellas*, ll. 225–6). Power generates a historical tale grounded in violence and war:

> Our hills and seas and streams – ,
> Dispeopled of their dreams –
> Their waters turned to blood, their dew to tears –
> Wailed for the golden years.
>
> *Hellas*, ll. 235–8

This lyric portrays the transition from pantheism to monotheism and the absolutes of sovereign power; the myriad possibilities – 'dreams' – available at one moment contract into a series of binary oppositions: full/empty, happiness/despair, past/present. The collective and individual dreams of people that looked forward to a new age now shrivel and become the nightmares of history, replete with blood and tears. The transubstantiation of water into blood and dew into tears yields not hope but despair. The only comfort that remains is a nostalgic lament 'for the golden years'.

The chorus produces one more lyric picture before Ahasuerus appears on stage. This image emblematically describes the history of the Greeks under Ottoman rule. The chorus is composed of slaves who can only imagine their freedom: 'Would I were the winged cloud [. . .] I would scorn [. . .] I would leave [. . .] I would flee' (*Hellas*, ll. 648–63). These conditional statements collect like drops of rain, forming into a philhellenic vision of Athens rising out of the sea like Botticelli's *Birth of Venus*: 'Athens arose! – around her born,/Shone like mountains in the morn/Glorious states, – ' (*Hellas*, ll. 684–6). Like the other lyrics, this picture is constructed through a series of binary oppositions. A scene of cultural emergence – 'Let there be light!' (*Hellas*, l. 682) – gives way to 'Ashes, wrecks, [and] oblivion' (*Hellas*, l. 687). The chorus then issues the command to 'Go,/Where [the] Thermæ and Asopus [rivers] swallowed Persia' (*Hellas*, l. 687–8). This site marks the Greek defeat of Xerxes on land. Rather than dwelling nostalgically on the Greek victories over Persia or the splendid 'Temples and towers,/Citadels and mart' (*Hellas*, ll. 692–3), the chorus again shifts its perspective, reproducing the historical moment of Greece's pre-eminence as one of civil and political collapse that extends from the Macedonian conquest to the present: 'Deluge upon deluge followed/[bringing] Discord, Macedon, and Rome:/And last Thou!' (*Hellas*, ll. 687–92). As in the 'Ode to the West Wind', Shelley focuses our attention on the paradoxical moment of autumnal ripeness and decay, which he also represents in *A Defence of Poetry* in terms of the 'fading coal' (*SPP*, 531) of creation that cools into ash or sparks into flame.[37] While the chorus sympathizes with the Greeks, it also criticizes those who would place 'Greece and her foundations [. . .] below the tide of war', and allow 'imperial spirits [to]/Rule the present from the past' (*Hellas*, ll. 696–701). This naïve vision of history can only result in destruction and annihilation:

> The crash as of an empire falling,
> The shrieks as of a people calling
> 'Mercy? Mercy!' how they thrill!
> Then a shout of 'Kill! Kill! Kill!'
> *Hellas*, ll. 724–7

The choral lyric concludes with 'a still small voice' of humanity, lamenting the 'revenge and wrong' perpetuated by those serving the 'unknown God in vain' (*Hellas*, l. 735).

Shelley's lyrics imitate the oppositional movement that structures the ode, tragedy and history. Each of these narrative and poetic constructions portrays the rise and fall of ideas, heroes and empires, but for Shelley these forms can also be reconfigured as a challenge to the conventional configurations of cultural and historical memories. Shelley momentarily 'fixes' these binary tensions in tableaux. Joanna Baillie and other dramatists radicalized historical drama through the theatrical practice of staging pictures.[38] Tableaux stilled the actor's movement in the moment of their most expressive poses. Baillie's tableaux in *Constantine Paleologus* – published in 1804 and first performed in 1808 – and Emma Hamilton's famous drawing room 'attitudes' represent two examples of this theatrical practice.[39] A former actress who had married Sir William Hamilton, England's envoy to Naples, Emma Hamilton was renowned for her drawing room performances where she and other women posed as figures from classical mythology, literature and history. Hamilton would don an evocative costume and would move rapidly through a variety of poses, giving expression to a range of emotional states.[40] The emotive force and the erotic allure of Hamilton's 'attitudes' parallels the affective bodily displays that defined melodrama and the ever-popular pantomime.

If Aeschylus' Persians marks the ascendancy of Greece as an imperial state, then Baillie's play, dramatizing the fifteenth-century fall of Constantinople, testifies to Greece's capitulation to the Ottoman Empire. Baillie's drama capitalized on the military crisis between British and Napoleonic forces in the aftermath of the Peace of Amiens in 1803. Baillie based Constantine Paleologus loosely on Edward Gibbon's account of Constantinople's fall in his The Decline and Fall of the Roman Empire, published in six volumes between 1776 and 1789. Like Gibbon's history, Baillie's play challenges the classical narrative of imperial history. Both Hellas and Constantine Paleologus offer a historic re-enactment that promotes public reflection on the possibilities for social and political reform. Baillie's tragedy portrays the Greek emperor, Constantine, and his loyal band of followers during the final days of the city's independence. Constantine's court espouses the values of the French Revolution – liberty, equality and fraternity. This cosmopolitan and Christian brotherhood of European soldiers stand together against the Muslim tyrant, Mahomet and his followers, which include depraved Greek citizens, the traitors, Petronius and Marthon and enslaved soldiers.[41] Baillie's drama envisions a pan-European alliance that would bring an end to the centuries of internecine conflict; it also reflects on the volatile historical situation in Constantinople between the collapse of the Peace of Amiens in 1803 and the assassination of the Sultan, Selim III, in 1808, when the city erupted into a massive open revolt. Baillie's construction of critical scenes as tableaux offers audiences a new way of viewing social and political relations. The drama's opening scene directions offers audiences an alternative historical perspective:

> A large platform on the roof of the palace of PETRONIUS, from which are seen spires and towers, and the broken roofs of houses, &c., with the general appearance of a ruined city, the distant part involved in smoke. ELLA is discovered with an attendant, standing on a balcony belonging to a small tower, rising from the side of the platform. As the curtain draws up the sound of artillery is heard.

In the midst of the sights and sounds of war, Ella and her attendant stand on a balcony overlooking a spectacle of devastation: broken roofs, a city in ruins and the skies filled with smoke. This prospect reproduces the conventional division between domestic (feminine) and national (masculine) spheres. However, as Greg Kucich argues, this visual segregation quickly dissolves as characters begin to move across the stage and women interpose themselves in scenes where men are preparing to fight. Emotional displays of affective sympathy shift the audience's focus away from the impassive masculine perspective reproduced in conventional histories.[42]

Baillie's drama weaves together masculine and feminine narratives until the final scene, which ends the play with an image of social dissolution:

> A secret spirit whispers to my heart,
> That in these walls your weaken'd wretched race,

Slaves of their slaves, in gloomy prison'd pomp
Shall shed each others blood, and make these towers
A place of groans and anguish, not of bliss.
Constantine Paleologus, V,iii; 478

The 'secret spirit' is the voice of history as Othus, the Greek historian who initially resists donning the soldier's armour, relates it to the audience. He tells a familiar tale: the rise and fall of empires and internecine wars between enslaved populations that produce nothing other than misery. Othus represents history as a tableau of martial exploits that are anything but valorous. Baillie's tableaux develop theatrical possibilities for her drama by exhibiting its potential to picture social and political reforms, but her work also reveals the form's ideological limitations. Melodrama's emphasis on the domestic sphere and its tendency to reconstruct historical narratives as domestic plots, often converts revolutionary impulses into socially acceptable norms.[43] Baillie's pictures of military destruction and domestic fidelity protest against the alluring spectacle of a thoroughly militarized and imperial culture but it also condemns the 'wondrous mixture [. . .] /Of woman's loveliness with manly state' as something 'Strange, and perplexing, and unsuitable' (*Constantine Paleologus*, V,iii; 477). Baillie's tableaux display the necessity of negotiating cultural oppositions but her plays ultimately tend to sustain these destructive cultural binaries that inhibit reform.

Shelley sets Baillie's tableaux into motion. Aware of the cultural clash over melodrama in the early nineteenth century and alert to melodrama's popularity as well as its deployment in the cultural production of a wartime sensibility, Shelley nonetheless experiments with the form and appropriates it for his own purposes. *Hellas* has a cinematic quality insofar as images are brought into focus but not allowed to congeal into a fully recognizable still. Demogorgon in *Prometheus Unbound* proclaims, 'the deep truth in imageless' (*PU*, II,iv,16). Shelley adheres to this principle throughout his dramatic and poetic works and foregoes representing either a fully articulate voice or a distinct, iconic image. In *Hellas* Mahmud repeatedly encounters amorphous figures in his dreams and in his visions. In the second dramatic scene Mahmud sits quietly as messengers bring him reports about the progress of the war. He cannot make these reports cohere into one image of either failure or success and frustrated he declares, 'I'll hear no more! Too long/ We gaze on danger through the mist of fear,/And multiply upon our shattered hopes/The images of ruin' (*Hellas*, ll. 640–43). Mahmud recognizes the news as nothing more than rumour and opinion and realizes he cannot discern anything clearly while in this 'mist of fear'.

Years earlier, when writing a letter to Thomas Jefferson Hogg in August 1815, Shelley identified Mahmud's dilemma as his own:

You will see in the papers the continuance of the same system which the Allies had begun to pursue: and a most spirited remonstrance of the king of France's ministers against the enormities of their troops. In considering the political events of the day I endeavour to divest my mind of temporary sensations, to consider them as already historical. This is difficult. Spite of ourselves the human beings which surround us infect us with their opinions: so much as to forbid us to be dispassionate observers of the questions arising out of the events of the age.

(Letters, 1. 430)

Here the young Shelley expresses a longing for what he perceives as the clarity of a dispassionate historical perspective. He is obviously frustrated by limited prospect of the present moment where opinions cloak truths and falsehoods equally, obscuring each and making it impossible to not be one of the infected multitude. Shelley wants to divest his mind of these 'temporary sensations' produced by the impassioned opinions of strangers, friends, political parties and even within literary circles. He endeavours to counter news about 'political events of the day' with the construction of a historical framework within his own imagination, but acknowledges the difficulty of sustaining such a paradigm. Mahmud shares Shelley's distrust of the news reports, and also attempts to place his confidence in the extended temporal perspective provided by history.

Mahmud cannot differentiate the rumours from the reports or resolve the information and the play of emotional turmoil that accompanies war into a viable account of unfolding events. Ahasuerus, Mahmud hopes, will provide him with the coherent image he longs to see. The ancient and mysterious wanderer, Ahasuerus embodies every perspective: the cosmopolitan, the religious, the historical, and as a prophet figure he also sees the future. His arrival inspires Mahmud with hope. Mahmud describes Ahasuerus as 'raised above thy fellow men/By thought, as I by power' (*Hellas*, ll. 738–9). Mahmud identifies Ahasuerus as his counterpart. But it quickly becomes clear that Ahasuerus will not provide the Sultan with a more coherent perspective or with a script for the role he must play to bring the present crisis to conclusion. Ahasuerus is 'no interpreter of dreams', and Mahmud soon realizes there exists no means of making the 'future present', except by letting 'it come' (*Hellas*, ll. 756–9). Ahasuerus grasps the significance of events very differently than Mahmud and the two characters speak at cross purposes until Ahasuerus exclaims,

> Sultan! Talk no more
> Of thee and me, the future and the past;
> But look on that which cannot change – the One [. . .]
> The future and the past are idle shadows
> Of thought's eternal flight – they have no being.
>
> Hellas, ll. 766–84

Ahasuerus rejects Mahmud's persistent construction of reality in terms of binaries. He conceives existence through the lens of Leibnitzian monism, which assumes a pre-established harmony between existing elements and perceives every moment as containing its past as well as its future.[44] Events unfold within one another: as a seed exists within a fruit for the purpose of recreating the plant that bears the fruit.

The seed collapses the distinction between the fruit and the plant into the materialized present. For Mahmud, this image is too abstract, in some ways, too concrete insofar as it does not respond to the many distractions that delineate the present crises. Ahasuerus soon realizes his only means of communicating meaningfully with Mahmud is through a recognizable framework: 'Would'st thou behold the future? – ask and have!/Knock and it shall be opened – look and lo!/The coming age is shadowed on the past/As on a glass' (*Hellas*, ll. 803–5). Ahasuerus repeats a familiar biblical injunction in Matthew 7.7 and Luke 11.9 that enjoins believers to engage their future through performative acts. Ahasuerus' proclamation does not usher in the future but takes Mahmud deeper into the past, where he encounters the 'imperial shade' (*Hellas*, l. 861) of Mahomet II.

Mahomet II represents a historical reference point around which Mahmud's dream and the contradictory reports can momentarily coalesce, but is he the *figure* missing from memory's glass earlier in the play? Ahasuerus tells Mahmud that Mahomet 'Is but the ghost of thy forgotten dream./A dream itself, yet, less, perhaps, than that/Thou callest reality [. . .] The Past/Now stands before thee like an Incarnation/Of the To-come; yet would'st thou commune with/That portion of thyself which was ere thou/Dids't start' (*Hellas*, ll. 842–4, ll. 852–6). Prior to this moment, Mahmud has viewed the inevitable collapse of his empire as the failure of the absolute, incontrovertible ideal that Islam (for Shelley, any religion) represents; he has clung to 'This gloomy crag of Time [, which] /Seemed an Elysian isle of peace and joy/Never to be attained' (*Hellas*, ll. 926–8). The ghost of Mahomet II teaches Mahmud the lesson he could not acquire under Ahasuerus' tutelage: that he is ruled by 'phantoms' of power – 'Mutinous passions, and conflicting fears' (*Hellas*, ll. 883–4) – and 'nought we see or dream/ Possess or lose or grasp at can be worth/More than it gives or teaches' (*Hellas*, ll. 921–3). History is not merely a narrative with heroic figures and battles won and lost. 'Thought [. . .] Will, Passion,/Reason, Imagination, cannot die' (*Hellas*, ll. 795–6) as people do; they exist as does the acorn falling in Dodona's forest, and, like the seed, 'these elements' follow a teleology. History can take form as either a static ideology or a dynamic process. It unfolds as a series of moments, each containing cherished ideals and the atrocities committed in the name of preserving those ideals.[45]

But the action of the play is relentless. Mahmud and the audience can just seize this concept before their attention is redirected toward the next scene. Just as the women panting in the first choral movement rouse Mahmud from his dream, so too shouts announcing the latest victory break Mahmud's trance. This signals the triumph of his imperial forces over the Greeks. However, Mahmud is no longer deluded by the transitory claims of victory or defeat and appoints himself the task of rebuking 'This drunkenness of triumph ere it die/And dying, bring despair' (*Hellas*, ll. 929–30). This series of lyric pictures and choral interludes concludes with Mahmud achieving a more radical historical awareness. Shelley has transformed a series of historical, literary and visionary moments into an epic stage. Unlike *Constantine Paleologus*, which ultimately reinscribes the radical nature of Baillie's vision within the traditional parameters of gender roles and so adheres to the domestic ideology of wartime melodrama, Shelley's *Hellas* reconfigures these familiar stage practices into a continuously moving framework: a cinematic reel.

Newsreel history

As the play shifts, mirroring and countering melodrama's wartime ideology as well as its stage practices, *Hellas* also moves steadily toward its final choral movement, which will fill the stage with a cacophony of voices. As Shelley informs his readers in his Preface, the plot is grounded in his 'newspaper erudition' (*SPP*, 431), and Shelley weaves this feature into the play's other components to produce his 'mere improvise' (*SPP*, 430) of melodrama. The reports Mahmud received from messengers before Ahasuerus' arrival will be depicted as disembodied voices after Mahomet's visitation. The *Voice without* imitates the newspaper's banner headlines. Its declarative statements attempt to captivate a distracted audience. The initial report describes the geo-political situation Ypsilanti created when he crossed into Wallachia and declared Greek independence in 1821. In the first of three bulletins, the *Voice without* proclaims: 'Russia's famished Eagles/Dare not to prey beneath the crescent's light' (*Hellas*, ll. 948–9). It had long been believed that the Greeks would not be capable of emancipating themselves from the Ottomans without European or Russian involvement; but as the drama's announcement makes clear, the Russians were in no position to go to war against the Ottoman Empire. Nonetheless, most Europeans believed it would take, as Byron writes in his notes to *Childe Harold*, 'the interposition of foreigners' (*CPW*, 2. 202) to liberate the Greeks. But as Byron also observes,

> Where is the human being that ever conferred a benefit on Greek or Greeks? They are to be grateful to the Turks for their fetters, and the Franks for their broken promises and lying counsels: they are to be grateful to the artist who engraves their ruins, and to the antiquary who carries them away; to the traveler whose janissary flogs them, and to the scribbler whose journal abuses them! This is the amount of their obligations to foreigners.
>
> (*CPW*, 2. 201)

Byron describes the impossible situation of the Greeks and many colonized and oppressed peoples, whose lack of independence makes it difficult for them to preserve their cultural heritage much less fashion meaningful alliances between countries with competing economic and political interests. Eton had observed in 1798 that the shared religion – Greek Orthodoxy – recommended Russian intervention on behalf of the Greeks, but the Russians had a history of deceiving and abandoning the Greeks. When Ypsilanti crossed the Russian frontier with a party of expatriate Greeks and announced he would liberate the Christian Greeks from the Turks, the Russians declared him a traitor, and it became clear they had no intention of invading Turkey on behalf of the Greeks.[46] As Byron notes, the Greeks were in the rather unenviable position of attracting the attention of many different interest groups: artists, antiquarians, politicians, traders and tourists. While some of these interests encouraged Russian intervention, others lobbied against it, voicing their concern that Russia might break ranks with Western imperial power and destabilize Europe. Shelley makes clear in his Preface that he suspected Russian rule would differ little from Turkish oppression:

> Russia desires to possess not to liberate Greece, and is contented to see the Turks, its natural enemies, and the Greeks, its intended slaves, enfeeble each other until one or both fall into its net. The wise and generous policy of England would have consisted in establishing the independence of Greece, and in maintaining it both against Russia and the Turk; – but when was the oppressor generous or just?
>
> (*SPP*, 432)

Shelley sees through the superficial play of national politics to the philosophical and cultural constructions of oppression, war and slavery. The real nemesis is not Russia, the Turks or even the British, but the pervasive practice of imperial conquest that perpetuates ethnic and religious intolerance.

The second report concerns France. While Napoleon was in power, many philhellenes shared Byron's view – again reflected in his notes to *Childe Harold* – that 'the subjugation of the rest of Europe will, probably, be attended by the deliverance of continental Greece' (*CPW*, 2. 202). After Napoleon's defeat at Waterloo and subsequent internal struggles, which resulted eventually in the restoration of the weakened Bourbon monarchs, France adapted to its new role as minor player on the world stage. The play's newspaper erudition depicts France as enjoying 'a partial exemption from the abuses which its unnatural and feeble government are vainly attempting to revive' (*SPP*, 432). Despite Napoleon's defeat and the restoration of the Bourbons, France remained a viable albeit tattered symbol of liberty, and while the struggle for freedom continued throughout Europe and the world, many like Shelley questioned whether France would be a 'poor shadow' of the liberty it had once proclaimed, or would become yet another 'tame Serpent' ready to strike when provoked by the radical cry for freedom.

Finally, the *Voice without* speaks about Great Britain. The 1790s brought the French to Egypt for cotton, grain and the Rosetta stone. The British followed them into the Mediterranean and in an attempt to protect their interests they reestablished their sixteenth-century alliance with the Ottoman Empire: setting up military bases and trading posts to safeguard their routes to India. During the first decade of the nineteenth century, as Napoleon's power waned in the region, Britain began to play a more significant role. The British were not overtly concerned with the internal politics of nations in this region, nor were they interested in playing the role of the liberator, except insofar as they portrayed themselves as liberating the world from the leviathan of French republican imperialism. They occupied the area primarily to preserve the Mediterranean as a safe corridor for international commerce. Malta and the Ionian islands came under British control at the end of the eighteenth century. In 1817, Thomas Maitland, the Governor of Malta and Lord High Commissioner of Iona, formalized the wartime autocracy with a constitution that instituted the domination of the Legislative Assembly by a Primary Council of men bound to the governor by a system of patronage. This system remained in place until the British left the Ionian Islands in 1863. Malta, however, continued to function as an autocratic state monopolized by British officials until 1887.[47] Frederick North, a former governor of Ceylon, did the most to promote Greek interests when he established a university on Corfu. But even North's schemes, effectively blocked by Maitland until 1823, underscored Britain's presence as Greece's protector, while all the while advocating for British commercial interests throughout the eastern Mediterranean.[48]

Shelley in his Preface identifies the tie between Britain and Greece as a secret alliance with tyranny. 'The English', he complains, 'permit their own oppressors to act according to their natural sympathy with the Turkish tyrant, and to brand upon their name the indelible blot of an alliance with the enemies of domestic happiness, of Christianity and civilization' (*SPP*, 432). In accord with this, the *Voice without* reports the Turkish victory over the Greeks as one in which the 'bought Briton' colluded with the Islamite, sending him the 'Keys of Ocean', and enabling an immediate reprisal. Newspaper erudition presents the Greek situation as part of a perpetual and global war. Essentially, it reproduces the wartime melodrama performed night after night on London's stages.

This section of *Hellas* recreates historical events as a cascading series of newsreel scenes. The *Voice without* reproduces these events as Astley's Royal Amphitheatre, Sadler's Wells or the Royal Circus would have done: as melodramatic theatrical spectacles. The patent theatres, which held a government-sanctioned monopoly on spoken-word drama and as such were subject to the censorship of the Lord Chamberlain's office, staged performances that often avoided dramatizing anything like a historical account of military campaigns, especially during the American Revolution and the early incursions of British military forces into the heart of the Indian sub-Continent. John Larpent, the inspector of plays for the Lord Chamberlain from 1778 until his death in 1824, enforced the Licensing Act (1737) by prohibiting productions that resonated too much with contemporary political situations. While this provided opportunities for unlicensed venues to stage such plays, they were of necessity radically transformed from spoken-word performances to entertainments, which relied upon illegitimate theatrical practices. This pioneering dramaturgy capitalized on the theatre's abilities to reconfigure legitimate theatrical productions effectively. It also marked the emergence of an alternative theatrical experience that appealed to mass audiences. Throughout the nineteenth century these theatrical practices converged to produce hybrid performances that deployed new technologies to create increasingly sophisticated illusions and spectacles. Forms like the melodrama produced pre-cinematic experiences that enabled audiences to *see* more of military conflict than the ordinary soldier.[49] These productions transformed the theatre into a space that simulated war and marked a revolution in the dramatization of nation and empire. This new dramaturgical form, as Moody points out, represents the confrontation between freedom and despotism, good and evil and 'implicitly reveals the failure of rationality, the inadequacy of rhetoric and the impossibility of benevolence'.[50] These performances effectively transformed audiences from a disparate collective of individuals into an amalgam of shared political and social interests.

Shelley's deployment of his newspaper erudition in this section is different than Coleridge and Southey's use of this type of information in their 1790s drama, *The Fall of Robespierre*, and in other productions, including the popular Tipu Sultan plays, which staged the Third and Fourth Mysore Wars in the 1790s. Daniel O'Quinn writes about these plays as productions of theatrical imperialism. They generated complex fantasies of global supremacy, enacted Britain's modern tactical superiority on the battlefield and depicted social and political capitulation in the terms of military paternalism.[51] These performances downplayed Britain's aggressive imperialist policies while at the same time they organized the cultural memories of war by shifting the emphasis from an act of identifying with particular actors to one that highlighted the visual experience of an increasingly mechanized war.[52] *Hellas* incorporates many of the tactics associated with melodramatic performances, but the drama's poetic form directs the audience to focus on its textual character as well. The variety of scenic possibilities compounded with the progression of the lyric's narrative does not privilege one formal framework more than another. The plot does not outstrip the presentation of information nor do images usurp the significance of the historical narrative. The disembodied *Voice without* attracts the audience's attention but it offers the audience no accompanying figure on the glass to which to affix a particular meaning. Shelley's drama captivates his audience to some extent like all theatrical performances but *Hellas* also attempts to liberate its audiences from the familiar wartime melodramas that were performed on and off stage. The drama's newsreel effect brings images *just* into focus but at that moment, the play moves forward, forcing the audience and each of the characters to abandon that particular framework for another one.

Hellas's next scene is that of the resurrection song, which begins with the line, 'The world's great age begins anew' (*Hellas*, l. 1060 ff.). This scene has received most of the drama's critical attention. A highly wrought hymn, this lyric recalls the golden age of Greece with a familiar litany of characters and images: ranging from the Argo to Orpheus and Ulysses. This lyric depicts the Hellenist ideal. The interplay of lyric and dramatic forms throughout the drama has, as with Mahmud, elicited the desire for a 'single voice'.[53] But the litany of voices and images repulse and contravene that yearning. Promising a 'brighter Hellas', a 'loftier Argo', 'Another Orpheus', a 'new Ulysses' and 'Another Athens', this lyric bespeaks a nostalgia for the lost Greek nation and its classical-era empire. Although the lyric betrays a wistful enthusiasm for Greek culture, it is only one part in a symphony of voices. This performance of multiple voices represents the core of *Hellas*: no singular voice is sustained. The tragic chorus depicting the Greek women's oppression, the melodramatic tableaux staging of the sights and sounds of war, and the newsreel of history, featuring the *Voice without*, cannot be reduced to the single voice of a unified subject. *Hellas* repeatedly transgresses the formal boundaries of Greek tragedy, melodrama and war dramaturgy, in each instance shifting the border that distinguishes between Eastern and Western imperialism to one that dilates between liberty and slavery and life and death.

Conclusion

Hellas presents audiences with a liberating performance, an alternative stage of imperialism whereon the rich and powerful Ottoman Sultan, Mahmud, is so haunted by dreams of slaves vying for love and revenge that he embarks on a liberating journey of self-discovery. In contrast with the poet figure in Shelley's *Alastor; or the Spirit of Solitude* (1816), this excursion does not involve travelling to foreign lands. Shelley creates the epic expanse in *Hellas* by incorporating melodramatic practices into Greek drama. Shelley capitalizes on the popularity of melodrama but he also reconfigures it for his own dramatic purposes. Instead of reproducing war reports and battle re-enactments as the almost inescapable experience of wartime that Mary Favret describes in her book, *War at a Distance*, Shelley recreates the classical stage of empire, transforming its tragedies into a lyric drama. *Hellas* intermixes choral movements with lyric pictures and dramatic episodes. His poetic drama is a series of moving pictures, representing different states of political consciousness and self-awareness. Juxtaposing Aeschylus' powerful dramatization of history in *The Persians* with the unfolding events tied to the Greek uprising against the Ottoman Empire (1821–1832), *Hellas* depicts the violent tensions that sustain the structures of sovereign and imperial power while it also requires its main character and its audience to negotiate and abandon this ideological complex.

In his notes to *Childe Harold* Byron poignantly describes the Greek cause as similar to that shared by the Catholics of Ireland, the Jews, and 'other cudgeled and heterodox people' (*CPW*, 2. 201). Their lives, he writes, are 'a struggle against truth; they are vicious in their own defence. They are so unused to kindness, that when they occasionally meet with it they look up upon it with suspicion, as a dog often beaten snaps at your fingers if you attempt to caress him' (*CPW*, 2. 201). Although Byron also declares that the 'Greeks will never be independent [. . .] and God forbid they ever should', he insists 'they may be subject without being slaves' (*CPW*, 2. 201). Bryon understood the political complexities that accompanied discussions about Greek independence. Britain played a key political role in the global politics of the post-Napoleonic world, but as an imperial power invested economically and militarily in the oppression of others, its identity as a liberator was compromised. Byron suggests that the Greeks and other oppressed and colonized peoples can be 'free and industrious' while at the same time being deprived of their independence (*CPW*, 2. 201). The colonized throughout the world existed as pawns in a chess game that included diplomats and politicians vying for territory, merchants vying for better prices and travellers eulogizing the artifacts and the ruins of destroyed nations and civilizations. Byron, like many British aristocrats whose education immersed them in the classical culture of Greece and Rome, expressed a strong sympathy with the Greeks and yet very few of them could imagine the Greeks or any of the world's oppressed peoples as free.

Byron's comments situate the question of Greek independence within the larger contexts of imperialism and global war. Writers like Baillie, Byron and Shelley realized that Britain's empire did not exist as isolated pockets of political and economic oppression but rather as a labyrinthine entity 'of overlapping territories, [and] intertwined histories'.[54] Throughout the Napoleonic wars, Britain cast its 'play of power' in the Mediterranean region as a war of liberation rather than as a contest for world resources and markets and imperial hegemony.[55] Britain's military bases on Malta and in occupied Sicily (1806–15) and on the Ionian islands (1809–14) did not exist because the British wanted to protect the Greeks from the Russians, who considered themselves the rightful governors of all Greek Orthodox populations inhabiting the Balkans and the Levant. Although the British attacked Egypt in 1801 and 1807 and exerted pressure on the Ottoman Porte to establish its influence in Northern Africa and throughout the Persian Gulf, this extension of British influence, including opening new markets in southern Europe and the Near East, was as a response to French imperialism. If the British could identify themselves as a liberator, so much the better, but ultimately their presence served to protect the empire's trading routes: nothing more, nothing less.

Aeschylus' *The Persians* is one of the earliest surviving Greek plays. A re-enactment of the Battle of Salamis (480 BCE), which the Greeks won against overwhelming odds, *The Persians* focuses on the horrors of war and can be read as the Ur-drama of Western imperialism. The play combines visual spectacle with lyric storytelling and its action is punctuated by choral singing and dancing. The plot begins with Xerxes' fateful invasion of Greece. Messengers return to the Persian court with disturbing news reports. Xerxes' mother cannot believe these reports and invokes the spirit of her dead husband in an attempt to discover the truth. The play's imperial vision is rife with contradictions: scenes of grief accompany victory celebrations. Although Shelley closely follows Aeschylus, he also rewrites the drama as a challenge to those Hellenists who venerated Greek culture so much that they effectively destroyed it by looting artifacts and turning a blind eye to ways in which they countenanced and justified Greek oppression. Shelley voiced his opposition to the idolization of Greek culture in 1812, when in a letter to William Godwin he reconsiders the pervasive cultural attitudes towards Greek and Latin literatures. Responding to Godwin's encomium to classical learning in an issue of his *Enquirer*, Shelley asks him a series of questions:

> Are not the reasonings on which your system [in *Political Justice*] is founded utterly distinct from & unconnected with the excellence of Greece & Rome? Was not the government of republican Rome, & most of those of Greece as oppressive & arbitrary, as liberal of encourag[e]ment to monopoly as that of Great Britain is at present? And what do we learn from their poets? as you have yourself acknowledged somewhere 'they are fit for nothing but the perpetuation of the noxious race of heroes in the world'. [. . .] their politics sprang from the same narrow & corrupted source – witness the interminable aggressions between each other and the states of Greece, & the thirst of conquest with which even republican Rome desolated the Earth. – they are our masters in politics because we are so immoral as to prefer self interest to virtue & expediency to positive good.
>
> (To William Godwin, 29 July 1812, *Letters*, 1. 317)

Shelley's enthusiasm for the Greek cause while living in Italy and his lifelong appreciation of Greek culture and its literary achievements did not blind him to the cultural politics promulgated in classical texts. The Greeks and the Romans may have espoused republican values and even republican systems of governance on occasion, but Shelley insists they were no less 'oppressive & arbitrary' than Britain in the early nineteenth century. They too 'desolated the Earth' in their pursuit of conquest. Shelley clearly sees how cultural productions reproduce political attitudes and practices. When writers and politicians adhere slavishly to these cultural models, they effectively replicate these values as those of the contemporary moment: becoming slaves to history.

Years later, in a letter written to Claire Clairmont just prior to composing *Hellas*, Shelley expresses his enthusiasm about the recent events in Greece: 'Greece has declared its freedom! [. . .] The Morea – Spirus – Servia', he writes, 'are in revolt. Greece will most certainly be free' (2 April 1821, *Letters*, 2. 278). These fervent declarations – recorded in his letters and in the Preface to *Hellas* – have been quoted by critics to argue, as David Ferris has, for Shelley's 'deference to a Greek past'.[56] The centrepiece of these arguments is Shelley's assertion in the Preface where he declares, 'We are all Greeks' (*SPP*, 431). Scholars place this statement routinely alongside Hunt's announcement: 'This is an age of Revolutions. The *Greeks* have risen in arms' (*The Examiner*, XIX, 15 April 1821, p. 231). This line of reasoning situates Shelley and *Hellas* as part of the philhellenic movement, which evolved from Hellenism: an eighteenth-century paradigm of European cultural achievement that identified Greece – its drama, its poetry, its political models and its cultural values – as the exemplar and the foundation of Western culture.

However when we examine these statements more closely, it is clear that both Hunt and Shelley question the efficacy of this cultural model. The complete passage from Shelley's Preface reads,

> We are all Greeks – our laws, our literature, our religion, our arts have their root in Greece. But for Greece, Rome, the instructor, their conqueror, or the metropolis of our ancestors would have spread no illumination with her arms, and we might still have been savages, and idolaters; or, what is worse, might have arrived at such a stagnant and miserable state of social institution as China and Japan possess.
>
> (*SPP*, 431)

Greece represents Hellenist ideals *and* the darker realities of imperialism that Hellenism obscures. Shelley introduces Rome and Greece as a peripatetic duo: the instructor and the conqueror. This is the nexus of power/knowledge, and as Michel Foucault has argued, this 'productive' relationship, which he traces back to the end of the classical era, involves the 'deployment of force and the establishment of truth'.[57] Shelley's familiarity with Bacon's 'power is knowledge', which identifies knowledge as an instrument of power and mechanical invention as the force that shapes history, leads him to this insightful discussion about cultural and historical reconfigurations of knowledge/power. The nodal point of power/knowledge for

Shelley is the imperial metropolis, where the government-sanctioned production of texts, theatrical performances and other art forms takes place. Shelley condemns this collusion by invoking a tradition of oriental satire, which startles the reader when Shelley contrasts the Greeks with those 'savages' and 'idolators' living in the 'stagnant and miserable' states of Japan and China. Shelley would have been familiar with oriental satires like Leigh Hunt's 'Account of the Remarkable Rise and Downfall of the late Great Kan of Tartary', where he deploys orientalist conventions to convey the despotic cruelty that defines the 'complete history of the present marvelous times'.[58] Hunt's satire comments on the treachery of war and empire building in the West. He is most concerned with the rise and fall of Napoleon but he also sees how British military forces and their systems of governance mirror Napoleon's tactics. Shelley's references to China and Japan provide a means of exploring the consequences of an imposed cultural isolation and how, similar to Greece, these places have been lifted, along with their history and their populations, out of the story of Western history, leaving them with no future and no past, but merely existing to function symbolically as representatives of political and social oppression.

Prior to this famous passage, Shelley identifies Greece as the root cause of Roman imperialism. Shelley deconstructs Hellenism with a satiric eye and with the finesse of a Greek philosopher. How, he asks, can we survey the cultural treasures of Greece without contemplating the horrors of war and conquest, which, in the first instance, established Greek cultural hegemony over the Persians, and, in the second, educated Rome and provided the new imperial power with its first spoils. Greek philosophy equipped Rome with its *raison d'être*, 'to spread [. . .] illumination with its arms'. From this perspective, the so-called 'savages and idolaters' are equated with the Greeks, the symbolic ideal of the West. This elision of East and West is central to the Greek conflict in 1821, because like the slave debate in Britain that resulted in the abolition of the trade in 1807 and emancipation in 1833, issues of race, ethnicity and national character defined the social dialogue that shaped Great Britain's stance on Greek independence. 'We are all Greeks' is not a rousing huzza for the Greek revolutionaries, but rather a somber realization, which Walter Benjamin echoed much later, about the assertions of civilization. 'There is no document [or paradigm] of civilization', Benjamin writes, 'which is not at the same time a document of barbarism. And just as such a document is not free of barbarism, barbarism taints also the manner in which it was transmitted from one owner to another'.[59] Shelley's Preface to *Hellas* interweaves satire with insightful observations about the nexus of power/knowledge and a Benjaminian critique. This satire of the public's enthusiasm for imperial cultural productions – ancient texts, philhellenic tracts and wartime melodrama – complicates our view of Shelley insofar as it invites us to read *Hellas* as an act of *imitatio*, creative imitation, that engages and complicates the debate about Greek independence. Instead of idolizing ancient Greek culture or, like Byron, condemning contemporary Greeks as barbarians and slaves, Shelley mounts a critique that identifies the cultural correspondence between nineteenth-century melodrama and classical tragedy. *Hellas* employs the innovative stagecraft of contemporary melodrama to subvert the British patriotic fervor and the philhellenic blindness that fuelled war and empire.

Jennifer Wallace in her discussion of *Hellas* encourages us to rethink Hellenism and its idealistic rhetoric in similar terms, although she does not consider melodrama in her study.[60] The fact that *Hellas* responds to and reflects on the outbreak of hostilities between the Greeks and the Ottoman Turks by invoking the earliest Greek tragedy, Aeschylus' *Persians*, has often been read as a signal of Shelley's Hellenism.[61] But *Hellas* abandons its tragic model by invoking melodramatic stage practices that do not idealize ancient Greece. A dramatic poetic production, *Hellas* provides its audiences and its characters with a fractured vision composed of sights and sounds, and although it collapses history into a Leibnizian monad where the past, the present and the future are embodied in one tale, namely, that of the Sultan, Mahmud II (1785–1839), it also follows Aeschylus' *Persians* in representing the unfolding conflict from the imperial perspective of the Ottomans. In contrast with Aeschylus' Xerxes, Mahmud's awareness of the future and his realization that he cannot effect the necessary changes to sustain his empire torment him. He mirrors Byron's eponymous character, Sardanapalus, who desires above all to absolve himself of power and the imperial trappings of his sovereign role and live with his Greek lover and slave, Myrrha. Mahmud and Sardanapalus are both overcome by revolutionary events; however, when confronted by his dreams and fears, Mahmud – and ideally the audience – struggles to comprehend this moment of historical transformation and attempts to achieve a perspective that abandons the simplistic ideology of war propaganda. Shelley's *Hellas*, with its melodramatic tactics, its lyric tableaux and newsreel history, provides an alternative to the closed world of tragedy, where the familiar 'tale of Troy', in the words of Erkelenz, 'bears the seeds of its own destruction'.[62]

Notes

1 Joseph Roach, *Cities of the Dead: Circum-Atlantic Performance* (New York, 1996), p. 33.
2 Stuart Curran, 'Lyrical Drama: *Prometheus Unbound* and *Hellas*', in Michael O'Neill and Anthony Howe (eds), *The Oxford Handbook of Percy Bysshe Shelley* (Oxford, 2012), pp. 289–98, p. 292; Jeffrey N. Cox, 'The Dramatist', in Timothy Morton (ed.), *The Cambridge Companion to Shelley* (Cambridge, 2006), pp. 65–84.
3 Jean-Luc Nancy, 'Abandoned Being', in *The Birth to Presence*, trans. Brian Holmes (Stanford, 1993). This term is critical to my interpretation of *Prometheus Unbound* and to a less extent, *Hellas*.
4 Mary Favret provides an inspiring and erudite study of wartime and its effects in *War at a Distance: Romanticism and the Making of Modern Wartime* (Princeton, 2010).
5 Nigel Leask, 'Byron and the Eastern Mediterranean: *Childe Harold* II and the "polemic of Ottoman Greece"', in Drummond Bone (ed.), *The Cambridge Companion to Byron* (Cambridge, 2004), p. 104.
6 Amongst Coleridge's writings on the theatre are his 'Satyrane Letters', originally published in *The Friend*, 7 December 1809, later reprinted in *Biographia Literaria*, chapter 22; his letters on drama to *The Courier*, dated 29 August, and 7, 9, 11, 19 September 1816, many parts of which were also printed in *Biographia Literaria*.
7 Daniel Vitkus writes about England's early relationship with the Ottoman Empire in '"The Common Market of All the World": English Theater, the Global System, and

the Ottoman Empire in the Early Modern Period', in Barbara Sebek and Stephen Deng (eds), *Global Traffic: Discourses and Practices of Trade in English Literature and Culture from 1550–1700* (New York, 2008), pp. 19–37, pp. 30–31.

8   Vitkus, '"The Common Market of All the World"', pp. 28–9.

9   Edward W. Said, *Orientalism* (New York, 1978).

10 Peter Brooks, *The Melodramatic Imagination: Balzac, Henry James, Melodrama, and the Mode of Excess* (New Haven, 1976).

11 Jane Moody, *Illegitimate Theatre in London, 1770–1840* (Cambridge, 2000), p. 88.

12 Leask, 'Byron and the Eastern Mediterranean', p. 107.

13 Jeffrey N. Cox discusses this in 'The Ideological Tack of Nautical Melodrama' in Michael Hays and Anastasia Nikolopoulou (eds), *Melodrama: The Cultural Emergence of a Genre* (New York, 1999), p. 171. Gillian Russell also provides an extensive account of these performances in *The Theatres of War: Performance, Politics, and Society, 1793–1815* (Oxford, 1995).

14 Russell, *Theatres of War*, p. 179.

15 Simon Bainbridge, *British Poetry and the Revolutionary and Napoleonic Wars: Visions of Conflict* (New York, 2004); David A. Bell, *The First Total War: Napoleon's Europe and the Birth of Warfare as We Know It* (New York: 2007); Jeffrey N. Cox, *Romanticism in the Shadow of War: Literary Culture in the Napoleonic War Years* (Cambridge, 2014). Mary Favret, *War at a Distance*); Philip Shaw, *Waterloo and the Romantic Imagination* (New York, 2002).

16 Favret, *War at a Distance*, p. 33.

17 Favret, *War at a Distance*, p. 39.

18 Jacky S. Bratton, 'British heroism and the structure of melodrama', in J.S. Bratton, Richard Allen Cave, et al. (eds), *Acts of Supremacy: The British Empire and the Stage, 1790–1930* (Manchester, 1991), pp. 18–61, p. 22.

19 Moody, *Illegitimate Theatre*, p. 10.

20 Jane Moody discusses Holcroft's play in *Illegitimate Theatre*, pp. 90–91. See also Bratton's more nuanced and positive interpretation of melodrama in 'British Heroism and Melodrama', and collections like *Melodrama: The Cultural Emergence of a Genre*. Jeffrey N. Cox aligns melodrama more clearly with reactionary politics, most recently, he and I make an argument along these lines in 'Melodramatic slaves', *Modern Drama* 55 (Winter, 2012), pp. 459–75.

21 Julie Carlson writes eloquently and persuasively about Coleridge, *Remorse*, and the theatre of remorse in *In the Theatre of Romanticism: Coleridge, Nationalism, Women* (Cambridge, 1994).

22 Jeffrey N. Cox elaborates on the destructive role of self anatomy in 'Shelley's *The Cenci*: The Tragedy of "Self-Anatomy"', *In the Shadows of Romance: Romantic Tragic Drama in Germany, England and France* (Athens, OH, 1987).

23 Michael Erkelenz, 'Inspecting the Tragedy of Empire: Shelley's *Hellas* and Aeschylus' *Persians*', *Philological Quarterly* 76.3 (Summer 1997), pp. 313–37, p. 330. I have also made this point in my 'Improvising on the Borders: Hellenism, History, and Tragedy in Shelley's *Hellas*', in Monika Class and Terry F. Robinson (eds), *Transnational England: Home and Abroad, 1780–1860* (Cambridge, 2009), pp. 42–57, p. 45.

24 Curran, 'Lyrical Drama', p. 290.

25 Curran, 'Lyrical Drama', p. 291.

26 Curran, 'Lyrical Drama', p. 290.

27 Curran, 'Lyrical Drama', p. 292.

28 Stephen Cheeke, 'Wrong-Footed by Genre: Shelley's *Hellas*', *Romanticism* 2.2 (1996): pp. 204–19, p. 206. Mark Kipperman, 'History and Ideality: The Politics of Shelley's *Hellas*', *Studies in Romanticism* 30 (Summer 1991): pp. 147–68.

29 Kipperman, 'History and Ideality', p. 161.

30 Nancy, 'Abandoned Being', *The Birth to Presence*, p. 37.

31 Alan Bewell writes extensively about this issue in *Romanticism and Colonial Disease* (Baltimore, 1999), pp. 209–41.

32 Cox and Van Kooy, 'Melodramatic Slaves', pp. 459–60. Key studies of melodrama include, Jacky Bratton, James Cook and Christine Gledhill, eds, *Melodrama: Stage Picture Screen* (London, 1994); Michael Booth, *English Melodrama* (London, 1965), Brooks, *The Melodramatic Imagination*; Elaine Hadley, *Melodramatic Tactics: Theatricalized Dissent in the English Marketplace, 1800–1885* (Stanford, 1995); Frank Rahill, *The World of Melodrama* (University Park, PA, 1967).

33 See the discussions of melodrama in my article, 'Darkness Visible: The Early Melodrama of British Imperialism and the Commodification of History in Sheridan's *Pizarro*', *Theatre Journal* 64.2 (May 2012), pp. 179–95.

34 See Susan Wolfson's discussion of *Sardanapalus* in *Borderlines: The Shiftings of Gender in British Romanticism* (Stanford, 2006), p. 149.

35 Moody, *Illegitimate Theatre*, p. 80.

36 Moody, *Illegitimate Theatre*, p. 82.

37 The full passage from *A Defense of Poetry* is instructive: 'The greatest poet even cannot say it: for the mind in creation is as a fading coal which some invisible influence, like an inconstant wind, awakens to transitory brightness: this power arises form within, like the colour of a flower which fades and changes [. . .] Could this force be durable [. . .], it is impossible to predict the greatness of the results: but when composition begins, inspiration is already on the decline [. . .]' (*SPP*, 531). James Chandler comments extensively on this 'case' in *England in 1819: The Politics of Literary Culture and the Case of Romantic Historicism* (Chicago, 1998), pp. 532–54.

38 Greg Kucich discusses this 'performance innovation' in 'Baillie, Mitford, and the "Different Track" of Women's Historical Drama on the Romantic Stage', in *Women's Romantic Theatre and Drama: History, Agency, and Performativity* (Farnham, 2010), pp. 21–42, p. 23.

39 Jeffrey N. Cox writes about Emma Hamilton's attitudes in *Poetry and Politics in the Cockney School: Keats, Shelley, Hunt and their Circle* (Cambridge, 1998), pp. 146–86.

40 Greg Kucich provides a detailed account of Emma Hamilton's performances in his article, 'Joanna Baillie and the re-staging of history and gender' in Thomas C. Crochunis (ed.), *Joanna Baillie, Romantic Dramatists: Critical Essays* (New York, 2004), pp. 108–29, p. 117. Kucich's article more fully explores the tableau motif in Baillie's dramas, however, he does not, as I suggest, tie this theatrical practice to the melodrama.

41 Joanna Baillie, *Constantine Paleologus; or, The Last of the Caesars* in *The Dramatic and Poetical Works of Joanna Baillie: Complete in One Volume* (London: Longman, Brown, Green, and Longmans, 1851). Rpt in *The Dramatic and Poetical Works of Joanna Baillie* (Hildesheim and New York, 1976). Because this edition does not have line numbers, I use this format (I,iii; 324) – act, scene, and page numbers – to reference the text.

42 Greg Kucich, 'Joanna Baillie and the re-staging of history and gender', p. 123.

43 Jeffrey N. Cox discusses this aspect of the melodrama in 'The Ideological Tack of Melodrama', p. 176.

44 For a concise explanation of Gottfried Wilhelm von Leibniz's theory about monads, see his short essay, 'Monadology', in *Monadology and Other Philosophical Essays*, trans. Paul Schrecker and Anne Martin Schrecker (New York, 1965), pp. 148–63.

45 Jeffrey N. Cox makes a similar point in his discussion of *Hellas* in 'The Dramatist', pp. 74–7.

46 William St Clair provides a more detailed account of these events and Russia's strained relationship with Great Britain and the Ottoman Turks throughout this period in *That Greece might still be Free: The Philhellenes in the War of Independence* (Oxford, 1972), pp. 2–3, pp. 134–5.

47 C.A. Bayly discusses Malta and the Ionian Islands in *Imperial Meridian: The British Empire and the World, 1780–1830* (London, 1989), pp. 196–202.

48 Bayly, *Imperial Meridian*, pp. 200–201.

49 See Gillian Russell, *The Theatres of War*, p. 78 and Daniel O'Quinn's *Staging Governance: theatrical Imperialism in London, 1770–1800* (Baltimore, 2005), pp. 342–3.
50 Moody, *Illegitimate Theatre*, p. 28.
51 O'Quinn, *Theatrical Imperialism*, pp. 325–6.
52 Russell, *Theatres of War*, pp. 77–8.
53 Cheeke, 'Wrong-Footed', p. 214.
54 Edward Said, *Culture and Imperialism* (New York, 1993), p. 61.
55 Bayly, *Imperial Meridian*, p. 105.
56 David Ferris, *Silent Urns: Romanticism, Hellenism, Modernity* (Stanford, 2000), p. 108.
57 Michel Foucault, *Discipline and Punish: The Birth of the Prison*, trans. Alan Sheridan (New York, 1977), p. 184. Significantly, Foucault does not equate power and knowledge as Frances Bacon does in his work, where he promotes the modern concept of technological progress, first in *The Advancement of Learning* (1605). Foucault contests Bacon.
58 Hunt's 'Account of the remarkable rise and downfall of the late Great Kan of Tartary, with the still more remarkable fancies that took possession of the heads of some of his antagonists: Very curious and necessary to be known in order to complete history of the present marvelous times' appeared in *The Examiner*, IX, 14 January 1816, pp. 17–20. Reprinted in *SWLH* 2. 40–49. This is an orientalized spoof of Napoleon, 'the Great Kan of Tartary'.
59 Walter Benjamin, 'Theses on the Philosophy of History', in *Illuminations*, trans. Harry Zohn (New York, 1968), p. 258.
60 Jennifer Wallace, *Hellas* in *Shelley and Greece: Rethinking Romantic Hellenism* (New York, 1997), p. 197.
61 Ferris, *Silent Urns*.
62 Erkelenz, 'Inspecting the Tragedy of Empire', p. 316.

5 'Is this the promised end? [. . .] or image of that horror?'

Promethean dramas of liberation

The abolition of personal slavery is the basis of the highest political hope that it can enter into the mind of man to conceive.

—Shelley, *A Defence of Poetry*, p. 525.

David Bell has described the Romantic period as a time when 'Europeans began to stare into the abyss of war and see not only something terrible but also something that held a terrible fascination, even a terrible sublimity'.[1] Despite the abolition of the slave trade in 1807 and Napoleon's defeat at Waterloo in 1815, conflicts across Europe and throughout the world continued to escalate. The magnitude of violence throughout the Romantic period – ranging from social and political manipulation to slavery and genocide – would be considered insupportable to any reasonable observer. Contemplating this scenario, Kant deemed it 'perfectly just for men who adopt this attitude to destroy one another, and thus to find perpetual peace in the vast grave where all the horrors of violence and those responsible for them would be buried'.[2] This apocalyptic vision of mutual destruction – similar to that depicted in Byron's 'Darkness' and in *The Cenci* – is, he later tells his readers, neither sensible nor does it provide solace. The more rational response is to confront the political violence and to insist that peace and liberty become moral imperatives. In Kant's words, the 'rights of man must be held sacred, however great a sacrifice the ruling power may have to make.[3] This philosophical insistence upon preserving right and simultaneously 'threatening or destroying an order of given right', namely the state, exposes the complex relationship between violence and right in the formation of the state and its governing systems.[4] Jacques Derrida picks up where Kant leaves off. Instead of focusing on the question of right, Derrida examines the paradoxical entanglements of politics in terms of the force of law, one where the powerful act to 'conserve the law' but consequently 'destroy it or suspend it'.[5] Attempting to preserve itself from real or imagined threats, the state abandons the law to enforce it. One could interpret these breaches as opportunities to 'reinvent [and] rejustify' the law, but who must endure the force of this law and for how long? And how does a society ultimately justify such acts?[6] Laws embody both a performative and an interpretive force; they act to regulate behaviour and without regulation of themselves. The character of the law is violent; one might say it is even tyrannical. Derrida invites us to consider the coexistence of justice and law. This paradox is not simply a philosophical conundrum, it defines human beings at every level and at every moment in time because it is inherently tied to the acts of war and revolution: both of which are waged and justified in the name preserving and/or enforcing the law. This discursive entanglement of revolutionary energies and despotic absolutes problematizes the political dichotomy between insurgence and totalitarian oppression.

In two 1817 articles published in the *Morning Chronicle*, entitled 'On the Spy-System', William Hazlitt addressed these 'moral paradoxes' in these terms:

> Lord Castlereagh, in the debate some evenings ago, appeared in a new character, and mingled with his usual stock of political common places, some lively moral paradoxes, after a new French pattern. According to his Lordship's comprehensive and liberal views, the liberty and independence of nations are best supported abroad by the point of the bayonet; and morality, religion, and social order, are best defended at home by spies and informers. It is a pretty system, and worthy of itself from first to last.
>
> (*SWWH*, 4.194)[7]

These lines are taken from Hazlitt's unsigned lead article. In early June there had been a number of uprisings in Yorkshire, Nottinghamshire and Derbyshire. The news about Derbyshire also included information about the role taken by a government spy, 'Oliver', to incite the riot. Soon thereafter more news became available about another spy, 'Castles', who had infiltrated, instigated and betrayed the Spa Fields rioters (December, 1816).[8] Hazlitt gives no quarter to 'moral paradoxes',[9] and as he writes two weeks later, Lord Castlereagh's assessment of the current situation 'will hardly satisfy most of our readers' because it is impossible to assent either to 'the accuracy of his statements, or the soundness of his logic' (*SWWH*, 4.196). Increasingly frustrated, Hazlitt drops many of the usual theatrical markers in his writing, which he employs in the first essay to identify Castlereagh as a character surrounded by the usual stock props and stock characters and to depict recent government action as yet another in a series of 'illegitimate' performances. But even as Hazlitt becomes more explicit in his charges against the government and in this taking a serious risk of being brought to trial for seditious libel, he again alludes to the theatre, making it clear to his readers that the minister's show of power is nothing more than a farce, where the government plays the role of a 'fine lady who wants to domineer over her credulous husband':

> He has suspended the laws of the country to save us from the danger of anarchy! We deny the danger, and deprecate the remedy. If ministers could afford to fan the flame of insurrection, to *alarm* the country into a surrender of its liberties, we contend that a danger that could be thus tampered with, thus made a convenient pretence for seizing a power beyond the law to put it down, might have been put down *without a power beyond the law*. If a Government's conspiring against itself were a sufficient ground for arming it with arbitrary

power, no country could for a moment be safe against ministerial treachery and encroachment, against real despotism founded on pretended disaffection. Government would be in perpetual convulsions and affected hysterics, like a fine lady who wants to domineer over her credulous husband. We deny that disaffection existed, except that kind which arose from extreme distress. Hunger is not disloyalty. Nor can we admit that a Government's having reduced a country to a state of unparalleled distress, and consequent desperation, is a reason for giving *carte blanche* to the Government, and putting people under military execution. [. . .] It is easy to keep the peace with a sword; [. . .] To reduce a people to the alternative of rebellion or of arbitrary sway, does not require the talents of a great statesman.

(SWWH, 4.196–7)

The 'danger of anarchy', as Shelley will reiterate in *The Mask of Anarchy*, stems from the government not from the people. It is not mass meetings or the formation of radical groups the ministry should fear, and suppressing them will do nothing to alleviate the real problems facing the country. In a moment of almost patriotic fervor, Hazlitt exclaims, 'We have put down the colossal power of Bonaparte' (*SWWH*, 4.196); we have overcome what appeared to be insurmountable odds to defeat Napoleon's forces and we cannot feed our own people? The country has dedicated its financial and military resources to keeping a peace that has been nothing more than 'the quiet re-establishment of the tyranny of the old Government', and has brought the 'nation to the brink of ruin' and plunged it 'into the depths of slavery' (*SWWH*, 2. 197). The real crisis, Hazlitt insists, has nothing to do with publishers, printers and public meetings. The country needs statesmen who will deal with the food shortages and address the dire state of the national economy. What good is a government that conspires 'against itself' and reduces 'the country to unparalleled distress [. . .] and desperation'? One can almost hear in Hazlitt's essays the resounding echo of Shelley and Beatrice Cenci's words: 'Something must be done . . . What yet I know not'.

Two years later Leigh Hunt opened *The Examiner* of 1819 with a very different assessment of the 'state of the world'. Presenting his readers with a millennial vision, Hunt embraces hope:

This is the commencement, if we are not much mistaken, of one of the most important years that have been seen for a long while. It is quiet; it seems peaceable to us here in Europe; it may even continue so, as far as any great warfare is concerned; but a spirit is abroad, stronger than kings, or armies, or all the most predominant shapes of prejudice and force.

(SWLH, 2. 175)

The spirit to which Hunt appeals is one that combines knowledge and hope. It represents that 'gigantic sense of the general good which has awaked for the first time in the known history of the world, and is stretching his earth-thrilling limbs from the Caucasus to the Andes' (*SWLH*, 2. 175). Hunt exhorts the mythic spirit, the Greek god, Prometheus to cross the threshold into history, where it can become an exemplum for confronting the combined destructive force of 'kings', 'armies' and 'prejudice'.

In 1819 Shelley too clasped this Promethean image in a hope-filled gesture. The rhetorical and moral didacticism associated with Hunt's Promethean spirit of knowledge morphs in Shelley's hands into the liberating cultural performance of *Prometheus Unbound*. Stuart Curran has identified Shelley's and Hunt's Promethean figure as 'a fundamentally political icon', which transforms an 'icon of despair' into 'an avatar of liberation'.[10] Adopting Prometheus as a culturally charged and politicized figure, Shelley's decision to write *Prometheus Unbound* reflects his desire to engage and respond to the increasingly familiar iconography associated with the eighteenth-century illustrated translations of Aeschylus' *Prometheus Bound*. Shelley appropriates and employs this protean imagery to awaken, as he writes in the Preface to *Laon & Cythna*, a 'nation from their slavery and degradation to a true sense of moral dignity and freedom' (*Poems*, 2. 33). In both texts, Shelley's purposes are aligned with those of the period's abolitionists who were also deploying Promethean iconography in their campaigns against trans-Atlantic slavery and the slave trade. *Prometheus Unbound* liberates its characters by challenging a literary and graphic tradition that focuses on the image of a fettered Prometheus.

Throughout the Romantic period, the Promethean myth was a cultural lens through which the dynamics of sovereignty, slavery and liberation were often depicted, performed and viewed. The story of Prometheus, which can be found in Hesiod's *Theogony* as well as Aeschylus' *Prometheus Bound* and in the fragmented references made by Homer and Pindar, is most clearly viewed as a tale of crime and punishment. Depicted as a defiant hero, Prometheus, as his name suggests, embodies forethought or the prophetic power to see the future. Prometheus emerges unscathed from the war between the Titans and the Olympians, but when Zeus overthrows his father, Cronus, he is given the task of creating humanity out of clay. Like Odysseus, Prometheus is a cunning trickster. At one point in Hesiod's text, he fools Zeus into choosing offal as his preferred sacrifice. When Prometheus steals fire from Olympus to comfort humanity, Zeus responds by sending his brother, Epimetheus, the first woman, Pandora, who unknowingly releases all the evil into the world. Prometheus' subversion transforms into open opposition when he refuses to tell Zeus how and when his reign will end. Zeus immediately sends Force and Power – in Greek, βία (Bia) and κράτος (Kratos) – to bind the Titan to a mountainside in the Caucasus where an eagle comes daily to torture him. According to Aeschylus' account, Prometheus finally capitulates to Zeus and is freed by Hercules. Prometheus represents a mythic complexity that identifies him as humanity's benefactor and protector while also being a secondary cause of its greatest ills. His character, with its imagery of sacrifice and eternal suffering, resonates with Christian theology, but as Curran's compelling argument makes clear, Promethean imagery provided a nexus point for political interest and aesthetic forms during the Romantic period. The entangled web of references and allusions is indicative of the perplexing relationships Shelley and others examine through

Figure 5.1 George Romney, *Prometheus Bound*, c. 1778–79, Courtesy of Thomas Agnew & Sons, Ltd.

Promethean lenses. How is revolution related to tyranny? Slavery to freedom? War to peace? These are not simply Orwellian paradoxes but refer to real issues that arise when the network of allusions tightens and transforms associative links into chains that bind.

Thomas Morell's first English translation of *Prometheus in Chains* was published in 1773 and made the Aeschylean tragedy more widely available to British readers. Four years later Richard Potter, the Norfolk abolitionist, published the entire Aeschylean corpus in a prose translation. While painting Potter's portrait, George Romney also began producing a series of chalk cartoons depicting scenes from Aeschylus (Figure 5.1). Richard Porson's 1795 translation was interleaved with John Flaxman's drawings (Figure 5.2). As Morell's title indicates, what often caught the public's imagination was the binding scene where Hephaestus or Vulcan, aided by Force and Power, chain Prometheus to a rock or mountainside. Romney and Flaxman produce a visual symmetry or parity between the figures of Force and Power. In Flaxman's drawing, Prometheus and Hephaestus with their beards are simultaneously linked to each other and contrasted. Romney's sketch in heavy black chalk underscores the violent movement and the force required to restrain Prometheus; the characters are more desperate and more emotive and the ominous nature of the contest is mirrored in the dark cloud above them. As in Flaxman's pen and ink drawing, the characters in Romney's picture are largely indistinguishable from one another. Their position indicates their identity. Flaxman, however, produces a more clearly discernable chiastic symmetry between his characters. Romney's figures embody the kind of emotional and

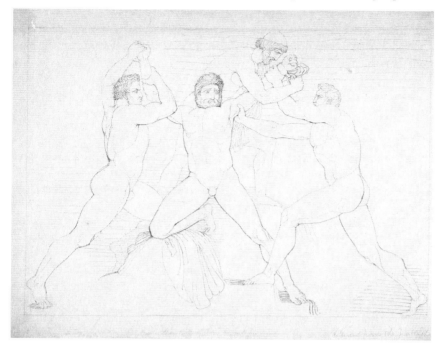

Figure 5.2 John Flaxman, R.A., *Prometheus Chained to the Rock*, 1792–94. Pencil, pen and ink on cream wove paper (275 × 363 mm). © Royal Academy of Arts, London: Photographer; Prudence Cuming Associates Limited

visceral performance that would later be linked to illegitimate dramatic forms like melodrama and the pantomime and wielded most effectively by the great actor, Edmund Kean (1787–1833). By way of contrast, Flaxman's characters embody a stilted classicism, reminiscent of the stage and eighteenth-century stage protocol where actors like John Philip Kemble (1757–1823), a generation earlier than Kean, would hold their position momentarily, creating a 'point' or a discrete moment that functioned often as a dramatic tableau.[11] Contemporary viewers of Flaxman's and Romney's work would have registered the physical and emotional struggle of the scene through what was ostensibly a theatrical lens. Both drawings serve as 'realizations' insofar as they manifest in a two-dimensional form that had only existed formerly in the words of a text or in the reader's mind. The next 'realization' to be performed, quite literally, was to effect the materialization of the picture into a dramatic tableau, which allowed the actors to bring the picture to life in the theatre. This final transition, as Martin Meisel points out, marked the theatre's role in affecting a 'literal re-creation and [a] translation' that was more 'real [and] physically present'.[12] This process depended upon the cultural intermixing of textual, visual and dramatic modes of representation to produce the incremental movement between what could only be imagined while reading a text and what could be seen on stage. The tableau format of Romney's and Flaxman's drawings suggests that they might have been thinking about the performative quality of their drawings. But, is this a desired outcome? What interest does society or the theatre have in making this scene real? While writing *Prometheus Unbound*, Shelley may well have been asking himself if it is possible to reverse this process? Can the theatre, a picture or a dramatic text de-realize tyranny? Can it liberate those who are chained? Can the chains of slavery be transformed into the ties that bind us one to another?

Richard Cosway's portrait of the bound Prometheus (Figure 5.3) shifts the viewer's attention away from the physical struggle of binding Prometheus toward the acts of suffering and endurance. Defiance and revolt are at best distant memories in Cosway's drawing, and they are most certainly no longer options the heroic figure can entertain. Power and Force are no longer necessary, but perhaps they have simply mutated into the figures of natural predators: the snake and the eagle. Once again the play of allusions is producing a discursive entanglement. Taking into account the imagery of the snake and eagle in Homer[13] and how Shelley deploys these figures in *Laon and Cythna*, it seems logical to identify these violent and conflicting forces as those that bind Prometheus too. The snake and the eagle cannot kill Prometheus because he is a god but they torture him relentlessly. Cosway's depiction of Prometheus' craggy musculature and his agonizing facial expression testify to an alternative range of emotions, which have altered from the arresting displays of perseverance and power in Flaxman's and Romney's drawings to a hopeless despair in this sketch. Throughout the period images of Promethean-like fettered bodies played a key role in the slave trade debates. The mythic experience of Promethean resistance and suffering in the illustrations of William Blake, Cosway, Flaxman, Henry Fuseli and Romney becomes increasingly and disturbingly resonant with these debates when these drawings are compared with those portraits that appear in John Gabriel Stedman's *Narrative of a Five Years Expedition Against the Revolted Negroes of Surinam* (1796).

Shelley's mythological drama is often read as enacting universal liberty, but it also speaks to the real conditions of trans-Atlantic slavery. Like many Romantic-period cultural productions, Shelley's *Prometheus Unbound* invites audiences to reconsider their preconceptions about the period's depictions of freedom and slavery. In 1762, Jean-Jacques Rousseau had boldly claimed: 'Mankind is born free, yet everywhere in chains'.[14] For Rousseau, freedom was a birthright and slavery was an imposed condition that required people to take political action. Twenty-five years later and just two years before the advent of the French Revolution, a group of British Quakers and Anglicans, including Thomas Clarkson, formed the Society for Effecting the Abolition of the Slave Trade. The society inaugurated a campaign to educate the public by means of writing and publishing books, circulating posters and sponsoring lectures. But it was Josiah Wedgewood's contribution that secured their success. The Wedgwood medallion featured the image of a black man (and later, a woman) in chains kneeling and pleading for his/her freedom. The bannered motto was simple and effective: 'Am I Not A Man And A Brother?' or alternatively, 'Am I Not A Woman And A Sister?'. The slave's supplicating posture on the medallion may demonstrate, as Srinivas Aravamudan argues, that

Figure 5.3 Richard Cosway, *Prometheus* c. 1785–1800. Pen and ink on paper. Print Collection, Miriam and Ira D. Wallach Division of Art, Prints and Photography, The New York Public Library, Astor, Lenox and Tilden Foundations

this man deserves his emancipation.[15] He is certainly willing to plead for it, but the fixity of his position and his chains also indicate there is something chillingly permanent about his situation. It is worth noting that this image was bought and sold as part of an extensive, nationwide, even global gift economy, when Wedgwood's company recreated it as a mass-produced ceramic cameo that was sold as a broach, a necklace or an inset piece for snuffboxes. A consumer item, this image, like the slaves it commemorated, supported the system of trade it appeared to challenge. This imagery and its accompanying mindset proliferated throughout the Atlantic region in successive emancipation movements and, quoting Marcus Wood, it represents a 'semiotic nexus [. . .] for containing the black male and female' within a racialized discourse.[16] To some extent the early translations of Aeschylus and the Promethean drawings fixed the image of the subjugated and the oppressed in the cultural imaginary whereas Stedman's *Narrative of a Five Years Expedition Against the Revolted Negroes of Surinam* placed those images within a specific geo-historical locale. But the Wedgwood medallion seemed to capitalize on the fact that people were kidnapped, bartered for, exchanged or sold and then transported out of Africa to another more obvious market place, the auction block, where a price tag was affixed permanently to a person's life and their freedom. Isolated and bound like Prometheus, the Wedgwood slave awaits the Herculean British government to strike off his/her chains. He/she will wait until 1833 for Britain to enact its emancipation legislation: for too many slaves more than their lifetime. In contrast with the Wedgewood image, which 'realized' slavery, Blake's etching, *Europe Supported by Africa and America*, a famous print he created for Steadman's *Narrative* that features three women in a scene of mutual aid and support, dissolves the iron chains of slavery. Blake's women stand together with their arms wrapped around one another and each holding a part of a cloth or a rope that emblematically links them to one another.

In writing *Prometheus Unbound*, Shelley confronted the many discursive entanglements and 'realizations' that undermined the political movements of reform and abolition. Was it possible or even desirable to 'unperplex', a word from Keats's *Lamia*, these cultural networks so as to unmoor a multi-valenced icon from its myriad ideological and cultural contexts? For Shelley and others in the period, the French Revolution – its promise and its failure – had demonstrated that no single event could bring about the necessary changes that would liberate a people from the prevailing power structures, religious beliefs and violent history. What was needed, Shelley realized when writing *A Defence of Poetry*, was a new kind of aesthetic that could kindle people's imaginations. This new formula, this magic spell, would function as a

> prismatic and many-sided mirror, which collects the brightest rays of human nature and divides and reproduces them from the simplicity of these elementary forms, and touches them with majesty and beauty and multiplies all that it reflects, and endows it with the power of propagating its like wherever it may fall.
>
> (*SPP*, 520)

In many ways the dramatic form and its accompanying theatrical praxes provided a cultural vehicle for this aesthetic 'mirror'. Exploring the tensions between the oppressed and the oppressor within the geo-historical contexts of the Atlantic slave trade as well as those of Asia – a character and a continent – Shelley's *Prometheus Unbound* creates a prismatic mirror that reflects on the oppressive and liberating manifestations of Promethean imagery. Shelley responded to the era's cultural, political and economic paradoxes by offering audiences an alternative means of conceiving revolution, history, slavery and freedom. *Prometheus Unbound* dramatizes the act of liberation and the effort it takes to liberate oneself and to maintain one's freedom as a continuous succession of actions. In an era when the intention to liberate oneself or others could be readily perceived in the negative terms of revolt or revolution, and freedom was increasingly commodified into 'something' that could be bought or sold and given as a gift, it is significant that Shelley represents liberation not as a single act taken by one person. In *Prometheus Unbound* each character moves – either imaginatively or physically – through multiple scenes where they enact their liberation step-by-step: *abandoning* their assumptions about themselves and the world in which they live.

Abandoning Aeschylus

Shelley opens his drama with a primordial scene. This is not the binding scene that Flaxman and Romney reproduce, but rather a picture that appears to be even darker than Cosway's drawing. This is the proverbial dark night of the soul. Unbeknownst to him, Prometheus has awakened to a dawn of revelation, but at this moment the mind-numbing daily torture, as Timothy Morton remarks, 'seems almost to have become part of his own body'.[17] Force and Power disappeared from this mountain crag eons ago, but Hephaestus' well-wrought manacles reaffirm Jove's unquestioned sovereignty. Prometheus has no future prospects other than futility and despair. The former contention between Prometheus and Jove/Jupiter (Shelley employs the Latinate forms of Zeus) has become nothing more than the stupefying state of total and endless war. A pervasive power, as Shelley writes in 'Mont Blanc', 'seems eternal now'. If, as A.W. Schlegel argues in his *Lectures on Dramatic Art and Literature* (translated into English in 1815), Aeschylus' *Prometheus Bound* celebrates the glorious triumph of subjection as never before, then at this point the festivities on Olympus have long since ended.[18] With the exception of his two faithful companions, Panthea and Ione, Prometheus has been abandoned.

This state or condition of Promethean torture represents what Giorgio Agamben terms 'a paradoxical threshold of indistinction'.[19] Prometheus embodies 'a limit-figure of life, a threshold in which life is both inside and outside the juridical order, and this threshold is the place of sovereignty'.[20] Jove's sovereign power is inextricably intertwined with rebelliousness and Promethean resistance. Since the Titan first rebelled, his defiance has constituted his and Jove's mutually constructed and destructive relationship. This paradigm of social conflict mirrors the struggle that marks the early stages of self-awareness that Hegel discusses in the Lordship and Bondage section of *The Phenomenology of Spirit*. Both parties have in their conflict repeatedly committed unlawful actions that 'justify' violence, if not the other's destruction. Prometheus initially acts because he considers himself to be just and Jove to be unjust. His continued defiance reinforces the distinctiveness of their identities and will not allow for any act of mutual recognition. The eagle's torturous appearance everyday re-enacts this symbolic antagonism. For some period of time both characters have repeatedly justified their actions, but at this point the past has collapsed into the present and the future and Prometheus no longer remembers what happened or how he defied Jove. Prometheus has existed for the past 3,000 years exposed and on the threshold between life and death. The binding scene, which enchained Prometheus and cast him as the bondsman or slave to Jupiter's role as the lord or master, was an act committed so long ago that it is now (mis)taken for an unchanging reality. This ghostly afterimage haunts the opening scene of Shelley's *Prometheus Unbound* because, as Derrida argues, it undermines any possibility for resolution in that it 'deconstructs from within any assurance of presence, any certitude or any supposed criteriology that would assure us of [. . .] justice'.[21]

The first scene of *Prometheus Unbound* reproduces Aeschylus' play and the political and historical dilemmas it represents as a dramatic tableau, a 'realization', as Meisel uses the term. The play and its characters remain haunted by the compromising paradoxes and discursive entanglements that the play re-enacts when, for example, the Phantasm of Jove appears in the first Act to reiterate Prometheus' curse. Notwithstanding this powerful binding of resistance to sovereign power, the play's purpose, as the title indicates, is to enact the Titan's release and his reunion with Asia. Over the course of the play, 'the baseless fabric of this vision [. . .] shall dissolve', as Prospero tells Ferdinand in *The Tempest* (IV,i, 151–5), but first, Prometheus will need to *recall* – to remember and to take back – his curse. The Titan's opening speech constitutes the play's initial performative gesture; this Act breaks the silence that has marked the interminable nightmare of history: the time when the earth has been 'made multitudinous with [. . .] slaves [who toil]/With fear and self-contempt and barren hope' (*PU*, I, 5–8). When Prometheus first speaks, he only repeats what we already know. He recreates the scene of his imprisonment, where he has been 'Nailed to this wall of eagle-baffling mountain,/Black, wintry, dead, unmeasured; without herb/ Insect, or beast, or shape or sound of life' (*PU*, I, 21–2). He has endured 'pain, pain ever, [and] forever!' (*PU*, I.20–24). 'No change', he insists, like a figure from one of Samuel Beckett's plays, 'no pause, no hope!' (*PU*, 1, 23). Alone and isolated, he wonders if anyone has 'felt', 'seen' or 'heard [his] agony' (*PU*, I, 25,27,29). Prometheus speaks 'in grief/Not exultation' (*PU*, 1.56–7). The situation has not changed but clearly Prometheus has. No longer defiant, the Titan is determined to remember what he said or did to deserve this existence. Schooled by Aeschylus, the audience may feel it knows what Prometheus did and perhaps there are some among them who believe that he deserves his fate. Others might identify him as the hero who defied omnipotent Jove.

For the Earth and the 'inarticulate people' within the play, the Titan's words have become a 'treasured spell' (*PU*, I,184), upon which they can 'mediate/In secret joy and hope [. . .]/But dare not speak' (*PU*, I, 184–6). Reflecting the final scene of Shakespeare's most heartbreaking tragedy, *King Lear*, 'the weight of this sad time' is palpable; however, instead of speaking what they feel, everyone, except Prometheus, remains constrained and silent. Prometheus may be a symbol of resistance, but he is not heard calling for revolt. No one is willing to repeat the curse. Like the taboos that structure Greek tragedy, Prometheus' curse has become verboten. Long ago, Prometheus' speech-act had empowered Jupiter 'to do thy worst [. . .]/To blast mankind, from yon ethereal tower [and] imprecate/the utmost torture of thy hate [on me and mine]' (*PU*, I,272–9). This state of being is, to quote John Locke, 'the perfect condition of slavery, which is nothing else but the state of war continued between a lawful conqueror and a captive'.[22] Locke's equation of slavery with the state of war is instructive. It points to the real, underlying history – the slave trade and the Napoleonic wars – that undergirds this mythological drama. Shelley's Promethean drama recognizes both the mythic and historical dimensions of Prometheus' condition. To effectively liberate Prometheus in his drama, Shelley must create a performance that reiterates these realities, recalling the violence of contemporary history, and also it must provide the audience with a means of 'abandoning' the paralytic hold these events have on culture and politics. Shelley's difficult task, like that of his Prometheus, is to never forget these atrocities but at the same time to unfetter his characters and his audience from the belief that violence and tyranny are a historical and a political necessity . . . that they simply represent the way things are. This is not an 'either/or' situation. Slavery, as we know, does not stop if people are legally emancipated; nor does the declaration of peace bring an end to war. Like Prometheus we would like to believe that there exists some magic word or deed that if recalled, would set things aright. What Shelley's first Act demonstrates is that the Promethean ideals of peace and love are not to be discovered in some apocalyptic future nor have they been irretrievably lost to history, but they exist in the marginalized, often silenced voices and in the stories of those who like Prometheus have endured too much for too long. After 3,000 years, Prometheus realizes that 'words are quick and vain; [and that]/Grief for a while is blind, and so was mine' (*PU*, I, 303–4). Inaugurating the dawn of a new age, Prometheus wishes 'no living thing to suffer pain' (*PU*, I, 305). Prometheus has begun the process of self-realization and the conflict is moving toward resolution, but in this play no single act will effect the desired transformation.

From the moment of Prometheus' opening monologue we are led to believe that the re-enactment of the curse will somehow rectify the situation. The appearance of the phantasm of Jupiter is momentous. The power that summons it and compels it to repeat the Titan's curse is obviously formidable but, as Carol Jacobs observes, 'not only does the repetition of the curse fail to solve the crisis of self-identity and authority, the revolution itself is not measurably closer at hand'.[23] Resuscitating the spectre of tyranny and reciting the curse prompts the immediate replay of mythic and historical scenes of terror and violence. Mercury and the Furies appear and mercilessly torment Prometheus with images of 'pain and fear' (*PU*, I, 452). Instead of liberating Prometheus, this spectral performance reanimates Jove's tyranny. The furies taunt Prometheus, calling out 'Immortal Titan!' and 'Champion of Heaven's Slaves' (*PU*, I, 442, 443). Prometheus claims he is 'the chained Titan' (*PU*, I, 445) and questions the identity of these new terrors: 'What and who are ye?' (*PU*, I, 446). 'Never yet', he tells the audience 'there came Phantasms so foul through monster-teeming Hell / From the all-miscreative brain of

Jove" (*PU*, I, 446–8). Prometheus' experience is both familiar and unfamiliar, and it prompts this realization: 'Methinks I grow like what I contemplate/And laugh and stare in loathsome sympathy' (*PU*, I, 450–451). The performance has created a moment of self-recognition. This 'realization' affirms a material distinction between Prometheus and Jupiter that has always existed, but Prometheus' new sympathy has supplanted his former defiance. Abhorrence mixes with laughter, revealing the absurdity of the situation, which Prometheus meets with something like indifference.

As the torturous scroll of history punitively unfurls before Prometheus, a fury, perhaps unconsciously or mistakenly, discloses 'the shadow of the truth' (*PU*, I, 655). Confounded by the pain of what he sees, Prometheus can at last claim to

> close my tearless eyes, but see more clear
> Thy works within my woe-illumed mind,
> Thou subtle Tyrant! . . . Peace is in the grave –
> The grave hides all things beautiful and good –
> I am a God and cannot find it there –
> Nor would I seek it.
>
> *PU*, 1.636–41

Closing his 'tearless eyes', Prometheus sees both himself and Jupiter more clearly. For irony to work there must be a double. There are several of what Paul de Man would have referred to as 'reflective disjunctions'[24] in this passage: blindness and insight, a 'woe-illumed mind', 'Peace is in the grave', and a god that either cannot find the beautiful and the good or will not seek it. Promethean language deploys irony to frame as absurd the 'heterogeneous material of experience' that does not 'fit' into a coherent worldview.[25] But as noted before in the discussion of the Hegelian dialectic, this language also represents the inscrutable processes of differentiation and self-definition.

The key enigmatic phrase is 'Peace is in the grave'. Kant begins his essay, 'Perpetual Peace: A Philosophical Sketch', with an anecdotal description of a Dutch innkeeper's sign, which features the words 'The Perpetual Peace' and below that the image of a cemetery. Kant's essay symptomatically reflects the real difficulties of mounting a philosophical critique of war and peace. Kant's and Shelley's humour is a bit perverse, but it is difficult not to laugh at how they represent the deep-rooted and 'grave' contradictions that sustain patriotic fervour and nationalism in the time of war, and which, even at the best of times, make peace only a virtual possibility. If death is the only means of finding 'the beautiful and the good' or peace, then one must begin, like Kant and Shelley, to question the values and the conditions of life.[26] Prometheus lies prostrate against the 'wall of eagle-baffling mountain' (*PU*, I, 20). The perplexities of place and identity multiply repeatedly throughout this scene. But the irony that delimits this world is akin to that which defines the realities of wartime and slavery. In a world where declarations of peace are succeeded by wars fought by other means or in other geographical locales, it is imperative to question, as David Clark does in relation to Kant, 'What comes *after*?'.[27] Just as the abolition of the slave trade in 1807 did not stop the forced transportation of African prisoners to the Americas, so too Napoleon's defeat at Waterloo and his exile did not bring an end to war. While each event undoubtedly brought with it some sense of relief, the requisite social and political institutions still did not exist to support either emancipation or peace.

The nightmarish conditions of history do not simply dissipate into thin air. In the midst of the furies' visions, Prometheus declares, 'This is defeat, Fierce King, not victory!' (*PU*, I, 642). This is the 'shadow of the truth' (*PU*, I, 655) that leads to Prometheus' final realization in the first Act: 'there is no agony and no solace left;/Earth can console, Heaven can torment no more' (*PU*, I, 819–20). Although these insights will lead to few if any material changes in the course of living in the real world, they prove to be enough in this drama to inaugurate a four-Act journey toward liberation. Prometheus has over the course of time challenged Jove, cursed him, endured psychological and physical torture; he has been a hero and a victim. He has played every available role and none of them have proved liberating. Act I concludes with a pageant of spirits that Earth sends to comfort Prometheus. She tells him they inhabit 'the dim caves of human thought' and 'behold/Beyond that twilight realm, as in a glass,/The future' (*PU*, I, 659, 661–3).

Throughout much of the first Act, Prometheus attempts to affect a revolution by reproducing the haunting tragedy of Aeschylus' *Prometheus Bound* and its historical legacies, imperial oppression and slavery. The closing scene marks the arrival of a chorus of spirits, which, Ione observes, are preceded by 'two shapes from the East and the West/[arriving] as two doves to one beloved nest' (*PU*, I, 752–3). This intermittent vision of love and world peace lasts for a moment and then, as Panthea notes, 'Only a sense/Remains of them' (*PU*, I, 802). Left with a similar sensation, Prometheus exclaims:

> How fair these air-born shapes! and yet I feel
> Most vain all hope but love, and thou art far,
> Asia! who when my being overflowed
> Wert like a gold chalice to bright wine
> Which else had sunk into the thirsty dust.
> All things are still – alas! how heavily
> This quiet morning weighs upon my heart;
> Though I should dream, I could even sleep with grief
> If slumber were denied not . . . I would fain
> Be what it is my destiny to be,
> The saviour and the strength of suffering man,
> Or sink into the original gulph of things. . . .
> There is no agony and so solace left;
> Earth can console, Heaven can torment no more.
>
> *PU*, I, 807–20

For Prometheus, the relentless and repetitious horrors of history have stopped. Prometheus once again glimpses a shadowy alternative to the seemingly interminable nightmare of history. The spirits have already declared 'Freedom! Hope!

Death! Victory!' (*PU*, I,701), but this chant is hardly convincing and the way forward remains unclear and fraught with indeterminacy. The pivotal stillness of the scene is further amplified by the ellipses which force Prometheus and the reader/observer to pause and pause again, suspending the drama's action within the constative dialectic. Prometheus, Ione and Panthea watch and listen, but Prometheus is not comforted. He has come to an impasse; torments and comforts are meaningless; he abandons everything but love.

The post-Napoleonic era was one of uncertainty. The destruction, the loss of life and the pain that followed Waterloo did not appear to represent peace. In fact, many Britons felt defeat more than the elation of victory. Their condition was not unlike that of a slave who has been finally liberated. Their transition from one social order to another is followed quickly by the realization that the requisite social and political institutions do not yet exist to sustain the conditions for peace or liberty. Those who have been oppressed have had no opportunity to shape society's values or its institutions. The awareness of one's freedom or peace is countermanded by the systemic injunctions and judicial restraints that invariably lead to what W.E.B. Du Bois referred to in *The Souls of Black Folk* as double consciousness: 'two souls, two thoughts, two unreconciled strivings; two warring ideals in one dark body whose dogged strength alone keeps it from being torn asunder'.[28] Moving into Acts II, III and IV, Shelley effectively drops the curtain on tragedy that sustained the charades of imperial and sovereign power. The ironies, the paradoxes and the discursive entanglements will not disappear but they will be reformulated and cast through different performance lenses. Relinquishing his role in the construction of sovereignty and in sustaining tyranny and establishing law and right, Prometheus begins the process of liberating himself from the prescriptions and decrees of power; he also opens himself to 'a profusion of possibilities'.[29]

The 'Æolian Modulations' of liberty

Shelley shifts the setting in *Prometheus Unbound* from Aeschylus' Georgian Caucasus to the Indian Caucasus and replaces the principal female protagonist, the Greek Io, with Asia.[30] Relocating his play further East in the Hindu Kush, in the mountains above Kashmir, Shelley deploys, as he did in *Alastor*, the sublime imagery which informs one of his favourite novels, Sydney Owenson's *The Missionary* (1811).[31] Setting his drama in India, arguably the most volatile and expansive geographical site within Britain's empire, Shelley stretches his canvas wider to reconsider the figure of Asia, both as a character and a continental landmass. Neither is foreign or unassimilable, and Shelley does not, as Theresa Kelley suggests in 'Reading Justice' insist upon 'an uneconomized singularity, difference and heterogeneity in the language of the play'.[32] British audiences, especially those myriads who attended the theatre, would have been quite familiar with how Asia was situated ideologically within the ever-expanding British Empire. Throughout the period there were numerous productions depicting Britain's ongoing struggle to subdue the Indian sub-continent: among those performed in the late eighteenth century were *Tippoo Saib, or British Valour in India* (1791), *Tippoo Sultan, or The Siege of Bangalore* (1792), *Tippoo Saib, or, East India Campaigning* (1792), *Tippoo Saib's Two Sons* (1792) and *The Siege and Storming of Seringapatam* (1800).[33] Shelley depicts Asia's plight as a quest for Prometheus: as a quest for liberation. In *Prometheus Unbound*, she is not subject, at least not directly, to imperial authority and although she finds it difficult, especially in the second Act, to conceive an alternative to sovereign power, her journey externalizes Prometheus' imaginative excursion in the first Act. Both characters move slowly towards a more nuanced and fraught 'realization' of their freedom. Given the contextual history of abolitionist tracts and slave drama in the first Act of Shelley's play, Asia's quest in Act II shifts the audience's focus from Britain's first empire in the Atlantic toward its increasingly successful attempts to control the colossal landmass of India in the nineteenth century. Britain's success in promulgating its imperial designs often relied on captivating audiences imaginatively and, through the theatrical performance of spectacles, reifying the cultural oppositions depicted through a British Orientalism.[34] Act I recreates the historical and tragic confrontation between the master and the slave and, as Jacobs argues, 'remains caught in the involutions of recalling the past'. Act II, again quoting Jacobs, progresses 'with a sense of momentum to the point of transformation and actual revolution'.[35] Asia's quest romance restructures the Promethean myth of liberation in terms other than those of tragedy.

Panthea joins Asia in Act II to pursue the elusive figure of spring that they have seen descending 'Cradled in tempests [. . .] as the memory of a dream[, which clothes]/The desert of our life. . . .' (*PU*, II,i, 6–12). The promise of spring cannot veil its tempestuous nature. This 'West Wind' appears to promise, like Shelley's sonnet, a liberating vision, but none of the characters we have met has the ability to bring this vision into focus. It shifts perpetually: reflecting, waning, gleaming forth and fading until "Tis lost!' (*PU*, II,i,24). When Panthea arrives, Asia anxiously awaits the news, but when Panthea attempts to relate her dreams, she confesses she cannot remember anything and that it cannot be heard or seen, but only felt (*PU*, II,i,79). Panthea's erotic dream, where she feels 'his presence flow and mingle through my blood' (*PU*, II,i,80), as she tells Asia, awakens Ione who considers this account as little more than her 'false' sister's sport. Their shared sexual desire is merely 'some inchantment [sic] old/Whose spells have stolen my spirit as I slept/And mingled it with thine;' (*PU*, II,i,100–102). Asia ignores Ione's commentary, reiterating her earlier demand, 'Thou speakest, but thy words/Are as the air. I feel them not. . . . oh, lift/Thine eyes that I may read his written soul!' (*PU*, II,i,108–10). Looking into Panthea's eyes, Asia glimpses 'a shade – a shape' she recognizes as Prometheus. William Keach describes this exchange as the visual 'recognition of one's self in another's eyes – a double recognition [. . .] defined by processes of reciprocal projection and mirroring that must be "read", not spoken or heard'.[36] Words prove incapable of affecting any 'realization'; the characters must abandon language, at least in part and rely upon the production of a mirroring spectacle or as Keach puts it, a 'constitutive perceptual change'.[37] But at this moment, another indiscernible 'shape' intervenes: one that obscures Prometheus and redirects Asia and Panthea to follow another 'vision', which manifests itself as Echo. Sound somehow becomes visible.

Led by Echo, it appears that Asia and Panthea are caught in a temporal interstice between the past and the present. Neither character can discern the direction from which Echo calls to them; does the voice solicit them to return to some moment already past, or do they pursue the untenable: are they somehow *following* Echo into the future? As with many a quest romance, the landscape through which they travel is an enchanted forest, in this instance, inhabited by two choruses and two talking fauns; hollow caverns and rocks provide additional topographic features for the stage. Asia and Panthea arrive at their destination at the beginning of scene three. Here the stage directions describe a terrain that is all too familiar: 'A Pinnacle of rock among Mountains'. Although Panthea identifies this as the realm of Demogorgon, the only ostensible distinction between this place and the site of Prometheus' torture is the existence of a portal, which Asia declares a 'Fit throne for such a Power!' (*PU*, II,i,310). By all appearances, this too is a site of sovereign power, but it does not invoke the paralysing stasis of the drama's first scene. The presence of the portal conveys the opportunity for continued mobility, something absent from the scene of Prometheus' tragic confinement and endless torture. As the scene comes into full view, the deserted mountaintop reveals its prospect overlooking 'Some Indian vale' (*PU*, II,iii,24). Lacking the innocence of an Edenic tableau, the panorama provides a sublime enchantment: a 'stream-illumined cave', 'wind-inchanted shapes of wandering mist', and 'sky-cleaving mountains' (*PU*, I,iii,26–8). Panthea and Asia do not consciously associate this uncanny scene with Promethean tragedy, but *we* have the opportunity to once again re-visit Prometheus' rock in light of this new prospect. Here, snow amasses 'Flake after flake, in Heaven-defying minds/As thought by thought is piled, till some great truth/Is loosened, and the nations echo round/Shaken to their roots:' (*PU*, II,iii,39–42). The imagery of thoughts amassing like snow promises revolutionary change. It may be glacial in its initial accretion, but the tipping point will produce an event of avalanche proportion that will materialize the revolution.

Spirits usher Panthea and Asia onward. This time, however, their direction is clear; they travel down into the abyss, where they quickly arrive at Demogorgon's cave. They encounter a veiled figure, but in this moment of discovery, the veil falls away – or so Asia tells us – but Panthea's vague description reproduces the insubstantial shows of power:

> I see a mighty Darkness
> Filling out the seat of power; and rays of gloom
> Dart round, as light from the meridian Sun,
> Ungazed upon and shapeless: – neither limb
> Nor form – nor outline
>
> *PU*, II,iv,2–6

The image of sovereignty permeates the landscape as its own shadow. It exists in the sublime mountaintop and in the cave's depths. Even as Panthea and Asia physically move across the stage, progressing from tragedy to quest romance, their actions appear to be guided by an absolute and arbitrary power. In the first Act, the conventions of Aeschylean tragedy cloak everything in the dark and oppressive garb of tyranny. But as the play yields to the expansive structure of romance, and Panthea and Asia's journey moves into an imaginative landscape filled with magical characters (speaking Fauns), the destructive conflict that defines tragedy shifts to the less threatening oscillations of romance. Indicating that romance simulates tragedy, this landscape is defined in terms of its shadows and echoes of power. The expansive stages of romance destabilize the static tableaus of tragedy, but liberty remains as elusive for Panthea and Asia as it was for Prometheus.

When Demogorgon invites them to 'Ask what thou wouldst know', Asia responds, 'What canst thou tell?' (*PU*, IV,iv,6–7). This scene suspends the action that has brought Asia and Panthea to this place. Demogorgon's cave represents the workings of a revolutionary mind. Does Demogorgon offer Asia a new epistemological framework or an alternative knowledge? If so, it will not be an easy task to uncover. Asia's initial questions merely follow the script of a religious catechism: 'Who made the living world?' Her questions appear to become more elaborate, but the answer remains essentially the same: 'God', 'God, Almighty God' and 'Merciful God' (*PU*, II,iv,8–18). Are Demogorgon's answers evasive or is Asia simply asking the wrong questions? This initial exchange parodies the catechism, which may lead to belief but will never reveal knowledge. Asia realizes that she is getting no closer to the truth she seeks and she suddenly demands, 'Utter his name' (*PU*, II,iv,29). Asia's demand for a name mirrors Prometheus' need to summon the phantasm of Jupiter and to recall his curse. Both characters are attempting to understand power as it is embodied by a particular entity and how its name structures their relationship with it. Dissatisfied with this reiterative performance that yields neither truth nor knowledge, Asia launches into an extensive history that retraces the steps taken by Prometheus in the first Act. Suddenly, she too comes to a more formidable realization and a more relevant question, 'Declare/who is his master? Is he too a slave?' (*PU*, II,iv,108–9). While this question alludes to the problematic dichotomy between self and other that melodrama superficially resolves through its rigid moral framework, it also potentially reveals the failures of these questions and of this dramatic form – quest romance – to liberate its characters from the shadows and echoes of sovereign power. Asia still cannot disavow the binary construction of power and once again asks, 'Who is the master of the slave?' (*PU*, II,iv,14). With this dialogical proof of Asia's inability to fathom the truth of power, Demogorgon abandons this exercise:

> – If the Abysm
> Could vomit forth its secrets: – but a voice
> Is wanting, the deep truth is imageless;
> For what would it avail to bid thee gaze
> On the revolving world? what to bid speak

> Fate, Time, Occasion, Chance and Change? – To these
> All things are subject but eternal Love.
> *PU*, II,iv,115–20

Kelley aptly refers to this catechistic exchange as a 'dance of circumlocution'.[38] Like Panthea in earlier scenes, Demogorgon now functions as Asia's mirror image. Whereas Panthea kept asking, 'what canst thou see/But thine own fairest shadow imaged' (*PU*, II,i,112–13), Demogorgon insists, 'I spoke only as ye speak' (*PU*, II,iv,113). Kelley argues that both interlocutors are passive. To the contrary, I believe each character, like those surrounding Prometheus in the first Act, reflects the cognitive and imaginative limitations of the generic framework, whether it be tragedy or romance.

The progress of romance is not dependent upon the characters' motivations but rather upon the deployment of dramatic or narrative machinery. Romance, according to Howard Felperin, encompasses action; the heroic figure must act to overcome impossible odds, often by means of some magical power.[39] Asia will not be able to realize her liberation until we see some evidence of a magical spectacle. In line with some philosophical and religious traditions, Asia's ability to discern the truth – and her liberation – cannot be fully realized until a fantastic or improbable incident gives material form to a new *weltanshauung* or worldview that embodies an objective force of metamorphosis.[40] Asia's final question has a performative quality that prompts immediate change: 'When shall the destined hour arrive?' (*PU*, II,iv,128). Invoking the future with her 'When' activates the drama's stage machinery like the magic phrase, 'open sesame'. Rocks begin to move, and the audience can see, as Asia does, 'Cars drawn by rainbow-winged steeds/Which trample the dim winds – in each there stands/A Wild-eyed charioteer, urging their flight' (*PU*, II,iv,129–32). The spectacle, Shelley and his contemporaries realized, is often more effective at evoking a response from the audience than words or a well-wrought character. Not only does it spark the audience's imagination, it also re-engages the audience in the unfolding quest romance, whose end in this case is the promised reunion of Asia and Prometheus. This Act concludes with a moment of abandon: Asia is astounded by the spectacle of 'Cars drawn by rainbow-winged steeds' and Demogorgon's insistence to 'Behold!' (*PU*, II,iv,128) rivets the audience's attention to the stage. Although the spectacle of the Hours affects Asia's awakening, her quest is far from over. Jupiter/Jove remains empowered, Prometheus still endures in the Caucasus, and the two lovers have not been reunited. To further effect a more complete transformation, Shelley shifts the drama's generic valence to pantomime and specifically the harlequinade where the slap of Harlequin's bat can transform a coach and horses into a balloon. Following this formal prompt, Asia's soul now morphs into 'an enchanted Boat' (*PU*, II,v,72) and her quest moves off stage.

David Mayer's account of the pantomime is useful here. The pantomime drew its subjects from popular legend, nursery fables, literary classics or fragments of classical mythology.[41] The settings were often remote or exotic and the stage was filled with giants, fairies, magicians and Greek or Roman gods. Regardless of the storyline, the plot unfolds as a power struggle, most often between a patriarchal figure and his daughter and her chosen suitor. The daughter's plight requires the intervention of a magical agent, whose stage appearance marks a pivotal transformation scene. At this point the pantomime becomes a harlequinade: the benevolent spirit transforms the young man into Harlequin and the young woman into Columbine. Other characters metamorphose into comic characters, most often taking form as Pantaloon (father), Lover (rival suitor) and Clown (father's servant or an official). Armed with a magical bat or sword, literally a slapstick, Harlequin and Columbine embark upon a quest where the primary activity is a game of hide and seek. Harlequin defeats Pantaloon and his forces after a long and entertaining escapade. When this is over the benevolent agent reappears and transforms and transports each character to the final scene – often a temple or a palace – where everyone lives happily ever after.

Act III opens on Mount Olympus. With its focus on Jupiter and the court, this new stage set suggests that the play has shifted away from the playfulness of the pantomime to the more ornate displays of power produced in Jacobean and Carolingian masques. The scene begins with Jove's declaration of power:

> Ye congregated Powers of Heaven who share
> The glory and the strength of him ye serve,
> Rejoice! henceforth I am omnipotent.
> All else has been subdued to me – alone
> The soul of man, like unextinguished fire,
> Yet burns towards Heaven with Fierce reproach and doubt
> And lamentation and reluctant prayer,
> Hurling up insurrection, which might make
> Our antique empire insecure though built
> On eldest faith, and Hell's coeval fear.
>
> *PU*, III,i,1–10

Throughout *Prometheus Unbound* the figures of sovereign power have been depicted as phantasms, shadows and echoes: all spectral presences. Finally, Shelley raises the curtain and deploys what appear to be the formal elements of the masque to realize this elusive and illusive figure as Jupiter. Unlike former revelations where the truth clearly remained imageless – a hint that we will not see truth here – this scene, like the conventional Jacobean masque, places Jupiter centre stage. Jupiter has haunted the play since its beginning, and his first stage appearance is initially striking but it does not take long for the audience to realize that this incarnation is little more than another mask, a body cloaked in a costume that (dis-)simulates and caricaturizes the power it represents. Giving shape to this indeterminate figuration that has motivated his characters in various ways, Shelley's masque quickly slips back into the realm of the harlequinade (the magical part of the pantomime) with its radical and satiric registers.

Throughout the first two Acts, Jupiter appears as a ghostly presence that represents the debilitating discursive entanglements that impede the formation of independent characters and thus block the theatrical realization of personal and communal liberty. The corporeal form of Jupiter in the third Act announces his intention to exert his power against 'the soul of man' that continues to hurl insurrection heavenward. Like Count Cenci, Swellfoot, Charles I and Mahmud, Jupiter believes that this is the dawn of a new age. He just needs to realize his 'darker purpose' (*King Lear*, I,i,34), which he asserts is possible now that Thetis has 'begotten a strange wonder' that will 'trample out the spark' of rebellion (*PU*, III,i,18–24). Confident and assured of his destiny, Jupiter cries out, 'Victory! Victory!' (*PU*, III,i,49). This scene is not an instance, as Stuart Sperry argues, 'where the visionary imagination outruns the means for expression'.[42] To the contrary, Jupiter's stage appearance represents the transformation of sovereign power from its depiction in tragedy, romance and myth into something more visually apprehensible. Jupiter's self-serving panegyric is deflated immediately by Demogorgon's appearance. The air is let out of the masque and like a balloon its collapse is marked by the popping sound of a slapstick that transforms the masque into a harlequinade. Proclaiming triumph in one moment, Jupiter is forced to descend with Demogorgon into 'the wide waves of ruin' (*PU*, III,i,71) in the next. Sperry describes Jupiter's fall as being subsumed 'into the eternity that Demogorgon represents',[43] but in terms of stage practice, the two figures simply disappear through the trap door, vanishing from the stages of myth, theatrical performance and human history. Viewed through the framework of the pantomime, Jupiter is nothing more than a blocking figure that separates Prometheus from Asia. The multiple dramatic forms Shelley deploys to produce different stages of awareness make clear how the theatre and the drama replicate despotism, but *Prometheus Unbound* reveals how the redeployment of these cultural performances through acts of playful abandonment can also prove liberating.

In the following scene, the emblematic and mythic figures of Ocean and Apollo encounter each other on the shores of Atlantis. Apollo reports to Ocean the news of Jupiter's fall and Ocean announces the end of the slave trade and the restoration of a more benign form of traffic and trade (*PU*, III,ii,18–34). Setting the scene's geographical and mythic locale as Atlantis, Shelley engages the drama's utopian 'archaeologies of the future', a phrase that Fredric Jameson employs to describe the generative possibilities of utopian discourses, which, he argues, are dependent upon the text's ability to assert 'its radical difference from what currently is'.[44] How a writer accomplishes this is critical to his/her success, which is marked, Jameson notes, by the text's ability to 'serve the negative purpose of making us more aware of our mental and ideological imprisonment'.[45] For Jameson, the fundamental dynamics of utopian politics mirror the Hegelian dialectic of identity and difference. As each scene produces a different formal framework, the underlying structural dynamic remains constant. In this scene Apollo initially directs the audience to concentrate of the image of Jupiter's fall as a historical and cognitive disruption that both interrupts and allows for the plot's progression. What follows must signal that change and produce a new, utopian realization that is somehow not unimaginable.

Act III was initially composed as the drama's final act and its utopian rhetoric does not lead to Meisel's realizations so much as it produces the affect of unravelling negations. The spirit of the Hour portrays the end of Jupiter's reign not an overt act of rebellion or conquest, but as the simple gesture of letting go. Tyranny is 'not o'erthrown, but unregarded' (*PU*, III,iv, 179). Also, humanity's 'realization' is not an evolutionary act of coming into being so much as it is a restoration or an unveiling:

> The loathsome mask has fallen, the man remains
> Sceptreless, free, uncircumscribed – but man:
> Equal, unclassed, tribeless and nationless,
> Exempt from awe, worship, degree, – the King
> Over himself; just, gentle, wise – but man:
> Passionless? no – [. . .]
> Nor yet exempt [. . .]
> From chance and death and mutability.
>
> *PU*, III,iv, 193–201

Even at this pinnacle of liberation, it seems impossible to completely abandon the language and the imagery of sovereignty. Like the contemporary cultural performances that Shelley viewed in London's theatres or alternatively in Italy, which compromised their audience's hopes for the future, *Prometheus Unbound* cannot seem to dissolve those linguistic ties to oppressive political structures and its language. Power permeates everything and it appears that the only available option is to abandon it, realizing that it is always present, always in some way threatening to manifest itself materially: from word to image and from image to full embodiment.

After working on *The Cenci*, Shelley returned to *Prometheus Unbound*, and wrote Act IV. Act III enacts the fantasy of liberation but it fails to actualize the critique that is necessary for the realization of freedom. Prometheus and Asia's new home is the site for the closing act's fantastic spectacle. Liberated from the play's haunting phantasms and shadows and Jupiter's more realistic albeit brief performance in the third Act, the two characters now begin the Promethean task of weaving a web of mystic measure (*PU*, IV,29). Shelley's characters watch and listen to a performance that re-enacts their freedom rather than their oppression. The fourth Act begins with a threnody or lament and marks the characters' abandonment of those dead and 'dark forms [. . .] to the past' (*PU*, IV,30, 39). The past is gone, but not forgotten. Weaving a new web of life and new consciousness has required that each character abandon all that they believed inviolable. As the Chorus of Hours chants, 'Break the dance, and scatter the song;/Let some depart and some remain' (*PU*, IV,159–60), we realize that the absence of permanence allows for continual renewal and revival. These 'Æolian modulations' (*PU*, IV,188) – random and as ungovernable as the wind blowing through an Aeolian harp – can unify Heaven and Earth, symbolized in the erotic dance of the Earth and Moon, but this 'perpetual Orphic song' (*PU*, IV,412) can also degenerate and be eclipsed, as Panthea relates, by

a mighty Power, which is as Darkness,
[. . .] rising out of Earth, and from the sky
[. . .] showered like Night, and from within the air
Bursts, like eclipse which had been gathered up
Into the pores of sunlight –
PU, IV, 510–14

At one moment, the 'bright Visions/Wherein the singing spirits rode and shone [now]/Gleam like pale meteors through a watery night' (*PU*, IV,511–13). In the next, Demogorgon reappears, as he did in Act II, as 'a mighty Darkness/Filling out the seat of power' (*PU*, II,iii,2–3). While Demogorgon is not necessarily equated with the shapeless spectre of sovereignty and power that haunts *Prometheus Unbound*, his disruptive appearance breaks up the celebratory dance and scatters the daedal song. Liberty and freedom are tenuous, at best; Demogorgon's presence easily destabilizes the creative harmony of the moment and reflects the human desire to fixate and idealize rather than to continuously act with abandon. 'Abandonment's only law', Nancy insists, 'like that of love, is to be without return and without recourse'.[46] Demogorgon's closing speech emphasizes the necessity of cultural memories and the recalling those curses even if they do evoke the frightening phantasm of sovereign power. The drama's final lines are Demogorgon's and they represent a 'spell' of self-realization:

These are the spells by which to reassume
An empire o'er the disentangled Doon.
To suffer woes which Hope thinks infinite;
To forgive wrongs darker than Death or Night;
To defy Power which seem Omnipotent;
To love, and hear; to hope, till Hope creates
From its own wreck the thing it contemplates;
Neither to change nor falter nor repent:
This, like thy glory, Titan! is to be
Good, great and joyous, beautiful and free;
This is alone Life, Joy, Empire and Victory.
PU, IV, 568–78

While Michael Scrivener has argued that Act IV 'provides a positive vision of realized idealism to inspire the post-Peterloo reform movement',[47] it also acknowledges the atrocities and myriad incidents of tyranny and oppression that marked the period. In these final words of the drama, Demogorgon portrays the world as it was and is and the relentless human struggle to simultaneously endure, forgive, defy and love. The magic 'spell' Demogorgon offers is no quick fix. His 'spell' against the false eternity of sovereignty is perpetual revolution, which as Franz

Fanon reminds us, is a vigilant, life-long praxis: 'a way of life' that embraces the 'struggle for human dignity'.[48] Shelley's drama of Prometheus' liberation is a hope-filled performance because it acknowledges the violent atrocities that have haunted history and dramatizes the transformation of the Promethean icon into an embodiment of those 'beautiful idealisms of moral excellence' (*SPP*, 209) that enable us to survive despair.

Conclusion

Shelley rewrites Aeschylus' *Prometheus Bound* by putting into play a gallimaufry of theatrical forms that stage the spectacle of Promethean liberation through acts of abandon. The conjunction of radical philosophical idealism with radical materialism in *Prometheus Unbound* creates a perceptual and a cognitive dialectic whose visionary purpose is reform. Shelley and Blake wrote with the purpose of re-envisioning the world, a world, they believed, that can and eventually will be transformed by a liberated imagination. As is the case with Blake's illuminated poetry, the central concern in Shelley's *Prometheus Unbound* is perception. His experimentation with 'characters & mechanism of a kind yet unattempted', as Shelley writes in a letter to Thomas Love Peacock, dramatizes the various modes of perceiving the world (6 April 1819; *Letters* 2. 94). The play's questions – 'Canst thou speak?' 'Hast thou beheld?' 'Hearest thou not?' 'Feelest thou not?' – depict the incessant struggle on the part of the drama's characters and its audiences to reconceive their experience through sensation and language. Richard Cronin has stated that *Prometheus Unbound* 'offers its readers not so much an object to look at as a lens to look with'.[49] Its myriad lenses coalesce in the spectacle of its universal dance of liberation that celebrates the discursive entanglements that so often reify oppressive power structures. Adapting and then abandoning Aeschylus' text of *Prometheus Bound*, Shelley reaffirms and reinvents the twinned concepts of freedom and liberty in line with Kant's moral imperative and Derrida's paradoxical counter-strategy. Abandoning everything but love, Shelley's drama advocates for the inexhaustible advent of life and its resurrection in myriad and seemingly infinite, albeit always entangled forms.

Notes

1 David A. Bell, *The First Total War: Napoleon's Europe and the Birth of Warfare as We Know it* (Boston, 2007), p. 6.
2 Immanuel Kant, 'Perpetual Peace: A Philosophical Sketch', in Hans Reiss (ed.) and H.B. Nisbet (trans.), *Kant: Political Writings* (Cambridge, 1991), pp. 93–130, p. 105.
3 Kant, 'Perpetual Peace', p. 125.
4 Jacques Derrida, 'Force of Law: The "Mystical Foundation of Authority"', in Drucilla Cornell, Michel Rosenfeld and David Gray Carlson (eds), *Deconstruction and the Possibility of Justice* (New York, 1992), pp. 3–67, p. 6.
5 Derrida, 'Force of Law', p. 23.
6 Derrida, 'Force of Law', p. 23.
7 William Hazlitt, 'On the Spy-System', *Morning Chronicle*, 30 June 1817 and 'On the Same Subject', *Morning Chronicle*, 15 July 1817. Reprinted in *SWWH* 4. 194–9.

8   I discuss the Spa Fields riots and government spies in chapters 1 and 2. 1817 proved to be an especially contentious year, with the public being made aware of the government's use of spies. The radical press had a field day. William Cobbett fled the country, fearing another round of prosecutions. T.J. Wooler and William Hone were brought to trial for blasphemous and seditious libel. Both men were acquitted. In 1819 the government passed more legislation in an attempt to silence the radical press. This crack down led to Peterloo and to a number of successful government prosecutions, including that of the radical publisher, Richard Carlile, who was sentenced to six years in prison for reprinting Paine's *Age of Reason*.

9   In *Romanticism, Nationalism, and the Revolt Against Theory* (Chicago, 1993), David Simpson traces the contrast between British common sense and French theory and considers some of the political consequences of this cultural distinction.

10 Stuart Curran, 'The Political Prometheus', in G.A. Rosso and Daniel P. Watkins (eds), *Spirits of Fire: English Romantic Writers and Contemporary Historical Methods* (Rutherford, NJ, 1990), pp. 260–284, p. 261 and p. 272. Initially printed in *Studies in Romanticism* 25 (Fall 1986), pp. 429–55.

11 Lisa A. Freeman discusses 'points' in *Character's Theater: Genre and Identity on the Eighteenth-Century English Stage* (Philadelphia, 2002), pp. 31–6. See also, Joseph R. Roach's *The Player's Passion: Studies in the Science of Acting* (1985; Rpt. Ann Arbor, 1993).

12 Martin Meisel, *Realizations: Narrative, Pictorial, and Theatrical Arts in Nineteenth-Century England* (Princeton, 1983), p. 30.

13 Homer, *The Illiad*, XII, 175–250.

14 Jean-Jacques Rousseau, *The Social Contract*, Maurice Cranston (trans.) (New York, 1968), p. 49.

15 Srinivas Aravamudan, *Tropicopolitans: Colonialism and Agency, 1688–1804* (Durham, NC and London, 1999), p. 5.

16 Marcus Wood, *The Horrible Gift of Freedom: Atlantic Slavery and the Representation of Emancipation* (Athens, GA, 2010), p. 61.

17 Timothy Morton, *Shelley and the Revolution of Taste* (Cambridge, 1994), p. 118.

18 August Wilhelm Schlegel, *Lectures on Dramatic Art and Literature*, trans. John Black (London, 1914): lecture IV, pp. 52–66. This text was available in England in 1815.

19 Giorgio Agamben, *Homo Sacer: Sovereign Power and Bare Life*, trans. Daniel Heller-Roazen (Stanford, 1998), p. 18.

20 Agamben, *Homo Sacer*, p. 27.

21 Derrida, 'Force of Law', pp. 24–5.

22 John Locke, *Two Treatises of Government*, Thomas Hollis (ed.) (London, 1764), Chapter IV. Of Slavery, paragraph 24. Accessed from http://oll.libertyfund.org/title/222/16265 on 2010–03–14.

23 Carol Jacobs, 'Unbinding Words: *Prometheus Unbound*', in Cynthia Chase (ed.), *Romanticism* (London, 1993), pp. 240–269, p. 244. This article is an edited reprint of a chapter in Carol Jacobs's *Uncontainable Romanticism: Shelley, Bronte, Kleist* (Baltimore, 1989), pp. 19–57.

24 Paul de Man, *Blindness and Insight: Essays in the Rhetoric of Contemporary Criticism* (Minneapolis, 1983), p. 213.

25 de Man, *Blindness and Insight*, p. 213.

26 David Clark, 'Unsocial Kant: the Philosopher and the un-regarded War Dead', *Wordsworth Circle* 41.1 (Winter 2010): pp. 60–68, p. 60. Some of these remarks are also inspired by conversations with David Clark.

27 Clark, 'Unsocial Kant', p. 61.

28 W.E.B. Du Bois, *The Souls of Black Folk*, (eds) Donald B. Gibson and Monica M. Elbert (New York, 1996), p. 5.

29 Nancy, 'Abandoned Being', p. 37.

30 Nigel Leask, *British Romantic Writers and the East: Anxieties of Empire* (1992; Cambridge, 2004), pp. 283–4.

31 In the summer of 1811, Shelley importuned his friend, Thomas Jefferson Hogg to read Owenson's *The Missionary*, writing at one point, 'Since I have read this book I have read no other – but I have thought strangely' (19 June 1811, *Letters*, 1.107). Other epistolary references to Owenson's work include a letter dated 20 June 1811, 1. 111–13 and one dated 28 July 1811, 1. 128–30.

32 Theresa Kelley, 'Reading Justice: From Derrida to Shelley and Back', *Studies in Romanticism* 46 (Summer/Fall 2007): pp. 267–87, p. 273.

33 Daniel O'Quinn discusses these and similar works in 'Theatre and Empire', in Jane Moody and Daniel O'Quinn (eds), *The Cambridge Companion to British Theatre, 1730–1830* (Cambridge, 2007), pp. 233–46. Also, O'Quinn's book, *Staging Governance: Theatrical Imperialism in London, 1770–1800* (Baltimore, 2005). Although O'Quinn's work focuses mostly on the eighteenth century, theatre managers of London's playhouses continued to produce dramas about India throughout the nineteenth century.

34 Leask of course has written about British Orientalism in his *British Romantic Writers and the East*. Andrew Warren has recently contributed to this discussion with his *The Orient and the Young Romantics* (Cambridge, 2014).

35 Jacobs, 'Unbinding Words', p. 248.

36 William Keach, 'The Political Poet', in Timothy Morton (ed.), *The Cambridge Companion to Shelley* (Cambridge, 2006), pp. 123–42, p. 133.

37 Keach, 'The Political Poet', p. 134.

38 Kelley, 'Reading Justice', p. 273.

39 Howard Felperin, *Shakespearean Romance* (Princeton, 1972), pp. 3–54.

40 Guy Debord, *The Society of the Spectacle*, trans. Donald Nicholson-Smith (1967; New York, 1994), pp. 12–13.

41 David Mayer, *Harlequin in His Element: The English Pantomime, 1806–1836* (Boston, 1969), p. 23.

42 Stuart Sperry, *Shelley's Major Verse: The Narrative and Dramatic Poetry* (Cambridge, MA, 1988), p. 108.

43 Sperry, *Shelley's Major Verse*, p. 109.

44 Fredric Jameson, *Archaeologies of the Future: The Desire Called Utopia and Other Science Fictions* (New York, 2005), p. xv.

45 Jameson, *Archaeologies of the Future*, p. xiii.

46 Nancy, 'Abandoned Being', p. 47.

47 Michael Scrivener, *Radical Shelley: The Philosophical Anarchism and Utopian Thought of Percy Bysshe Shelley* (Princeton, 1982), p. 240.

48 Franz Fanon, *A Dying Colonialism*, trans. Haakon Chevalier (New York, 1965), p. 1 and p. 13.

49 Richard Cronin in *Shelley's Poetic Thoughts* (New York, 1981), p. 133.

Epilogue
'Scenic potions'

Our bard, who full of antiquated notions,
Intends to cure the world by scenic potions,
Gravely resolves to set the nation right,
If your applause should crown his hopes to night.
—Thomas Holcroft, *Duplicity*, Epigraph

Shelley's decision to respond to Aeschylus' *Prometheus Bound* was linked to his desire to engage and re-deploy Promethean imagery as a rhetoric of liberation. Like *Swellfoot* and *Hellas*, *Prometheus Unbound* is more than a remix of classical drama. *Prometheus Unbound* depicts an expansive and alternative epic stage of liberation: one that offers audiences 'spells by which to reassume/An empire o'er the disentangled Doom' (*PU*, IV,568–69). A counter-drama to *The Cenci*, wherein individuals and their stories remain locked in the vault of history and bound within the closed world of tragedy, *Prometheus Unbound*, more than Shelley's other dramas, transvalues the cognitive frameworks of slavery and liberty by creating a world where characters constantly move, sequentially abandoning one position after another until they consciously *manifest* their freedom. In contrast with the period's slave dramas[1] and much of the iconography associated with abolition and emancipation, especially post-1807, when the British Parliament's Act to abolish the slave trade inaugurated the cultural myth that freedom could be granted by a governing body, Shelley embraces and then redeploys the 'visual rhetorics of disempowerment, stereotypification, and passivity'.[2]

While all of Shelley's dramas point to the destructive cultural construction of Hegelian binaries, they do not reify this opposition as did many of the circulated prints, narratives, dramas and other forms of memorabilia that portrayed emancipation as a simple or swift negation of slavery. Throughout his oeuvre, we see Shelley trying to think beyond the patriotic conception of the nation and empire and the popular reduction of freedom to the absence of slavery. As in *Prometheus Unbound*, Shelley time and again takes up conventional images in order to challenge them; he recalls them in acts of reinvention. Reflecting on another of his dramas, *Swellfoot the Tyrant*, where Shelley examines the construction and the ideological paradoxes of Liberty, and then turning to *The Masque of Anarchy*, where he explicitly formulates the poignant question of freedom that haunts

British identity and British history, we can see how Shelley challenges the passivity that accompanies an acceptance of the way things are. 'What is Freedom?', he writes in *The Mask of Anarchy*,

>   – ye can tell
> That which slavery is, too well –
> For its very name has grown
> To an echo of your own.
> *   *   *   *
> What are thou Freedom? O! could slaves
> Answer from their living graves
> This demand – tyrants would flee
> Like a dream's dim imagery:
> > *The Mask of Anarchy,*
> > ll. 156–9, ll. 209–12

This virulent response to the Peterloo massacre embodies Shelley's uncompromising, even, as Michael Scrivener adds, his militant spirit.[3] Shelley's poem promotes a radical agenda and it does so by engaging popular culture and reproducing the satiric iconography that rhetorically frames the radical caricatures of William Hone, George Cruikshank and other nineteenth-century artists. The poem depicts and critiques the 'despotic system of self-multiplication', what Steven Jones refers to as 'mimetic violence'.[4] The 'idols' and 'phantasms' of power that Shelley confronts in 'Charles the First', *Hellas* and *Prometheus Unbound* and parodies in *Swellfoot the Tyrant* function as empty vessels that reconfigure any content to its own form and purposes. Sovereign power reproduces everything as a mirror of itself. The 'prismatic and many-sided mirror' (SPP, 520) that represents Shelley's politically and historically radical dramaturgy reflects and refracts any singular 'truth' into its many components and possibilities. Isaac Cruikshank's 1820 '*REFLECTION – to be or not to be?*' (Figure 2.4) visually disrupts the self-replicating imagery of the monarchy by placing the Queen Caroline's reflection in the Prince's mirror. This radical praxes that Shelley adapts in his poetry and his drama implicates and subverts the systemic and systematic horrors perpetrated under the guises of Liberty and Britannia, amongst other mythic, nationalistic and imperial figurations circulating in the period. In these lines from *The Mask of Anarchy*, the repeated query fixates on slavery. Slavery, like the King's image, is everywhere. It *appears* to be a universal condition just as the monarch *appears* to be sovereign. During the early nineteenth century, a person looking into a mirror might see the reflection of a slave, or what British society might have identified as a slave. Theatre, politics and other cultural performances too often 'realized – as Martin Meisel uses the term – the horrors of tyranny, oppression and slavery.[5]

To reconfigure the oppressive presence of these idols and phantoms represented by the King's portrait (Chapter 3) and by prevailing images of enchained figures (Chapter 5), Shelley often incorporates a 'shape' into his work: Demogorgon appears in *Prometheus Unbound*, Cythna is described as a 'radiant shape' (*Poems,*

XI.4248), *Swellfoot* features its shape, 'England in 1819' has its phantom and finally *The Triumph of Life* has 'A shape all light' (*The Triumph of Life*, l. 352). Each of these figures can be interpreted as perilously mirroring the singularity of sovereign power. The semiotic crosscurrents are difficult to navigate in all of Shelley's work, but it is clear that a Shape appears, and it rises up like Shelley's 'glorious Phantom' in his sonnet, 'England in 1819' to 'illumine our tempestuous day'. This Shape, which appears in line 110, is Freedom, not the more compromised figure of Liberty or the equally problematic Britannia. An amorphous 'presence' that can be intuited but not perceived – 'they knew the presence there,/And looked, – but all was empty air' (*The Masque of Anarchy*, ll. 120–121) – Shelley's Shape, like Demogorgon in *Prometheus Unbound*, is no lithesome beauty or a benevolent agent that appears in the popular pantomime to liberate at a stroke the threatened lovers.[6] '[A]rrayed in mail/Brighter than the Viper's scale' (*The Mask of Anarchy*, ll. 110–11), its appearance is more akin to Richard Cosway's Promethean figure (Figure 5.3) or William Cullen Bryant's 'bearded man,/Armed to the teeth [. . .] [and] scarred/With tokens of old wars'.[7] My point is that Shelley's conception of freedom may be one of the 'beautiful idealisms of moral excellence', but it is not a pretty or an eroticized image and it is never attained easily.

Shelley and his works have often been described as mythic, utopian and idealistic. It would prove a fruitless task to deny this but what readers often overlook is his gritty historical realism and his pragmatism in the struggle for political reform. The Romantic period was an age of intense cultural surveillance. Censorship, Jane Moody writes, was a 'collective enterprise'.[8] Dramas were not only subject to the censorship of the Lord Chamberlain's office they also were subjected to the regulative control of an intensely politicized reviewing culture that sharpened the audience's critical acuity as it mesmerized them with fear and conflated political and cultural registers into a polarized network of discursive entanglements. Thomas Holcroft was one of the period's most radical and most prominent playwrights. His comedies provoked visceral responses from reviewers and from theatrical audiences alike. In 1794 Holcroft was brought to trial as one of four defendants in the famous Treason Trials of that year. Although he and the others were acquitted, life afterwards proved exasperating when he was forced to submit his plays anonymously and found few who would support his theatrical and dramatic efforts. Eventually, he left the country and worked in France until 1802. When he returned to London, he transformed the English stage with his Covent Garden production of the first melodrama, *A Tale of Mystery*, a translation of Guilbert de Pixérécourt's *Coelina, ou, L'Enfant du mystére*. Melodrama did not evolve into a liberating dramaturgy, although it certainly reflected the knotty conundrums posed by British imperialism.

I turn to Holcroft in these final pages because his dramas were radical stages insofar as they were performed repeatedly in London's theatres and afterwards sustained the attention of more readers than Shelley or any Shelleyan could ever imagine. In 1781, nine years before the French Revolution and more than 20 years before he would face the British jury on charges of treason, Holcroft printed his comedy, *Duplicity*, where he refers to his plays as 'scenic potions'.[9] These 'potions', like Shelley's 'spells' in *Prometheus Unbound* were designed, as Moody notes, to 'act as catalysts for moral and political reform'.[10] Holcroft's criticism of aristocratic privilege and government corruption were, much like Shelley's, direct and uncompromising, and as Holcroft stresses in his Preface to this play, contemporary political tensions were compounding the 'difficulties and dangers [. . .] in vast proportion' to former eras.[11] Holcroft voices his concern [about] 'commit[ing] any thing to paper',[12] for fear that when it is read repeatedly and reconsidered it will lose it performative charge. And yet, he persistently restored speeches in the printed versions of his plays that had been censored by the Lord Chamberlain's office, potentially challenging the more robust and punitive laws that covered print publications.[13] Holcroft and Shelley both understood the power of print culture to 'sentence'[14] an author in printed reviews and his printer or publisher to prison. In the final lines of *Prometheus Unbound*, Demogorgon 'spells' out the script for liberation, but this notion like Holcroft's 'scenic potions' realizes the very limits of its emancipatory politics. Shelley's final words in his most liberating drama – 'Empire, and Victory' – rematerialize the very constructions that shacked not only the drama and its theatrical performances but real people. It is easy to overstate the efficacy of Shelley's dramas as radical stages, but as much as they attempt to take us forward they also incessantly hurl us back to those discursive entanglements for which there is no spell or potion.

Notes

1 Jeffrey N. Cox and I discuss the period's slave drama in 'Melodramatic Slaves', *Modern Drama* 55.4 (Winter 2012): pp. 459–75.
2 Marcus Wood, *The Horrible Gift of Freedom: Atlantic Slavery and the Representation of Emancipation* (Athens, GA and London, 2010), p. 17. Wood works with Lewis Hyde's *The Gift: Imagination and the Erotic Life of Property* (New York, 1999) to reconsider the visual rhetoric of abolition and emancipation and how freedom came to be depicted within and through a gift economy in popular culture.
3 Michael Scrivener, *Radical Shelley: The Philosophical Anarchism and Utopian Thought of Percy Bysshe Shelley* (Princeton, 1982), p. 198.
4 Andrew Warren, *The Orient and the Young Romantics* (Cambridge, 2014), p. 222. Steven Jones, *Shelley's Satire: Violence, Exhortation, and Authority* (DeKalb, IL, 1994), p. 110.
5 Martin Meisel, *Realizations: Narrative, Pictorial, and Theatrical Arts in Nineteenth-Century England* (Princeton, 1983). Linda Colley, *Britons: Forging the Nation 1707–1837* (New Haven, 1992). As Linda Colley points out, 'By 1815, the boundaries of the British empire were so extensive that they included one in every five inhabitants of the globe. The question of how these millions of men and women who were manifestly not British, but who had been brought under British rule by armed force should be treated and regarded thus became inescapable. What responsibilities, if any, did the mother country have towards them? Did they have any claim on those vague but valuable freedoms that so many Britons considered to be peculiarly their own?' (323).
6 Jones, *Shelley's Satire*, p. 117.
7 Here, I follow Wood who in his *The Horrible Gift of Freedom*, p. 39, compares the conventional figure of Liberty to William Cullen Bryant's depiction of Freedom in 'The Antiquity of Freedom', *The Poetical Works of William Cullen Bryant*, ed. Parke Godwin (2 vols, New York, 1882), 2. 305–7, pp. 305–6.

8 Jane Moody, 'Inchbald, Holcroft and the Censorship of Jacobin Theatre', in Maria Crisafulli and Keir Elam (eds), *Women's Romantic Theatre and Drama: History, Agency, and Performativity* (Farnham, 2010), pp. 197–211, p. 198.

9 Thomas Holcroft, *Duplicity* (London, 1781), Epilogue.

10 Jane Moody, 'Inchbald, Holcroft and the Censorship of Jacobin Theatre', p. 206.

11 Holcroft, *Duplicity*, Preface, p. v.

12 Holcroft, *Duplicity*, Preface, p. iv.

13 Moody, 'Inchbald, Holcroft and the Censorship of Jacobin Theatre', pp. 208–9.

14 Holcroft, *Duplicity*, Preface, p. vii.

Bibliography

All quotations from Shakespeare's dramas are taken from *The Norton Shakespeare*, Stephen
  Greenblatt, Walter Cohen, Jean E. Howard, Katherine Eisaman Mauss (eds) (New York:
  W.W. Norton, 1997).
Unless otherwise noted in the text, quotations of Percy Shelley's dramas and poetry are
  from *Shelley's Poetry and Prose*, Donald H. Reiman and Neil Fraistat (eds), 2nd edn.
  New York: Norton, 2002.

Printed primary sources

Aeschylus, *Aeschylus: Persians and Other Plays*, Christopher Collard (trans.) (Oxford:
  Oxford University Press, 2008).
The Annual Register, or a View of the History, Politics, and Literature, for the Year 1794,
  2nd edition (London: R. Wilks for the proprietors of Dodsley's Annual Register, 1806).
Bacon, Francis, *Francis Bacon: Selected Philosophical Works*, Rose-Mary Sargent (ed.)
  (Indianapolis: Hackett Publishing Company, Inc., 1999).
Baillie, Joanna, *Plays on the Passions*, Peter Duthie (ed.) (Peterborough, Ontario: Broad-
  view Press, 2001).
———, *Constantine Paleologus; or, The Last of the Caesars* in *The Dramatic and Poetical
  Works of Joanna Baillie: Complete in One Volume* (London: Longman, Brown, Green,
  and Longmans, 1851).
———, *The Dramatic and Poetical Works of Joanna Baillie: Complete in One Volume*
  (London: Longman, Brown, Green, and Longmans, 1851); 2nd edn, repr., *The Dramatic
  and Poetical Works of Joanna Baillie* (Hildesheim and New York: Georg Olms Verlag,
  1976).
Barbauld, Anna Letitia, *Selected Poetry and Prose*, William McCarthy and Elizabeth Kraft
  (eds) (Peterborough, Ontario: Broadview Press, 2002).
Barcus, James E., *Shelley: The Critical Heritage* (New York and London, Routledge and
  Kegan Paul, 1975).
Barrymore, William, *El Hyder, or, The Chief of the Ghaut Mountains* (1818; London:
  Lacy's Acting Edition, 1852).
Bell, John, *Bell's British Theatre, Consisting of the Most Esteemed Plays* (34 vols, London,
  1797).
The Black Dwarf, A London Weekly Publication, 1817–19.
Blake, William, *The Complete Poetry and Prose of William Blake*, David V. Erdman (ed.)
  (1965; Rev. ed. Berkeley: University of California Press, 1982).

Brecht, Bertolt, *A Short Organum for the Theatre* (1949), in John Willett (ed. and trans.), *Brecht on Theatre: The Development of an Aesthetic* (New York: Hill & Wang, 1964), pp. 179–205. Rpt. in *Marxist Literary Theory*, Terry Eagleton and Drew Milne (eds) (London: Blackwell Publishing, 1996), pp. 107–135.

Bryant, William Cullen, *The Poetical Works of William Cullen Bryant*, Parke Godwin (ed.) (2 vols, New York: D. Appleton and Company, 1882).

Burke, Edmund, *A Philosophical Enquiry into the Origins of our Ideas of the Sublime and the Beautiful*, Adam Philips (ed.) (1990 Oxford: Oxford University Press, 2008).

———, *Reflections on the Revolution in France: A Critical Edition*, J.C.D. Clark (ed.) (Stanford: Stanford University Press, 2001).

Charles I, *The trial and execution of King Charles I; facsimiles of the contemporary official accounts contained in The charge of the Commons of England against Charl Stuart; King Charls, his tryal [and] King Charles, his speech made upon the scaffold* (Leeds, England: Scolar Press, 1966).

Cobbett, William, *William Cobbett: Selected Writings*, Leonora Nattras (ed.), James Epstein (Consulting ed.) (6 vols, London: Pickering & Chatto Publishers, 1998).

——— (ed.) with T.B. Howell, *Cobbett's Complete Collection of State Trials . . . from the Earliest Period to the Present Time* (London, 1809–1826).

Coleridge, Samuel Taylor, *Consciones ad Populum*, Jonathan Wordsworth (ed.) (Oxford: Woodstock Books, 1992).

De Quincey, Thomas, *Collected Writings of Thomas De Quincey*, David Masson (ed.) (13 vols, 1890; Edinburgh and London: A. and C. Black, 1897).

Earle, Jr, William, *Obi or; The History of Three-Fingered Jack*, Srinivas Aravamudan (ed.) (Peterloo, Ontario: Broadview Press, 2005).

Eton, William, *A Survey of the Turkish Empire* (London, 1798).

The Examiner, 1808–22.

Fawcett, John, *Obi; or Three-Finger'd Jack: A Serio-Pantomime, in Two Acts* http://www.rc.umd.edu/praxis/obi/obi_pantomime_act1.html

Forman, H. Buxton, 'The Improvvisatore Sgricci in relation to Shelley', *The Gentleman's Magazine* 248 (1880): pp. 115–23.

Godwin, William, *An Enquiry Concerning Political Justice* (Oxford: Oxford University Press, 2013).

———, *Essay on Sepulchres: or, A Proposal for Erecting some Memorial of the Illustrious Dead in all Ages on the Spot where their Remains have been Interred*, in Mark Philip (ed.), *The Political and Philosophical Writings of William Godwin* (7 vols, London: William Pickering, 1993), Vol. 6, pp. 1–30.

Havard, William, *King Charles the First: an Historical Tragedy. Written in Imitation of Shakespear. As it is Acted at the Theatre-Royal in Lincoln's-Inn-Fields* (Dublin, 1737). Copy retrieved from *ECCO*.

Hazlitt, William, *Hazlitt on Theatre*, William Archer and Robert Lowe (eds) (New York: Hill & Wang, 1895).

Hegel, G.W.F., *Hegel on Tragedy*, Anne and Henry Paolucci (eds) (Smyrna, DE: Bagehot Council [Griffon House Publications], 2001).

———, *Phenomenology of Spirit*, A.V. Miller (trans.) (Oxford: Oxford University Press, 1977).

Holcroft, Thomas, *Duplicity: A Comedy* (London: Printed for G. Robinson, 1781).

Hogg, James, *The Private Memoirs and Confession of a Justified Sinner*, Adrian Hunter (ed.) (Peterborough, Ontario: Broadview Press, 2001).

Hume, David. *The History of England from the Invasion of Julius Caesar to the Revolution in 1688*, Forward by William B. Todd (6 vols, Reprint, Indianapolis: Liberty, 1983).

Hunt, Leigh, *Hunt's Dramatic Criticism, 1808–1831*, Lawrence H. and Carolyn Washburn Houtchens (eds) (New York: Columbia University Press, 1949).

Hurd, Richard, *Letters on Chivalry and Romance (1762)*, Hoyt Trowbridge (ed.), Augustan Reprint Society (Los Angeles: University of California Press, 1963).

Jeffrey, Francis, 'The Corsair: a Tale and the Bride of Abydos: a Turkish Tale', *Edinburgh Review* 23 (1814): pp. 198–229. Reprinted in *Byron: The Critical Heritage*, Andrew Rutherford (ed.) (New York: Barnes and Noble, 1970), pp. 53–64.

Kant, Immanuel, *Perpetual Peace: A Philosophical Sketch*, in Hans Reiss (ed.), H.B. Nisbet (trans.), *Kant: Political Writings* (Cambridge: Cambridge University Press, 1970), pp. 93–130.

Keats, John, *John Keats: Complete Poems*, Jack Stillinger (ed.) (1978; Cambridge, MA: Belknap Press at Harvard University Press, 1985).

von Leibniz, Gottfried Wilhelm, 'Monadology', *Monadology and Other Philosophical Essays*, Paul Schrecker and Anne Martin Schrecker (trans.) (New York: Bobbs-Merrill Educational Publishing, 1965), pp. 148–63.

Locke, John, *Two Treatises of Government*, Thomas Hollis (ed.) (London: A. Millar et al., 1764).

Lockhart, John Gibson, *Peter's Letters to his Kinsfolk* (3 vols, Edinburgh: Blackwoods, 1819).

Marx, Karl, *The Eighteenth Brumaire of Louis Bonaparte* (1963; New York: International Publishers, 1994).

———, *Capital: A Critique of Political Economy*, Vol. 1, Ben Fowkes (trans.) (New York: Penguin, 1990).

Milner, H.M. *Tippoo Saib; Or, The Storming of Seringapatam* (1823; London: Hodgson's Juvenile Drama, [1825?]).

Milton, John, *Eikonoklastes*, in Merritt Y. Hughes (ed.), *The Complete Prose Works of John Milton* (8 vols, New Haven: Yale University Press, 1962), Vol. 3 (1648–49), pp. 337–600.

Mitford, Mary, *Charles the First: An Historical Tragedy in Five Acts.* London: John Duncombe and Co., 1834. Reprinted and edited by Thomas C. Crochunis for *British Women Playwrights around 1800.* 15 January 2001. http://www.etang.umontreal.ca/bwp1800/essays/mitford_charles_preface.html

Montogomery, James (ed.) with others, *Poems on the Abolition of the Slave Trade; written by James Montgomery, James Grahame, and E. Benger. Embellished with Engravings from Pictures Painted by R. Smirke, Esq. R.A.* (London, 1809).

Moseley, Benjamin, *A Treatise on Sugar with Miscellaneous Observations*, 2nd ed. (London: John Nichols, 1800).

Murray, William H., *Obi; or Three-Fingered Jack, A Melodrama in Two Acts* http://www.rc.umd.edu/praxis/obi/obi_melodrama_act1.html

Owenson, Sydney, *The Missionary*, Julia M. Wright (ed.) (Peterborough: Broadview Press, 2002).

Paine, Thomas, *Paine: Political Writings*, Bruce Kuklick (ed.) (Cambridge: Cambridge University Press, 1989).

Prynne, William. *Histrio-mastix. The players scourge, or, actors tragœdie, divided into two parts. Wherein it is largely evidenced, by divers arguments, by the concurring authorities and resolutions of sundry texts of Scripture . . . That popular stage-plays . . . are sinfull, heathenish, lewde, ungodly spectacles, and most pernicious corruptions; condemned in all ages, as intolerable mischiefes to churches, to republickes, to the manners, mindes, and soules of men. And that the profession of play-poets, of stage-players; together with the penning, acting, and frequenting of stage-playes, are unlawfull, infamous and misbeseeming Christians. All pretences to the contrary are here likewise fully answered; and the unlawfulnes of acting, of beholding academicall enterludes, briefly discussed; besides sundry other particulars concerning dancing, dicing, health-drinking, &c. of which the table will informe you. By William Prynne, an vtter-barrester of Lincolnes Inne.* London: Printed by E[dward] A[llde, Augustine Mathewes, Thomas Cotes] and W[illiam] I[ones] for Michael Sparke, and are to be sold at the Blue Bible, in Greene Arbour, in little Old Bayly, 1633. Accessed through *EBBO.*

Reeve, Clara, *The Progress of Romance and the History of Charoba, Queen of Aegypt.* Reproduced from the Colchester Edition of 1785, Esther M. McGill (ed.) (New York: The Facsimile Text Society, 1930).

Robinson, Henry Crabb, *Henry Crabb Robinson on Books and Their Writers*, Edith Morley (ed.) (3 vols, London: J.M. Dent & Sons Ltd., 1938).

Rousseau, Jean-Jacques, *The Social Contract*, Maurice Cranston (trans.) (New York: Penguin, 1968).

Schlegel, August Wilhelm, *Lectures on Dramatic Art and Literature*, John Black (trans.) (London: G. Bell and Sons, Ltd, 1914).

Schlegel, Friedrich, *Dialogue on Poetry and Literary Aphorisms*, Ernst Behler and Roman Struc (trans.) (University Park: The Pennsylvania State University Press, 1968), pp. 94–227.

———, *Philosophical Fragments*, Peter Firchow (trans.) (Minneapolis: University of Minnesota Press, 1991).

Scott, Walter, *Essays on Chivalry, Romance, and The Drama* (London: Frederick Warne and Co., 1887).

Scott, Walter Sidney (ed.), *The Athenians: Being a Correspondence between Thomas Jefferson Hogg and his Friends Thomas Love Peacock, Leigh Hunt, Percy Bysshe Shelley, and Others* (London: Cockerel Press, 1943).

Shelley, Mary Wollstonecraft, *The Letters of Mary Wollstonecraft Shelley*, Betty T. Bennett (ed.) (3 vols, Baltimore: Johns Hopkins University Press, 1980).

Shirley, James, *The Triumph of Peace*, in Clifford Leech (ed.), *The Book of Masques* (Cambridge: Cambridge University Press, 1967).

Sophocles, *Antigone*, in David Grene and Richmond Lattimore (eds), Richmond Lattimore (trans.), *Sophocles I*, Second Edition (Chicago: University of Chicago Press, 1991).

Walpole, Horace, *Mysterious Mother*, in Paul Baines and Edward Burns (eds), *Five Romantic Plays, 1768–1821* (Oxford: Oxford University Press, 2000).

Whitelocke, Bulstrode, *Memorials of the English affairs: or, an historical account of what passed from the beginning of the reign of King Charles the First, to King Charles the Second his happy restauration. . . . with the private consultations and secrets of the cabinet. A new edition: with many additions never before printed* (London, 1732). Retrieved from *ECCO.*

Wollstonecraft, Mary, *A Vindication of the Rights of Woman*, Carol H. Poston (ed.), Second Edn., (1975; New York: W.W. Norton, 1988).

Wordsworth, William and Samuel Taylor Coleridge, *Lyrical Ballads 1798 and 1800*, Michael Gamer and Dahlia Porter (eds) (Peterborough, Ontario: Broadview Press, 2008).

Secondary sources

Abrams, M.H., *Natural Supernaturalism: Tradition and Revolution in Romantic Literature* (New York: W.W. Norton, 1973).

Adorno, Theodor W, *Aesthetic Theory*, Gretel Adorno and Rolf Tiedemann (eds), Robert Hullot-Kentor (trans.), Theory and History of Literature, Volume 88 (Minneapolis: University of Minnesota Press, 1997).

———, *The Culture Industry: Selected Essays on Mass Culture* (1991; New York: Routledge, 2002).

——— and Max Horkheimer, *Dialectic of Enlightenment*, John Cumming (trans.) (New York, Continuum, 1993).

Agamben, Giorgio, *Homo Sacer: Sovereign Power and Bare Life*, Daniel Heller-Roazen (trans.) (Stanford: Stanford University Press, 1998).

———, *The Open: Man and Animal*, Kevin Attell (trans.) (Stanford: Stanford University Press, 2003).

———, *State of Exception*, Kevin Attell (trans.) (Chicago: University of Chicago Press, 2005).

Altick, Richard, *The Shows of London* (Cambridge, MA: Belknap Press of Harvard University Press, 1978).

Anderson, Benedict, *Imagined Communities: Reflections on the Origin and Spread of Nationalism* (New York: Verso, 1991).

Aravamudan, Srinivas, *Tropicopolitans: Colonialism and Agency, 1688–1804* (Durham, NC and London, Duke University Press, 1999).

Austin, J.L., *How to do Things with Words*, J.O. Urmson and Marina Sbisà (eds) (Cambridge: Harvard University Press, 1962).

Baer, Marc, *Theatre and Disorder in Late Georgian London* (Oxford: Clarendon Press Oxford, 1992).

Bainbridge, Simon, *British Poetry and the Revolutionary and Napoleonic Wars: Visions of Conflict* (New York and Oxford: Oxford University Press, 2003).

Bakhtin, Mikhail, *The Dialogic Imagination: Four Essays by M.M. Bakhtin*, Michael Holquist (ed.), Caryl Emerson and Michael Holquist (trans.) (Austin: University of Texas Press, 1981).

Bann, Stephen, *Romanticism and the Rise of History* (New York: Twane Publishers, 1995).

Barrell, John, ' "An Entire Change of Performances?": The Politicisation of Theatre and the Theatricalisation of Politics in the mid 1790s', *Lumen* XVII (1998), pp. 11–50.

———, *Imagining the King's Death: Figurative Treason, Fantasies of Regicide, 1793–1796* (Oxford: Oxford University Press, 2000).

———, *Exhibition Extraordinary!! Radical Broadsides of the Mid 1790s* (Nottingham: Trent Editions, 2001).

Baudrillard, Jean, *The Spirit of Terrorism and Requiem for the Twin Towers*, Chris Turner (trans.) (London: Verso, 2002).

Bayly, C.A., *Imperial Meridian: The British Empire and the World, 1780–1830* (London and New York: Longman, 1989).

Bell, David A., *The First Total War: Napoleon's Europe and the birth of Warfare as We Know It* (New York: Houghton Mifflin Co., 2007).

Benjamin, Walter, 'Theses on the Philosophy of History', in *Illuminations*, Harry Zohn (trans.) (New York: Harcourt, Brace & World, Inc., 1968).

———, 'The Work of Art in the Age of Mechanical Reproduction', in *Illuminations*, Harry Zohn (trans.) (New York: Harcourt, Brace & World, Inc., 1968).

———, *The Origin of German Tragic Drama*, John Osborne (trans.) (New York: Verso, 1998).

———, 'On the Image of Proust', in Michael W. Jennings, Howard Eiland and Gary Smith (eds), Rodney Livingstone et al. (trans.), *Walter Benjamin: Selected Writings* (1927–34), volume 2 (2 vols, Cambridge, MA: Belknap Press of Harvard University Press, 1999), pp. 237–47.

Bewell, Alan, *Romanticism and Colonial Disease* (Baltimore: The Johns Hopkins University Press, 1999).

Bhabha, Homi, 'Of Mimicry and Man: The Ambivalence of Colonial Discourse', in Philomena Essed and David Theo Goldberg (eds), *Race Critical Theories* (London and Malden, MA: Blackwell Press, 2000), pp. 113–22.

Bloom, Harold, *Shelley's Mythmaking* (New Haven: Yale University press, 1959).

———, *The Visionary Company: A Reading of English Romantic Poetry* (Ithaca: Cornell University Press, 1971).

———, *The Anxiety of Influence: A Theory of Poetry* (New York: Oxford University Press, 1973).

Bolton, Betsy, 'Farce, Romance and Empire: Elizabeth Inchbald and Colonial Discourse', *The Eighteenth Century* 39.1 (1998): pp. 3–24.

Booth, Michael, *English Melodrama* (London: Herbert Jenkins, 1965).

Botkin, Frances R., 'Being Jack Mansong: Ira Aldridge and the History of Three-Fingered Jack', in Paul Youngquist (ed.), *Race, Romanticism, and the Atlantic* (Farnham, England: Ashgate, 2013), pp. 145–61.

Bourdieu, Pierre, *Outline of a Theory of Practice*, Richard Nice (trans.) (Cambridge: Cambridge University Press, 1977).

Bratton, Jacky S. et al. (eds), *Acts of Supremacy: The British Empire and the Stage, 1790–1930* (Manchester: Manchester University Press, 1991).

———, 'British Heroism and the Structure of Melodrama', in J.S. Bratton et al. (eds), *Acts of Supremacy: The British Empire and the Stage, 1790–1930* (Manchester: Manchester University Press, 1991), pp. 18–61.

———, James Cook and Christine Gledhill (eds), *Melodrama: Stage Picture Screen* (London: British Film Institute, 1994).

———, *New Readings in Theatre History* (Cambridge: Cambridge University Press, 2003).

Brooks, Peter, *The Melodramatic Imagination: Balzac, Henry James, Melodrama, and the Mode of Excess* (1976; New Haven: Yale University Press, 1985).

Bryant-Bertail, Sarah, *Space and Time in Epic Theater: The Brechtian Legacy* (Rochester, NY: Camden House, 2000).

Butler, Judith, 'Performative Acts and Gender Constitution: An Essay in Phenomenology and Feminist Theory', *Theatre Journal* 40.4 (December 1988): pp. 519–31.

———, *Gender Trouble: Feminism and the Subversion of Identity* (1990; New York: Routledge, 1999).

———, *Antigone's Claim: Kinship Between Life and Death* (New York: Columbia University Press, 2000).

———, *Precarious Life: The Powers of Mourning and Violence* (London: Verso, 2004).

Butler, Marilyn, *Romantics, Rebels and Reactionaries: English Literature and its Background, 1760–1830* (1981; New York and Oxford: Oxford University Press, 1990).

Butler, Martin, *The Stuart Court Masque and Political Culture* (Cambridge: University of Cambridge Press, 2001).

Cameron, Kenneth Neill, *Shelley: The Golden Years* (Cambridge: Harvard University Press, 1974).

Canfield, J. Douglas, 'The Ideology of Restoration Tragicomedy' *English Literary History* 51.3 (Autumn 1984): pp. 447–64.

Cantor, Paul A, ' "A Distorting Mirror": Shelley's *The Cenci* and Shakespearean Tragedy', in G.B. Evans (ed.), *Shakespeare: Aspects of Influence* (Cambridge: Harvard University Press, 1976), pp. 91–108.

———, 'Part One: *Coriolanus*', *Shakespeare's Rome: Republic and Empire* (Ithaca: Cornell University Press, 1976), pp. 55–124.

Carlson, Julie A., *In the Theatre of Romanticism: Coleridge, Nationalism, Women* (Cambridge: Cambridge University Press, 1994).

———, Race and profit in English theatre', in Jane Moody and Daniel O'Quinn (eds), *The Cambridge Companion to British Theatre 1773–1830* (Cambridge: Cambridge University Press, 2007), pp. 175–88.

———, 'Fancy's History', *European Romantic Review* 14.2 (2003): pp. 163–76.

Chandler, James, *England in 1819: The Politics of Literary Culture and the Case of Romantic Historicism* (Chicago: University of Chicago Press, 1998).

Cheeke, Stephen, *Byron and Place: History, Translation, Nostalgia* (New York: Palgrave, 2003).

———, 'Wrong-footed by Genre: Shelley's *Hellas*', *Romanticism* 2.2 (1996): pp. 204–19.

Clark. Anna, 'Queen Caroline and the Sexual Politics of Popular Culture in London, 1820', *Representations* 31 (Summer 1990): pp. 47–68.

Clark, David L., 'Schelling's wartime: philosophy and violence in the age of Napoleon', *European Romantic Review* 19.2 (April 2008): pp. 139–48.

———, 'Unsocial Kant: the Philosopher and the Un-regarded War Dead', *Wordsworth Circle* 41.1 (Winter 2010): pp. 60–68.

Colley, Linda, *Britons: Forging the Nation, 1707–1837* (New Haven and London, Yale University Press, 1992).

Cox, Jeffrey N., *In the Shadows of Romance: Romantic Tragic Drama in Germany, England, and France* (Athens, OH: Ohio University Press, 1987).

——— (ed.), *Seven Gothic Dramas, 1789–1825* (Columbus: Ohio State University Press, 1992).

———, 'The ideological Tack of Melodrama', in Michael Hays and Anatasia Nikolopoulou (eds), *Melodrama: The Cultural Emergence of a Genre* (1996; New York: St Martin's Press, 1999), pp. 167–89.

———, 'Staging Hope: Genre, Myth, and Ideology in the Dramas of the Hunt Circle', *Texas Studies in Language and Literature* 38:3/4 (Fall/Winter 1996): pp. 245–64. See also *Poetry and Politics*, pp. 123–45.

———, *Poetry and Politics in the Cockney School: Keats, Shelley, Hunt and their Circle* (Cambridge: Cambridge University Press, 1998).

——— (ed.), *Slavery, Abolition & Emancipation: Writings in the British Romantic Period*, (8 vols, vol. 5, Drama, London: Pickering and Chatto, 1999).

——— with Michael Gamer (eds), *The Broadview Anthology of Romantic Drama* (Peterborough: Broadview Press, 2003).

———, 'Staging Baillie', in Thomas C. Crochunis (ed.), *Joanna Baillie, Romantic Dramatist: Critical Essays* (London: Routledge, 2004), pp. 146–67.

———, 'The Dramatist', in Timothy Morton (ed.), *Cambridge Companion to Shelley* (Cambridge: Cambridge University Press, 2006), pp. 65–84.

———, 'The Death of Tragedy; or, the Birth of Melodrama', in Tracy C. Davis and Peter Holland (eds), *The Performing Century: Nineteenth-Century Theatre's History* (New York: Palgrave Macmillan, 2007), pp. 161–81.

——— with Dana Van Kooy, 'Melodramatic Slaves', *Modern Drama* 55.4 (Winter 2012): pp. 459–75.

———, *Romanticism in the Shadow of War: Literary Culture in the Napoleonic War Years* (Cambridge: Cambridge University Press, 2014).

Crisafulli, Lilla Maria and Keir Elam (eds), *Women's Romantic Theatre and Drama: History, Agency, and Performativity* (Farnham, England: Ashgate, 2010).

Crook, Nora, 'Caluminated Republicans and the Hero of Shelley's "Charles the First"', *Keats-Shelley Journal* 56 (2007): pp. 155–72.

———, 'Shelley's Late Fragmentary Plays: "Charles the First" and the "Unfinished Drama"', in Alan M. Weinberg and Timothy Webb (eds), *The Unfamiliar Shelley* (Farnham, England: Ashgate, 2009), pp. 297–312.

Cronin, Richard, *Shelley's Poetic Thoughts* (New York: St Martin's Press, 1981).

Curran, Stuart, *Shelley's Cenci: Scorpions Rings with Fire* (Princeton: Princeton University Press, 1970).

———, *Shelley's Annus Mirabilis: The Maturing of an Epic Vision* (San Marino, CA: Huntington Library, 1975).

———, *Poetic Form and British Romanticism* (New York: Oxford University Press, 1986).

———, 'The Political Prometheus', *Studies in Romanticism* 25 (Fall 1986), pp. 429–55. Rpt. in G.A. Rosso and Daniel P. Watkins (eds), *Spirits of Fire: English Romantic Writers and Contemporary Historical Methods* (Rutherford, NJ: Farleigh Dickenson University Press, 1990), pp. 260–284.

———, 'Lyrical Drama: *Prometheus Unbound* and *Hellas*', in Michael O'Neill, Anthony Howe, with the Assistance of Madelieine Callaghan (eds), *The Oxford Handbook of Percy Bysshe Shelley* (Oxford: Oxford University Press, 2012), pp. 289–98.

Dawson, P.M.S., 'Shelley and the *Improvvisatore* Sgricci: An Unpublished Review', *Keats-Shelley Memorial Bulletin* 32 (1981): pp. 19–29.

Debord, Guy, *The Society of the Spectacle*, Donald Nicholson-Smith (trans.) (1992; New York: Zone Books, 1999).

De Certeau, Michel, *The Practice of Everyday Life*, Steven Rendall (trans.) (Berkeley: University of California Press, 1984).

Deleuze, Gilles and Félix Guattari, *A Thousand Plateaus: Capitalism and Schitzophrenia*, Brian Massumi (trans.) (Minneapolis: University of Minnesota Press, 1987).

de Man, Paul, *Blindness and Insight: Essays in the Rhetoric of Contemporary Criticism*, Second Edition, Revised (1971; Minneapolis: University of Minnesota Press, 1983).

Derrida, Jacques, 'Force of Law: The "Mystical Foundation of Authority"', in Drucilla Cornell, Michel Rosenfeld, David Gray Carlson (eds), *Deconstruction and the Possibility of Justice* (New York: Routledge, 2002), pp. 3–67.

———, *On Cosmopolitanism and Forgiveness*, Mark Dooley and Michael Hughes (trans.) (2001; New York: Routledge, 2004).

———, *Specters of Marx: The State of the Debt, the Work of Mourning, and the New International*, Peggy Kamuf (trans.) (New York: Routledge, 1994).

Dick, Alexander and Angela Esterhammer (eds), *Spheres of Action: Speech and Performance in Romantic Culture* (Toronto: University of Toronto Press, 2009).

Dollimore, Jonathan, *Radical Tragedy: Religion, Ideology, and Power in the Drama of Shakespeare and his Contemporaries*, Second Edition (1984; Durham: Duke University Press, 1993).

Donkin, Ellen, 'Mrs. Siddons Looks Back in Anger: Feminist Historiography for Eighteenth-Century British Theater', in Janelle G. Reinelt and Joseph R. Roach (eds), *Critical Theory and Performance* (Ann Arbor: University of Michigan Press, 1992), pp. 276–90.

Du Bois, W.E.B., *The Souls of Black Folk*, Donald B. Gibson and Monica M. Elbert (eds) (New York, Penguin, 1996).

Duff, David, *Romance and Revolution: Shelley and the Politics of a Genre* (London: Cambridge University Press, 1994).

———, 'From Revolution to Romanticism', in Duncan Wu (ed.), *A Blackwell Companion to Romanticism* (London: Blackwell, 1999), pp. 23–34.

———, '"The Casket of My Unknown Mind": The 1813 Volume of Minor Poems', in Alan M. Weinberg and Timothy Webb (eds), *The Unfamiliar Shelley* (Farnham, England: Ashgate, 2009), pp. 41–67.

Duncan, Ian, *Modern Romance and Transformations of the Novel: The Gothic, Scott, Dickens* (London: Cambridge University Press, 1992).

———, *Scott's Shadow: The Novel in Romantic Edinburgh* (Princeton: Princeton University Press, 2007).

Dyer, Gary, *British Satire and the Politics of Style, 1789–1832* (Cambridge: Cambridge University Press, 1997).

Eliot, T.S., 'Tradition and Individual Talent', in *Selected Essays* (New York: Harcourt, Brace and Company, 1950).

Epstein, James, A., *Radical Expression: Political Language, Ritual, and Symbol in England, 1790–1850* (New York: Oxford University Press, 1994).

Erdman, David V., *Blake: Prophet Against Empire* (1954; New York: Dover, 1977).

Erkelenz, Michael, 'The Genre and Politics of Shelley's *Swellfoot the Tyrant*', *Review of English Studies* 47.188 (November 1996): pp. 500–520.

———, 'Inspecting the Tragedy of Empire: Shelley's *Hellas* and Aeschylus' *Persians*', *Philological Quarterly* 76.3 (Summer 1997): pp. 313–37.

Esterhamer, Angela and Alexander Dick (eds), *Spheres of Action: Speech and Performance in Romantic Culture* (Toronto: University of Toronto Press, 2009).

———, 'The Cosmopolitan *Improvvisatore*: Spontaneity and Performance in Romantic Poetics', *European Romantic Review* 1.2 (April 2005): pp. 153–65.

———, 'Improvisational Aesthetics: Byron, the Shelley Circle, and Tommaso Sgricci', *Romanticism on the Net* 43 (August 2006) <http://www.erudit.org/revue/ron/2006/v/n43/013592ar.html>

Fanon, Franz, *Black Skin, White Masks*, Richard Philcox (trans.) (1952; New York: Grove Press, 2008).

———, *A Dying Colonialism*, Haakon Chevalier (trans.) (New York: Grove Press, 1965).

Favret, Mary, 'Everyday War', *English Literary History* 72 (2005): pp. 605–33.

———, *War at a Distance: Romanticism and the Making of Modern Wartime* (Princeton: Princeton University Press, 2010).

Felperin, Howard, *Shakespearean Romance* (Princeton: Princeton University Press, 1972).

Felsenstein, Frank (ed.), *Trader, Indian Maid: Representing Gender, Race, and Slavery in the New World – An Inkle and Yarico Reader* (Baltimore: Johns Hopkins University Press, 1999).

Ferris, David S., *Silent Urns: Romanticism, Hellenism, Modernity* (Stanford: Stanford University Press, 2000).

Ferris, Suzanne, 'Percy Bysshe Shelley's *The Cenci* and the Rhetoric of Tyranny', in Terence Allan Hoagwood and Daniel P. Watkins (eds), *British Romantic Drama: Historical and Critical Essays* (Madison: Farleigh Dickinson University Press, 1998), pp. 208–28.

Foley, Helene P. and Jean E. Howard, 'The Urgency of Tragedy Now', printed in a special issue of *PMLA* 129.4 (October 2014): pp. 617–33.

Foster, Hal (ed.), *The Anti-Aesthetic: Essays on Postmodern Culture* (Port Townsend, WA: Bay Press, 1983).

Foucault, Michel, *The Archeology of Knowledge* and *The Discourse on Language*, A.M. Sheridan Smith (trans.) (1969; New York: Pantheon, 1972).

———, *The Order of Things, An Archaeology of the Human Sciences* (1970; New York: Vintage, 1973).

———, *Discipline and Punish: The Birth of the Prison*, second edition, Alan Sheridan (trans.) (New York: Vintage, 1977).

———, *The History of Sexuality: An Introduction*, Robert Hurley (trans.) (1978; New York: Vintage, 1990).

Freeman, Lisa A., *Character's Theater: Genre and Identity on the Eighteenth-Century English Stage* (Philadelphia: University of Pennsylvania Press, 2002).

Fumerton, Patricia, *Cultural Aesthetics: Renaissance Literature and the Practice of Social Ornament* (Chicago: University of Chicago Press, 1991).

Gamer, Michael, 'Authors in Effect: Lewis, Scott, and the Gothic Drama', *English Literary History* 66 (1999): pp. 831–61.

———, *Romanticism and the Gothic: Genre, Reception, and Canon Formation* (Cambridge: Cambridge University Press, 2000).

———, 'A Matter of Turf: Romanticism, Hippodrama, and Satire', *Nineteenth-Century Contexts*, 28.4 (December 2006): pp. 305–34.

Garber, Marjorie, *Shakespeare After All* (New York: Anchor Books, 2004).

Gaull, Marilyn, 'Pantomime as Satire: Mocking a Broken Charm', in Steven E. Jones (ed.), *The Satiric Eye: Forms of Satire in the Romantic Period* (New York: Palgrave, 2003), pp. 207–24.

George, Mary Dorothy, *Catalogue of Political and Personal Satires* (11 vols, London: British Museum, Department of Prints and Drawings, 1870–1954).

Gladden, Samuel, *Shelley's Textual Seductions: Plotting Utopia in the Erotic and Political Works* (New York and London: Routledge, 2002).

———, 'Shelley's Agenda Writ Large: Reconsidering *Oedipus Tyrannus; or, Swellfoot the Tyrant*', in 'Reading Shelley's Interventionist Poetry, 1819–1820', Michael Scrivener (ed.), a special edition of *Romantic Praxis*. Available at http://www.rc.umd.edu/praxis/interventionist/gladden/gladden.html

Glen, Heather and Paul Hamilton (eds), *Repossessing the Romantic Past* (Cambridge: Cambridge University Press, 2007).

Goldberg, Jonathan, *James I and the Politics of Literature: Jonson, Shakespeare, Donne, and their Contemporaries* (Baltimore: Johns Hopkins University Press, 1983).

Greenblatt, Stephen, 'Introduction', in Stephen Greenblatt (ed.), *The Power of English Forms in the Renaissance* (Norman: University of Oklahoma Press, 1982), pp. 3–6.

———, *Shakespearean Negotiations: The Circulation of Social Energy in Renaissance England* (Berkeley and Los Angeles: University of California Press, 1988).

Groseclose, Barbara, 'The Incest Motif in Shelley's *The Cenci*', *Comparative Drama*, 19.3 (Fall 1985): pp. 222–39.

Guillory, John, *Cultural Capital: The Problem of Literary Canon Formation* (Chicago: University of Chicago Press, 1993).

Hadley, Elaine, *Melodramatic Tactics: Theatricalized Dissent in the English Marketplace, 1800–1885* (Stanford: Stanford University Press, 1995).

Hall, Edith, 'The Problem with Prometheus: Myth, Abolition, and Radicalism', in Edith Hall, Richard Alston, and Justine McConnell (eds), *Ancient Slavery and Abolition: From Hobbes to Hollywood* (Oxford: Oxford University Press, 2011), pp. 209–46.

Hamilton, Paul, 'Literature and Philosophy', in Timothy Morton (ed.), *Cambridge Companion to Shelley* (Cambridge: Cambridge University Press, 2006), pp. 166–84.

———— and Heather Glen (eds), *Repossessing the Romantic Past* (Cambridge: Cambridge University Press, 2007).

Harrison, Margot, 'No Way for a Victim to Act?: Beatrice Cenci and the Dilemma of Romantic Performance', *Studies in Romanticism* 39 (Summer 2000): pp. 187–211.

Hays, Michael and Anastasia Nikolopoulou, (eds), *Melodrama: The Cultural Emergence of a Genre* (1996; New York: St Martin's Press, 1999).

Henderson, Jeffrey, *The Maculate Muse: Obscene Language in Attic Comedy*, Second Edition (Oxford: Oxford University Press, 1991).

Hendrix, Richard, 'Popular Humor and "The Black Dwarf"', *The Journal of British Studies* 16.1 (Autumn 1976): pp. 108–28.

Heydt-Stevenson, Jillian, *Austen's Unbecoming Conjunctions: Subversive Laughter, Embodied History* (New York: Palgrave, 2005).

Hill, Christopher, *Milton and the English Revolution* (1977; New York: Penguin Books, 1979).

Hilton, Nelson, 'An Original Story', in Nelson Hilton and Thomas A. Volger (eds), *Unnam'd Forms: Blake and Textuality* (Berkeley: University of California Press, 1986).

Hogle, Jerrold E., *Shelley's Process: Radical Transference and the Development of His Major Works* (New York: Oxford University Press, 1988).

————, '"Gothic" Romance: Its Origins and Cultural Functions', in Corrine Saunders (ed.), *A Companion to Romance: From Classical to Contemporary* (Malden, MA: Blackwell Publishing, 2004), pp. 216–32.

Hone, J. Anne, *For the Cause of Truth: Radicalism in London, 1796–1821* (Oxford: Clarendon Press, 1982).

Hunt, Alastair and Matthias Rudolf, 'Introduction: The Romantic Rhetoric of Life', in Alastair Hunt and Matthias Rudolf (eds), *Romanticism and Biopoitics: A Romantic Circles* PRAXIS Volume, http://romantic.arhu.umd.edu/praxis/biopolitics/HTML/praxis.2012.hunt-rudolf.html

Hyde, Lewis, *The Gift: Imagination and the Erotic Life of Property* (New York: Vintage, 1999).

Jacobs, Carol, 'Unbinding Words: *Prometheus Unbound*', in Cynthia Chase (ed.), *Romanticism* (London: Longman, 1993), pp. 240–69.

————, *Uncontainable Romanticism: Shelley, Bronte, Kleist* (Baltimore: Johns Hopkins University Press, 1989).

Jacobus, Mary, '"The Great Stage where Senators Perform": *Macbeth* and the Politics of Romantic Theatre', *Romanticism Writing and Sexual Difference: Essays on* The Prelude. (Oxford: Clarendon Press, 1989), pp. 33–68.

Jameson, Fredric, *The Political Unconscious: Narrative as a Socially Symbolic Act* (Ithaca: Cornell University Press, 1981).

————, 'Postmodernism and Consumer Society', in Hal Foster (ed.), *The Anti-Aesthetic: Essays on Postmodern Culture* (Port Townsend, WA: Bay Press, 1983), pp. 111–25.

————, *Archaeologies of the Future: The Desire Called Utopia and Other Science Fictions* (New York: Verso, 2005).

Janover, Michael, 'The Limits of Forgiveness and the Ends of Politics', *Journal of Intercultural Studies* 26.3 (August 2005), pp. 221–35.

Jones, J. Jennifer, 'Absorbing Hesitation: Wordsworth and the Theory of the Panorama', *Studies in Romanticism* 45.3 (Fall 2006): pp. 357–75.

Jones, Steven E., *Shelley's Satire: Violence, Exhortation, and Authority* (DeKalb: Northern Illinois University Press, 1994).

———, ' "Choose Reform or Civil War": Shelley, the English Revolution, and the Problem of Succession', *Wordsworth Circle* (Summer 1994): pp. 145–9.

——— (ed.), *The Satiric Eye: Forms of Satire in the Romantic Period* (New York: Palgrave Macmillan, 2003).

Kantorowicz, E.H., *The King's Two Bodies* (Princeton: Princeton University Press, 1957).

Karr, David, ' "Thoughts that Flash like Lightning": Thomas Holcroft, Radical Theater, and the Production of Meaning in 1790s London', *Journal of British Studies* 40 (July 2001): pp. 324–56.

Keach, William, *Arbitrary Power: Romanticism, Language, Politics* (Princeton: Princeton University Press, 2004).

———, 'The Political Poet', in Timothy Morton (ed.), *The Cambridge Companion to Shelley* (Cambridge: Cambridge University Press, 2006), pp. 123–42.

Kelley, Theresa M., 'Reading Justice: From Derrida to Shelley and Back', *Studies in Romanticism* 46 (Summer/Fall 2007): pp. 267–87.

Kipperman, Mark, 'History and Ideality: The Politics of Shelley's *Hellas*', *Studies in Romanticism* 30 (Summer 1991): pp. 147–68.

Koselleck, Reinhart, *Futures Past: On the Semantics of Historical Time*, Keith Tribe (trans.) (Columbia: Columbia University Press, 1985).

Kucich, Greg, 'Inventing Revolutionary History: Romanticism and the Politics of Literary Tradition', *Wordsworth Circle* (Summer 1994): pp. 138–45.

———, ' "This Horrid Theatre of Human Sufferings": Gendering the Stages of History in Catharine Macaulay and Percy Bysshe Shelley', in Thomas Pfau and Robert F. Gleckner (eds) *Lessons of Romanticism: A Critical Companion* (Durham: Duke University Press, 1998), pp. 448–65.

———, 'Mary Shelley: Biographer', in Esther Schor (ed.), *The Cambridge Companion to Mary Shelley* (Cambridge: Cambridge University Press, 2003), pp. 226–41.

———, 'Joanna Baillie and the re-staging of history and gender', in Thomas C. Crochunis (ed.), *Joanna Baillie, Romantic Dramatist: Critical Essays* (New York: Routledge, 2004), pp. 108–29.

———, 'Baillie, Mitford, and the "Different Track" of Women's Historical drama on the Romantic Stage', in Lilla Maria Crisafulli and Keir Elam (eds), *Women's Romantic Theatre and Drama: History, Agency, and Performativity* (Farnham, England: Ashgate, 2010), pp. 21–41.

Lang, Andrew, *The Life and Letters of John Gibson Lockhart* (2 vols, London: Nimmo, 1897).

Laqueur, Thomas W, 'The Queen Caroline Affair: Politics as Art in the Reign of George IV', *Journal of Modern History* 54 (September 1982): pp. 417–66.

Leask, Nigel, *British Romantic Writers and the East: Anxieties of Empire* (1992; Cambridge: Cambridge University Press, 2004).

———, 'Byron and the Eastern Mediterranean: *Childe Harold* II and the 'polemic of Ottoman Greece', in Drummond Bone (ed.), *The Cambridge Companion to Byron* (Cambridge: Cambridge University Press, 2004): pp. 99–117.

Lévi-Strauss, Claude, *The Elementary Structures of Kinship*, Rodney Needham (ed.), James Harle Bell and John Richard Von Sturmer (trans.) (Boston: Beacon Press, 1969).

Lindenberger, Herbert, *Historical Drama: The Relation of Literature and Reality* (Chicago: University of Chicago Press, 1975).

Lipking, Joanna, 'The New World of Slavery – An Introduction', in Aphra Behn's *Oroonoko*, Joanna Lipking (ed.) (New York: Norton, 1997), pp. 75–89.

Liu, Alan, ' "Shapeless Eagerness": The Genre of Revolution in Books 9–10 of *The Prelude*', *Modern Language Quarterly* 43 (1982): pp. 3–28.

———, *'Wordsworth: The History in "Imagination" '*, *English Literary History* 51 (1984): pp. 505–48.

Lochhead, Marion, *John Gibson Lockhart* (London: John Murray, 1954).

Loewenstein, David, *Milton and the Drama of History: Historical Vision, Iconoclasm, and the Literary Imagination* (Cambridge: Cambridge University Press, 1990).

Maguire, Nancy Klein, 'The Theatrical Mask/Masque of Politics: The Case of Charles I', *Journal of British Studies* 28 (January 1989): pp. 1–22.

Makdisi, Saree, *William Blake and the Impossible History of the 1790s* (Chicago: University of Chicago Press, 2003).

Marsden, Jean I., 'Sex, Politics, and She-Tragedy: Reconfiguring Lady Jane Grey', *Studies in English Literature 1500–1900*, 42.3 (Summer 2002): pp. 501–22.

Martineau, Jane, et al. (eds), *Shakespeare in Art* (London: Merrell Publishers, Ltd, 2003).

Mastrosilvestri, Vita M., 'Elizabeth Inchbald: Translation as Mediation and Re-writing', in Lilla Maria Crisafulli and Keir Elam (eds), *Women's Romantic Theatre and Drama: History, Agency, and Performativity* (Farnham, England: Ashgate, 2010), pp. 159–68.

Maus, Katherine Eisaman, 'Coriolanus', in Stephen Greenblatt, Walter Cohen, Jean E. Howard and Katherine Eisaman Maus (eds), *The Norton Shakespeare.* (New York: WW Norton and Co., 1997), pp. 2785–92.

Mayer, III, David, *Harlequin in His Element: The English Pantomime, 1806–1836* (Cambridge: Harvard University Press, 1969).

Mazzeo, Tilar J., *Plagiarism and Literary Property in the Romantic Period* (Philadelphia: University of Pennsylvania Press, 2007).

McCole, John, *Walter Benjamin and the Antinomies of Tradition* (Ithaca: Cornell University Press, 1993).

McGann, Jerome, *The Romantic Ideology* (Chicago: University of Chicago Press, 1983).

McPherson, Heather, 'Picturing Tragedy: *Mrs. Siddons as the Tragic Muse* Revisited', *Eighteenth-Century Studies* 33.3 (2000): pp. 401–30.

Medwin, Thomas, *The Life of Percy Bysshe Shelley* (Oxford: Oxford University Press, 1913).

Meisel, Martin, *Realizations: Narrative, Pictorial, and Theatrical Arts in Nineteenth-Century England* (Princeton: Princeton University Press, 1983).

Meyer, Eric, ' "I Know Thee not, I Loathe Thy Race": Romantic Orientalism in the Eye of the Other', *English Literary History* 58.3 (Autumn 1991): pp. 657–99.

Mitchell, W.J.T., *Iconology: Image, Text Ideology* (Chicago: University of Chicago Press, 1986).

———, *Picture Theory: Essays on Verbal and Visual Representation* (Chicago: University of Chicago Press, 1994).

———, *What Do Pictures Want? The Lives and Loves of Images* (Chicago: University of Chicago Press, 2005).

———, *Seeing Through Race* (Cambridge, MA: Harvard University Press, 2012).

Moody, Jane, ' "Fine Word, Legitimate!": Toward a Theatrical History of Romanticism', *Texas Studies in Literature and Language* 38.3/4 (Fall/Winter 1996): pp. 223–44.

———, *Illegitimate Theatre in London, 1770–1840* (Cambridge: Cambridge University Press, 2000).

———, 'Romantic Shakespeare', in Stanley Wells and Sarah Stanton (eds), *The Cambridge Companion to Shakespeare on Stage* (Cambridge: Cambridge University Press, 2002), pp. 37–57.

——— and Daniel O'Quinn (eds), *The Cambridge Companion to British Theatre, 1730–1830* (Cambridge: Cambridge University Press, 2007).

Moretti, Franco, ' "A Huge Eclipse": Tragic From and the Deconsecration of Sovereignty', in Stephen Greenblatt, (ed.), D.A. Miller (trans.), *The Power of Forms in the English Renaissance* (Norman: University of Oklahoma Press, 1982), pp. 7–40.

Morton, Timothy, *Shelley and the Revolution in Taste: The Body and the Natural World* (Cambridge and New York: Cambridge University Press, 1994).

———, *The Poetics of Spice: Romantic Consumerism and the Exotic* (Cambridge and New York: Cambridge University Press, 2000).

——— (ed.), with Nigel Smith, *Radicalism in British Literary culture, 1650–1830: From Revolution to Revolution* (Cambridge: Cambridge University Press, 2002).

———, 'Shelley, Nature and Culture', in Timothy Morton (ed.), *The Cambridge Companion to Shelley* (Cambridge and New York: Cambridge University Press, 2006).

——— (ed.), *The Cambridge Companion to Shelley* (Cambridge: Cambridge University Press, 2006).

———, 'Porcine Poetics: Shelley's *Swellfoot the Tyrant*', in Alan M. Weinberg and Timothy Webb (eds), *The Unfamiliar Shelley* (Farnham, England: Ashgate, 2009), pp. 279–95.

Mulhallen, Jacqueline, *The Theatre of Shelley* (Cambridge: Open Book Publishers, 2010).

Myers, Victoria, 'Blasphemy Trials and *The Cenci*: Parody as Performative', in Alexander Dick and Angela Esterhammer (eds), *Spheres of Action: Speech and Performance in Romantic Culture* (Toronto: University of Toronto Press, 2009), pp. 100–123.

Nancy, Jean-Luc, *The Birth to Presence*, Brian Holmes and others (trans.) (Stanford: Stanford University Press, 1998).

Negri, Antonio, 'The Specter's Smile', in Michael Sprinker (ed.) and Patricia Dailey and Constantino Costantini (trans.), *Ghostly Demarcations* (1999; New York: Verso, 2008).

———, *The Porcelain Workshop: For a New Grammar of Politics*, Noura Wedell (trans.) (Los Angeles: Semiotext(e), 2008).

Nora, Pierre, 'Between Memory and History: *Les Lieux de Mémoire*', *Representations* 26 (Spring 1989): pp. 7–25.

O'Neill, Michael, Anthony Howe with the Assistance of Madeleine Callaghan (eds), *The Oxford Handbook of Percy Bysshe Shelley* (Oxford: Oxford University Press, 2012).

O'Quinn, Daniel, 'Elizabeth Inchbald's *The Massacre*: Tragedy, Violence and the Network of Political Fantasy', *British Women Playwrights around 1800*, 1 June 1999, 8 pars. http://www.etang.umontreal.ca/bwp1800/essays/oquinn_massacre.html

———, 'Scissors and Needles: Inchbald's *Wives as They Were, Maids as They Are* and the Governance of Sexual Exchange', *Theatre Journal* 51 (1999): pp. 105–25.

———, *Staging Governance: Theatrical Imperialism in London, 1770–1800* (Baltimore: Johns Hopkins University Press, 2005).

———, 'Theatre and empire', in Jane Moody and Daniel O'Quinn (eds), *The Cambridge Companion to British Theatre 1773–1830* (Cambridge: Cambridge University Press, 2007), pp. 233–46.

——— and Jane Moody (eds), *The Cambridge Companion to British Theatre 1773–1830* (Cambridge: Cambridge University Press, 2007).

———, 'Fox's Tears: The Staging of Liquid Politics', in Alexander Dick and Angela Esterhammer (eds), *Spheres of Action: Speech and Performance in Romantic Culture* (Toronto: University of Toronto Press, 2009), pp. 194–221.

Orgel, Stephen, *The Illusion of Power: Political Theater in the English Renaissance* (Los Angeles and Berkeley: University of California Press, 1975).

———, and Roy Strong (eds), *Inigo Jones: The Theatre of the Stuart Court, including the complete designs for productions at court for the most part in the collection of the Duke of Devonshire together with their texts and historical documentation* (2 vols, Berkeley: University of California Press, 1973).

Patterson, Annabel, *Shakespeare and the Popular Voice* (Cambridge: Basil Blackwood, 1989).

Phillips, Mark Salber, *Society and Sentiment: Genres of Historical Writing in Britain, 1740–1820* (Princeton, New Jersey: Princeton University Press, 2000).

Potkay, Monica Brzezinski, 'Incest as Theology in Shelley's *the Cenci*', *Wordsworth Circle* 35.2 (Spring 2004): pp. 57–65.

Rahill, Frank, *The World of Melodrama* (University Park: Pennsylvania State University Press, 1967).

Redfield, Marc, 'Aesthetics, Sovereignty, Biopower: From Schiller's *Über die ästhetische Erziehung des Menschen* to Goethe's *Unterhaltungen deutscher Ausgewanderten*', in Alastair Hunt and Matthias Rudolf (eds), *Romanticism and Biopoitics: A Romantic Circles* PRAXIS volume http://romantic.arhu.umd.edu/praxis/biopolitics/HTML/praxis.2012.redfield.html

Roach, Joseph R., *The Player's Passion: Studies in the Science of Acting* (1985; Rpt Ann Arbor: University of Michigan Press, 1993).

———, 'Introduction', in Janelle G. Reinelt and Joseph R. Roach (eds), *Critical Theory and Performance* (Ann Arbor, 1992), pp. 293–8.

———, 'Slave Spectacles and Tragic Octoroons: A Cultural Genealogy of Antebellum Performance', *Theatre Journal* 33 (November 1992): pp. 167–87.

———, *Cities of the Dead: Circum-Atlantic Performance* (New York: Columbia University Press, 1996).

Roberts, Hugh, 'The Communicative Strategies of Shelley's Prefaces', in Alan M. Weinberg and Timothy Webb (eds), *The Unfamiliar Shelley* (Farnham, England: Ashgate, 2009), pp. 183–98.

Robinson, Jeffrey C., 'Romantic Poetry: The Possibilities for Improvisation', *Wordsworth Circle* 38.3 (Summer 2007): pp. 94–100.

Roe, Nicholas, *John Keats and the Culture of Dissent* (Oxford: Clarendon at Oxford University Press, 1997).

Rogers, Nicholas, *Crowds, Culture, and Politics in Georgian Britain* (Oxford: Oxford University Press, 1998).

Rossington, Michael, 'Shelley's Republics', in Heather Glen and Paul Hamilton (eds), *Repossessing the Romantic Past* (Cambridge: Cambridge University Press, 2007), pp. 63–79.

Russell, Gillian, 'Playing at Revolution: The Politics of the O.P. Riots of 1809', *Theatre Notebook* 44 (1990): pp. 16–26.

———, *The Theatres of War: Performance, Politics, and Society, 1793–1815* (Cambridge: Cambridge University Press, 1995).

———, 'Burke's Dagger: Theatricality, Politics and Print Culture in the 1790s', *British Journal for Eighteenth-Century Studies* 20 (1997): pp. 1–16.

——, 'The Eighteenth Century and the Romantics on War', in Kate McLoughlin (ed.), *The Cambridge Companion to War Writing* (Cambridge: Cambridge University Press, 2000), pp. 112–25.

——, *Women, Sociability and Theatre in Georgian London* (Cambridge: Cambridge University Press, 2007).

Said, Edward W., *Orientalism* (New York: Vintage Books, 1978).

——, *Culture and Imperialism* (New York: Vintage Books, 1993).

Schama, Simon, *The Power of Art* (New York: Ecco, 2006).

Schechner, Richard, *Between Theater and Anthropology* (Philadelphia: University of Pennsylvania Press, 1985).

Schmid, Thomas H., ' "England Yet Sleeps": Intertextuality, Nationalism, and Risorgimento in P.B. Shelley's *Swellfoot the Tyrant*', *Keats-Shelley Journal* 53 (2004): pp. 61–85.

Scrivener, Michael Henry, *Radical Shelley: The Philosophical Anarchism and Utopian Thought of Percy Bysshe Shelley* (Princeton: Princeton University Press, 1982).

——, 'The Discourse of Treason, Sedition, and Blasphemy in British Political Trials, 1794–1820', *Romantic Circles* (March 1999), http://www.rc.umd.edu/print/praxis/law/scrivener/mscrv.htm, 19 paragraphs.

——, 'John Thelwall and the Revolution of 1649', in Timothy Morton and Nigel Smith (eds), *Radicalism in British Literary Culture, 1650–1830, From Revolution to Revolution* (Cambridge: Cambridge University Press, 2002), pp. 119–32.

Shaw, Philip, *Waterloo and the Romantic Imagination* (New York: Palgrave Macmillan, 2002).

Shohet, Lauren, *Reading Masques: The English Masque and Public Culture in the Seventeenth Century* (Oxford: Oxford University Press, 2010).

Simpson, David, *Romanticism, Nationalism, and the Revolt against Theory* (Chicago: University of Chicago Press, 1993).

——, *9/11: The Culture of Commemoration* (Chicago: University of Chicago Press, 2006).

——, *Wordsworth, Commodification, and Social Concern: The Poetics of Modernity* (Cambridge: Cambridge University Press, 2009).

Smith, E.A., *A Queen on Trial: The Affair of Queen Caroline* (Phoenix Mill, UK: Alan Sutton Publishing Ltd., 1993).

Smith, Nigel, 'Radicalism and Replication', in Timothy Morton and Nigel Smith (eds), *Radicalism in British Literary Culture, 1650–1830 From Revolution to Revolution* (Cambridge: Cambridge University Press, 2002), pp. 45–63.

—— and Timothy Morton (eds), *Radicalism in British Literary Culture, 1650–1830 From Revolution to Revolution* (Cambridge: Cambridge University Press, 2002).

——, *Literature and Revolution in England, 1640–1660* (1994; New Haven: Yale University Press, 1997).

Sperry, Stuart M., *Shelley's Major Verse: The Narrative and Dramatic Poetry* (Cambridge, MA: Harvard University Press, 1988).

St Clair, William, *That Greece Might Still be Free: The Philhellenes in the War of Independence* (London: Oxford University Press, 1972).

Steiner, George, *The Death of Tragedy* (New Haven: Yale University Press, 1961).

Stevenson, John, 'The Queen Caroline Affair', in John Stevenson (ed.), *London in the Age of Reform* (Oxford: Basil Blackwell, 1977), pp. 117–48.

Suleri, Sara, *The Rhetoric of English India* (Chicago: University of Chicago Press, 1992).

Thomas, Sophie, *Romanticism and Visuality: Fragments, History, Spectacle* (New York: Routledge, 2008).

Thompson, E.P., *The Making of the English Working Class* (1963; New York: Vintage Books, 1966).

Tillyard, E.M.W., *The Elizabethan World Picture* (1943; New York: Vintage Books, 1959).

Turner, Victor, *From Ritual to Theatre: The Human Seriousness of Play* (New York: Performing Arts Journal Publications, 1982).

Van Kooy, Dana, 'Improvising on the Borders: Hellenism, History, and Tragedy in Shelley's *Hellas*', in Monika Class and Terry F. Robinson (eds), *Transnational England: Home and Abroad, 1780–1860* (Cambridge, Cambridge Scholars Publishing, 2009), pp. 41–57.

———, 'Darkness Visible: The Early Melodrama of British Imperialism and the Commodification of History in Sheridan's *Pizarro*', *Theatre Journal* 64.2 (May 2012): pp. 179–95.

———, with Jeffrey N. Cox, 'Melodramatic Slaves', *Modern Drama* 55.4 (Winter 2012): pp. 459–75.

Virilio, Paul, *Speed and Politics: An Essay on Dromology*, Mark Polizzotti (trans.) (1977; Los Angeles: Semiotext(e), 2006).

———, *War and Cinema: The Logistics of Perception*, Patrick Camiller (trans.) (New York: Verso, 1989).

Vitkus, Daniel, ' "The Common Market of All the World": English Theater, the Global System, and the Ottoman Empire in the Early Modern Period', in Barbara Sebek and Stephen Deng (eds), *Global Traffic: Discourses and Practices of Trade in English Literature and Culture from 1550–1700* (New York: Palgrave Macmillan, 2008), pp. 19–37.

Wallace, Jennifer, *Shelley and Greece: Rethinking Romantic Hellenism* (New York: St Martin's Press, 1997).

Warren, Andrew, *The Orient and the Young Romantics* (Cambridge: Cambridge University Press, 2014).

Wasserman, Earl, *Shelley: A Critical Reading* (Baltimore: The Johns Hopkins Press, 1971).

Watkins, Daniel P., *Keats's Poetry and the Politics of the Imagination* (Rutherford: Fairleigh Dickinson University Press, 1989).

Webb, Timothy, *Shelley: A Voice not Understood* (Atlantic Highland, NJ: Humanities Press, 1977).

———, *English Romantic Hellenism, 1700–1824* (Manchester: Manchester University Press, 1982).

———, 'Romantic Hellenism', in Stuart Curran (ed.), *The Cambridge Companion to British Romanticism* (Cambridge: Cambridge University Press, 1993), pp. 148–76.

——— and Alan M. Weinberg (eds), *The Unfamiliar Shelley* (Farnham, England: Ashgate, 2009).

Weinberg, Alan M. ' "These Catchers of Men": Imposture and Its Unmasking in "A Philosophical View of Reform" ', in Alan M. Weinberg and Timothy Webb (eds), *The Unfamiliar Shelley* (Farnham, England: Ashgate, 2009), pp. 257–76.

Weinberg, Alan M. and Timothy Webb (eds), *The Unfamiliar Shelley* (Farnham, England: Ashgate, 2009).

Weston, Rowland, 'History, Memory, and Moral Knowledge: William Godwin's *Essay on Sepulchres* (1809)', *The European Legacy*, 14.6 (2009): pp. 651–65.

White, Hayden, *Metahistory: The Historical Imagination in Nineteenth-Century Europe* (1973; Baltimore: Johns Hopkins University Press, 1985).

White, Newman Ivey, *The Unextinguished Hearth: Shelley and His Contemporary Critics* (New York: Octagon Books, Inc., 1966).

Wolfson, Susan, *Borderlines: The Shiftings of Gender in British Romanticism* (Stanford: Stanford University Press, 2006).

Wood, Marcus, *Radical Satire and Print Culture, 1790–1822* (Oxford: Oxford University Press, 1994).

———, *The Horrible Gift of Freedom: Atlantic Slavery and the Representation of Emancipation* (London and Athens, GA: The University of Georgia Press, 2010).

Woodring, Carl, *Politics in English Romantic Poetry* (Cambridge, MA: Harvard University Press, 1970).

Worrall, David, *Harlequin Empire: Race, Ethnicity and the Drama of the Popular Enlightenment* (London: Pickering & Chatto, 2007).

Youngquist, Paul, *Monstrosities: Bodies and British Romanticism* (Minneapolis: University of Minnesota Press, 2003).

——— (ed.), *Race, Romanticism, and the Atlantic* (Farnham, England: Ashgate, 2013).

Žižek, Slavoj, *The Sublime Object of Ideology* (New York: Verso, 1989).

———, *Tarrying with the Negative: Kant, Hegel, and the Critique of Ideology* (Durham, NC: Duke University Press, 1993).

———, *Looking Awry: An Introduction to Jacques Lacan through Popular Culture* (1992; Cambridge, MA: MIT Press, 2000).

———, *Welcome to the Desert of the Real: Five Essays on September 11 and Related Dates* (London: Verso, 2002).

———, *Violence: Six Sideways Reflections* (New York: Picador, 2008).

Index

*Page numbers in **bold** refer to illustrations.*